PEERLESS

The Life and Times of Sugar Ray Robinson

By Brian Hughes M.B.E. and Damian Hughes

First Published 2007

Damian Hughes
16 West Grove
Sale
Manchester
M33 3AS

ISBN:
0-9551848-1-9 (10 digit)
978-0-9551848-1-9 (13 digit)

Printed in the UK by
Cromwell Press, Trowbridge, Wiltshire

Contents

Acknowledgements

The authors would like to extend their heartfelt gratitude to the following individuals for their incredible help, support, encouragement and advice: Lindy Lindell, Clay Moyle, Donald Koss, George Zeleny, Jack Cashill, Jack Shehan, Johnny Bos, Mike Casey, Quinten Brown, Ralph Brown, Ralph Cathcart, Richard Hernandez, John A. Bardelli, Sam Gregory, Tom Donelson, Stephen Gordon, Ernest 'Gino' Morales, Harold Lederman, Iris Bates, Harry Otty (author of the excellent 'Charley Burley and the Black Murders' Row') and Andrew Searle.

They would also like to offer a very special thank you to Angelo Dundee for his help, wise counsel and advice and for contributing the foreword and to Britain's leading promoter, Frank Warren, whose generosity and help has made it possible for this book to be published.

They would also like to issue their enduring gratitude for the photographs which were kindly supplied by John Redfern, Lee Woods, Raymond McCormack and the great Carmen Basilio.

Finally, both authors would like to thank Rosemarie and Geraldine, Anthony, Christopher, Rachael and Joseph for their continued love, patience and support.

We hope you enjoy the book.

Foreword

by Angelo Dundee

I have been fortunate enough to see some of boxing's greatest fighters from the halcyon period of the Forties and Fifties through to the modern day and have been privileged to work with a number of them. I feel well qualified, therefore, to declare that Sugar Ray Robinson was an absolute phenomenon.

He was, without question, the best welterweight to rule the division in the 1940s; an era which included Fritzie Zivic, Maxie Shapiro, Marty Servo, Jackie Wilson, Chuck Taylor, George Costner, Tommy Bell, and Kid Gavilan, to name just a few. I was fortunate to work with Carmen Basilio, who was a great and courageous fighter, which gave me close up access to his rival, Robinson, when Basilio beat him to claim his title in one of the sport's most thrilling and exciting fights.

Robinson offers a great example for any aspiring youngsters who may consider taking up boxing. He was a totally dedicated and diligent trainer who would listen to his coaches and constantly worked on striving to improve on his natural talent.

Brian and Damian Hughes are successful in taking you on a thrilling journey through the golden years of boxing in this excellent autobiography of Sugar Ray Robinson and I am confident that, like me, you will enjoy reading about this great fighter and his stunning achievements.

Sit back and enjoy the story of the great Sugar Ray.

Angelo Dundee

Introduction

by Frank Warren

Having been involved with boxing for more than 25 years, I'm proud to say that I've worked alongside some of the greatest names in the sport.

There's little I regret, but there are a handful of fighters I would loved to have worked with. It's easy to look at the past through rose-tinted glasses and claim today's fighters aren't a patch on those who have long since hung up their gloves. There are contemporary boxers who could have competed with the best in history, but few could have lived with arguably the greatest of all time, Sugar Ray Robinson. While most fighters have resilience, dedication and determination, fewer have the power and ring craft to complement it, and fewer still the grace to turn what is the ultimate trial of mental and physical strength into an art form. And only one or two in a generation have an almost indefinable spark of magic which separates these immortal warriors from their peers. Robinson had it all.

The heavyweights Muhammad Ali and Joe Louis may be better known, but in the pound-for-pound stakes, even they may have had to give way to Robinson.

As a promoter I've always dreamed of discovering the new Sugar Ray Robinson, and I know Brian Hughes, one of Britain's great trainers, shares the same hopes every time a new face walks through the doors at his gym.

The search goes on, but in the meantime, Brian has brought his rich stream of boxing knowledge to this book - along with a deep understanding of the history and social conditions of the 1940s and 1950s - to ensure the real Sugar Ray Robinson comes alive on these pages.

Happy reading and best wishes.

Frank.

Frank Warren

Preface

IN MODERN DAY boxing polls determined to discover the greatest ever pound for pound fighter, it is a remarkable phenomenon that one man's name still tends to stand out as arguably the finest exponent: Sugar Ray Robinson.

Without wishing to debate the merits of Robinson over Muhammad Ali or Joe Louis to name two other favourites of the perennial list-makers, it is interesting to think about what a boxer of Robinson's calibre would be valued at in today's multi-million dollar age. In a sport dominated by money and where promoters like Don King, Bob Arum or Frank Warren command equal column inches to the athletes, how much would they pay a boxer with Robinson's sublime skill and boxing intelligence? The mind boggles at the potential.

It was boxers like Sugar Ray who helped make boxing a major sporting attraction and helped fill newspapers with stories every day of the week during its halcyon days in the middle of the last century. Boxing was renowned for its exciting fighters and Sugar Ray Robinson had the necessary style and flourish allied with a flawless technical ability.

Before we look at the man, it is worth dwelling a while on the statistics of his 25-year career. His amateur record was an amazing precursor of what was to come as he racked up 85 wins, 0 defeats and 69 early stoppages (49 in the first round) before his professional career record of 202 fights and 175 wins, with an amazing 109 of them coming before the scheduled ending. Many journalists and boxing followers believed that such was Robinson's natural ability that he never had to work hard at his chosen profession. They were wrong; he spent hours in the gym where he practiced with a thoroughness which his trainers, George Gainford and Harry Wiley, had devised with him.

He was also a man of his time and we must consider the context of the age which he emerged. In 1940, when Sugar Ray commenced his boxing career, boxing was a thriving business. Mike Jacobs was the biggest power in boxing and Sugar Ray had his first professional contest in Madison Square Garden on a Jacobs promotion. It was also a sport which attracted powerful mobsters such as Frankie Carbo and Frank 'Blinky' Palermo, the two most notorious of some of the underworld's biggest names. Despite being a favourite of these reptiles, Robinson wanted to be independent and would resist their siren calls throughout this career.

Unfortunately, like many who are touched by genius, Sugar Ray's character had a dark side. Towards the end of his career, there were disturbing reports of his vicious assaults on his second wife, Edna Mae, as well as his growing dependence on the drug marijuana, as well as the sadly inevitable money problems after earning an estimated four-million dollars through boxing until he ended up destitute in the middle 1960s.

We all need heroes and so I would like to welcome you to a book about one of my heroes. Sugar Ray Robinson. He is still at the top of my own list of the greatest fighters ever to have lived.

1.

Birth of a Legend

THERE HAS BEEN sufficient information written about the early life of Sugar Ray Robinson which highlights how the conditions of this period helped to shape the man and so let us look in brief detail at this era.

His mother and father originated from Dublin, Georgia. Leila Hurst, his mother, came from a large family of eight boys and eight girls. His father, Walker Smith, was raised on a farm. Details of how they met are unclear but they were married in 1917 when Leila was just 17 and Walker, slightly older.

Walker was described by neighbours as being "a lively looking fellow with the proportions of a welterweight" and possessing a roving eye for the ladies, a trait which his son inherited.

After their marriage, the young couple moved into a small dilapidated farm which was furnished with an old bed and a chair which was given to them by Leila's mother. Shortly after this move, they celebrated the birth of their first child, a beautiful daughter named Marie. Another daughter, Evelyn, followed a year later. For Walker, these were highlights of his life on the farm, which was centred on the hard toil of growing cotton, corn and peanuts for $10 wages.

A couple of years earlier, Leila's sister, Lillie, and her husband, Herman Heyes, had packed up their belongings and took up residence in Detroit. Lillie had sent word to her sister that there were plenty of jobs in Detroit, mainly in the motor industry, which paid good money. This was enough incentive for both Leila and Walker to try their luck in the Motor City.

On 3rd May 1920, Leila gave birth to a 7 pound 12 ounce son who they decided to name Walker Smith Junior. Incidentally, there is a discrepancy about whether he was born in 1920 or 21. Sugar Ray himself claims that it was 1921; however his views cannot be assumed to be entirely accurate as he had a record for inventing dates, places or anything else he felt was needed to be able to portray the image he wanted at any given time or place.

Another area of uncertainty centres on where he was actually born. For most of his life, Robinson believed that he was born in Detroit, Michigan and he stated this with some pride in his autobiography. However, in 2006, his cousin, Ms Cannida-Farmer, threw doubts on this claim by recounting that in 1987 she had requested a certified copy of Robinson's birth certificate from the Montgomery County Courthouse in Mount Vernon. To her surprise, the details stated that Walker Smith Jr. was actually born at 312 North Railroad Street - now Martin Luther King Jr Drive East - in Ailey, Georgia.

Although the tiny farm in Georgia was bad, at least it possessed wide open spaces to play. Conditions in Detroit, however, were the pits. "Where we lived in Detroit, which was officially called Paradise Valley, but was better known as Black Bottom by the residents, because that's exactly what it was. Black because we lived there, and Bottom because that's where we were at," said Sugar Ray years later when recalling his early life.

The family lived in abject poverty and Walker didn't help matters due to his fondness for drink and this, along with other minor problems, saw him in and out of work more than was good for him. At one stage, events became so bad that Walker was forced to swallow his pride and apply for dole from the relief agency. Leila, however, refused to pursue this option and found herself a job as a seamstress at the General Linen Company in Detroit during the day and as a chambermaid at the plush Statler Hotel on Washington Boulevard at night as well as working in shops and laundries when there were opportunities.

Walker's drunken rages and regular flirting with women didn't help matters and so there were increasingly regular arguments between the young parents until, eventually, Leila reached breaking point and decided that she would have to make a change.

One morning in 1927, when her husband had left the house, Leila roused the three children and helped them pack their sparse belongings. Junior, who was six years old, asked his mother where they were going so early in the morning. Leila explained that they were going to their grandmother's farm in Glenwood, which was situated in Georgia where she took them and ensured that they were safe and settled before she headed back to Detroit to continue her work commitments.

Junior loved his new life on the farm where his uncle, Herschel Hurst, would take him hunting and fishing and he started to excel at the outdoor life. A year later, however, Leila returned to the farm and took them on the return trip back to the Motor City. Despite her best intentions, however, nothing had changed in the year-long absence. "Black Bottom was bleaker than when we left it a year before," remarked Sugar Ray.

These events would leave a deep mark on him throughout his life. When he would recall his childhood he remembered "the abject poverty", which left him with a real sense of fear about losing money. This fear, it was often said, was a major reason for his attitude to negotiating with promoters for the amount of money he considered he was worth.

To help their mother, the three Smith children helped neighbours with various tasks and other menial jobs. Junior enjoyed running errands, washing windows and shining shoes, whilst his sisters became known as reliable babysitters. Leila would not allow these activities to detract from the education she was determined they should enjoy, but Junior considered school to be a boring distraction. When he wasn't playing truant, he would entertain himself in the playground by doing his favourite trick of walking on his hands or racing his friends or playing his favourite sport, baseball. He idolised Babe Ruth and Ty Cobb despite being a huge fan of the Detroit Tigers. He was also renowned as being an adept card player with hands that moved as fast and tricky as a professional card dealer in a casino; something that would prove extremely useful a little later in his life.

In his spare time, he was a regular visitor to the Brewster Recreation Centre, a two-story building that had recreation facilities designed to keep local youngsters occupied and out of trouble. It was regarded as a God-send for the poor kids of the area as it contained a swimming pool, basketball court, table-tennis room and a boxing ring.

Legend has it that one day a big, wide-shouldered lad passed through carrying a training bag. All the kids shouted "Hiya Joe" and the big fellow would smile and acknowledge their greeting with a wave of his hand. "Who's that," Junior asked a friend. "Oh, that's Joe Barrow," came the reply, "He's a boxer." Junior was intrigued and sidled over to watch him box a few rounds. This is often described as being the moment Junior became smitten by the boxing bug.

Joe Barrow was an idol to all the local black kids, who would walk behind him wherever he went. He lived around the corner from the Smiths' humble residence and attended the same school as Marie, Junior's sister. It was a great source of pride to Junior that, in later years, he would become close friends with his early idol, who became known to the world as Joe Louis. In later years, Junior loved to recall his younger days and regularly recounted the occasions that, "Whenever Joe was in the gym, so was I" and boasted about carrying his bag.

As with many things in his life, all was not necessarily how it seems and this recollection appears to be one of them. In his excellent book, 'Metro Detroit Boxing', Lindy Lindell pours cold water on the ideas that these legends ever shared a gym at such a young age. "Although Robinson was born in Detroit, he left for New York with his family at age seven. It is highly unlikely, therefore, that he ever carried Joe Louis' bag when he went to train at Brewster Recreation Center," said Lindy.

Dave Clark was a loyal stablemate of Joe Louis throughout the 1930s and achieved a number ranking as a light-heavyweight contender during this period. After his retirement, he became a trainer and whenever Robinson later fought as a professional in Detroit, Clark would be hired as an assistant to George Gainford. He keenly recalled seeing Junior as an eight-year old.

"Walker Smith, as he was, was brought into the Brewster Gym by a trainer named Wesley Davies. I never saw him train or put on the gloves or even consider being a fighter but I do remember him as a kid in the gym." Clark suggested that Junior's interest in boxing only sparked once he had moved to New York.

Walter Smith, a contemporary of Louis when he trained at the centre and later, a well respected trainer at Detroit's Kronk Gym, supports this view. "Nobody knew who Sugar Ray was before he left town, and Joe Louis didn't have a bag," he said. In fact, Leila Smith herself scoffed at these stories and suggested that they were a figment of her son's over-active imagination.

Whether he attended the gym or not, there is little doubt that it was Louis who attracted him to the sport, yet at the same time there was another focus of his admiration.

The Purple Gang were a group who roamed Detroit and were constantly being hounded by the police. Junior, like most black youngsters, looked up to this gang and admired them immensely. Leila would pray every night that he would not follow their lead and her two daughters ensured that her prayers were answered by making sure that he kept on the straight and narrow by give him a smack whenever they suspected that he was being led astray.

Most of his behaviour though was to try and gain attention from his peers rather than from the police. At Duffield School, he would walk on his hands down the corridor, which delighted the other children but annoyed the staff. Leila was regularly requested by the principal to come and hear about her son's antics. Once back home she would deliver stern lectures to him and he would promise with absolute sincerity that he would not upset the teachers again. The next day, he would flash his endearing smile to the teacher complete with profuse apologies, before promptly leaving the room and doing it all over again!

In 1932, Leila was finding it harder and harder to survive in Detroit. She had, by now, divorced her hapless husband, who did strive to keep in touch and visit regularly. The depression, however, bit hard and the motor industry suffered as bad as any industry and so, once again, the Smiths were on the move. They packed up their belongings and moved to New York City. "We were like gypsies," recalled Leila, "always on the move from the landlord."

They situated themselves at West 53rd Street, near Broadway, but like their life in Detroit, this was a tough environment for a woman on her own with three young children. To help earn money, Junior took to dancing on the sidewalks near Broadway, where his nimble footwork was so good people would throw money on the floor for him.

The famous black dancer, Bill 'Bojangles' Robinson, spotted the youngster and he encouraged him to strive to make something of himself as a tap dancer. Even Leila thought her son was quite talented at dancing and would somehow find a dollar a week for dancing lessons at the Roy Scott Studios. He would keep the dollar and stay on the street trying to earn more money.

After a short time on West 53rd Street, Leila moved again, the destination - Harlem. This area was the home of many thousands of black families and over the years would produce its fair share of characters. Unfortunately, it didn't take the hyperactive Junior too long to start running with different gangs. He was 14 years old and stood almost 5 foot 11 inches and weighed about eight stone. He was finely proportioned with long ballet dancer's legs, long sinewy arms and the build of young thoroughbred colt. Additionally, his bright personality and charming smile shone through radiantly. Although he wasn't a juvenile delinquent or a criminal in the accepted sense, there was a feeling amongst his sisters and mother that he was beginning to get out of control; fighting in the streets and petty thieving were his main crimes but he was becoming too big to physically punish and the verbal admonishments were too frequent to have enough impact.

One dark night Benny Booksinger, a young local man who worked as the neighbourhood Police Athletic League organizer, gathered a number of kids underneath a street light and began matching them up accordingly. Junior was matched against a boy named Harmon, who was 15 and physically bigger than Junior, but by employing his considerable speed, Junior, or 'Smitty' as he was sometimes called by his new neighbours, licked his opponent with ease.

Feeling on top of the world and buoyed by his easy victory, Junior began bragging about his prowess around the neighbourhood. Aggrieved, Harmon's 17-year-old brother, Lee, pushed forward and told Junior that since he had beaten his brother he would now naturally have to defeat him. It was agreed. There could be no backing down from this challenge and the two of them went at each other with an unrestrained fury.

To Junior's enduring horror, Leila happened to see her son fighting and dashed across the street and stopped the fight. She demanded to know who arranged it and poor Benny Booksinger received a fearful thrashing.

The damage to his street credibility didn't stop him returning and it was a source of great pride to him that in all of these contests he was unbeaten except for once, which was to Billy Graham, a white lad who actually went on to become a top level professional. Graham, it is alleged, was often referred to as the 'uncrowned world welterweight champion', but they never fought each other as professionals and so Robinson had no chance to avenge his loss.

Whilst Junior was officially registered as attending Cooper Junior High School on 116th Street on Madison Avenue, his pattern of repeated truancy endured. It was here that he met his close friend, Warren Jones, who was obsessed with boxing and was a good influence on his friend. On one occasion the pair of them played truant together and visited the famous Empire State Building. When Junior walked into the elevator, he was violently sick and this was the first and last experience of using elevators. He would walk up the stairs, no matter how many floors, to his destination.

Warren Jones' uncle was George Gainford. George was the chief trainer at the Salem - Crescent Amateur Club, which boasted the best amateur fighters in New York and which was a beacon of light for hundreds of youngsters in the suburban slums of Harlem, where crime, delinquency and hardship were a permanent feature of daily life. The club offered the chance to all local kids to try boxing as a route by which they might escape to a better way of life.

Warren was forever trying to get Junior, or 'Smitty' as he affectionately called him, to join his uncle's team of boxers. Eventually, he did go along with his friend to meet George. As soon as he walked into the gym, which was situated in the basement of an old church, his stomach turned because of the stale smell of liniment and the sweaty odour of bodies that populated the gym. Gainford was a huge man, standing well over six feet and weighing about 16 stone. He had a big, round melodious face, and twinkling eyes and a hearty deep-throated laugh which could be heard all around. He had a loud, commanding, booming voice which he used to great effect while coaching his boxers, and later, when arguing on his boxers' behalf. Born in Charleston, South Carolina, he had moved to Harlem many years before and was well renowned in the area. He claimed he boxed as a professional middleweight under the name 'Kid Ford'. He warmly welcomed his nephew and his friend.

Junior got the impression, when shaking hands with Gainford for the first time, that the big man was looking straight through him and he was afraid of him. Normally quick with his tongue, he was left scrabbling for words. Eventually, he managed to explain that he wanted to start boxing. Gainford couldn't have been less impressed with a potential prospect, but he handed him a pair of old boxing shorts and a battered pair of boxing boots and a well worn protector. He instructed him to come back the next night and try the sport. However, once outside the gym, Junior quickly renounced his desire to learn the sport and decided that he would pawn the loaned boxing gear and after giving his mother some of the cash, he used the rest of the money in a card school.

The following evening, he didn't show up at the gym and Gainford, used to seeing dozens of youngsters come and go as quickly as little Junior, was unconcerned. When he did see his nephew Warren, he asked him to get the equipment back off his friend. Warren did as asked but his request was met with a smile and a nonchalant shrug of the shoulders

Birth of a legend

Months later, and with the incident long forgotten by him, Junior was rolling dice near the African Mission Church on 129th Street and 7th Avenue in Harlem. Appalled at the gambling, he was grabbed by the local Reverend Cullen, who frog-marched him down to the cellar of the Salem-Crescent gym, where he asked Gainford to deliver a stern lecture about gambling. It was the first time the big trainer had seen him since loaning the gear.

Gainford never smiled or spoke a direct word to him but made him get into the ring. His intention was to teach the youngster a painful lesson. However, to his surprise, the kid shaped up well against some more experienced fighters. He had beautiful footwork, lightning fast speed and actually looked like he had some potential. Big George told Junior that if he was serious about learning to fight, he would teach him. But, he said in a stern, loud voice: "You have to learn to take orders. My orders!"

Gainford later admitted that although he did not show any obvious enthusiasm to Junior, he was impressed. There was some spark about the youngster that made him think that he just might have found that someone special that most trainers dream about constantly.

The next night, he turned up for training at the gym and Gainford began crafting his skills. He observed immediately that he was 'right-hand crazy', throwing his right all the time as if trying to knock somebody out. In an effort to teach him not to be solely reliant on a right hand punch, Gainford tied his right hand to his side and made him concentrate on using his left instead. Time would show that the wily trainer did a masterful job as boxing connoisseurs would marvel at his marvellous use of this weapon - the straight left jab!

Inevitably for someone of his nature, after a week of training young Junior became bored and the lure of his friends proved stronger than his desire to be in the gym learning the craft of boxing. Despite being disappointed Gainford didn't go chasing him. He had about thirty other youngsters training and because the Salem Crescent boys were all good fighters they appeared on tournaments most nights of the week. George was a busy man.

During this absence from the gym Junior had a street fight against Sonny Leacock. Leacock was an all-round sportsman and fought a number of times in the Police Athletic League bouts. Junior did not want to fight Leacock, whom he considered a friend, but he was egged on by the other kids and his vanity got the better of him. Within a couple of minutes the fight was over with Leacock out to the world courtesy of Junior's lightning fast punches. It was at this moment that he admitted that he first began to think deeply about becoming a boxer, perhaps a professional.

A few days later, Bill 'Pop' Miller, a friend and neighbour, called to speak to Junior's mother. Miller, who had managed and trained the world middleweight champion Theodore 'Tiger' Flowers in 1926 and still helped

15

coach the Salem Crescent boxing team alongside Gainford and had also witnessed the fight with Leacock, thought Junior could be a potentially good fighter. He asked Leila for her permission to look after her son. Miller also coached Cedric Harvey, who became a Golden Gloves champion.

Leila was surprised to hear what Mr Miller had told her. She wasn't aware that her son had even attempted to start boxing. She knew Junior was always talking about Joe Louis and other famous boxers. In fact, she gave her son some money for his fare to visit Pompton Lakes, where Louis was training to fight Primo Carnera. He claimed that the Brown Bomber had remembered him from their days in Detroit and back in Harlem; he had told everyone who would listen about how the heavyweight champion remembered him. She was, however, delighted and agreed to Miller's request.

Soon afterwards, an amateur tournament was taking place. It was a neighbourhood event which was filled mainly by relatives coming to support. The Smith women, Leila, Evelyn and Marie, were all present. It was the first boxing tournament they had attended and they were proud to see their youngest apply himself.

As the bell rang to start the first round his opponent rushed straight at him like a tank. Junior was confused; he hadn't yet learnt how to handle this kind of aggression and he was hammered all around the ring. He burned up with embarrassment and humiliation as his mother had to watch him get a thrashing in the ring. At one stage, he was hit by thundering punches which spun him against the ropes, looking out into the crowd.

He later recalled seeing the distraught look on his mother's face. He thought of the courage and determination that she had shown in trying to support her family alone and he used these feelings to motivate and acquit himself well. He dug deep inside to find the necessary resolve to win the keenly contested bout and redeem himself. He did exactly that by smashing his opponent all over the ring. He eventually won his bout and redeemed himself.

Although Robinson claims that his first official amateur fight was with Pete Mello at the Sacred Heart Church in Jackson Heights, Queens, New York City, official records show that he actually fought a boy named Albert DeMathies in a three round contest first. He won on points but found it hard going. In the opening round he could hardly touch DeMathies. When he returned to his corner at the end of the first, he was advised to forget looking for a knockout and just concentrate on outpointing the tough kid in front of him. Junior followed orders and won. A couple of weeks later he travelled with Gainford and some other fighters to Kingston, New York for a tournament. He was not scheduled to box but went for the ride.

Birth of a legend

At amateur tournaments the weighing-in ritual is always fraught with bad temper and arguments. The club matchmaker might get let down by certain clubs or a certain boxer. The weights might not be correct and a hundred and one other problems usually crop up. It was no different at this tournament held in Kingston.

When the Salem Crescent boxers arrived the matchmaker, a man named Ben Becker, was agitated and approached Gainford immediately. He explained that he had a local kid who had sold the venue out almost single-handed. The kid's father helped sponsor the tournaments and brought much needed money into the club funds. His opponent had withdrawn and he had to have someone in the opposite corner. "I've been let down George," he said with a worried frown on his face. "I've just got to get this kid on the bill tonight, no matter what it costs."

Those were the words big George wanted to hear: 'No matter what it costs!' The beleaguered matchmaker knew Gainford always had spare boxers with him, and he beseeched George to allow one of his lads to box this local favourite. Gainford was a cunning man and knew the matchmaker would pay considerably more money to get the local favourite a contest. He played it cool and told him he had nobody in the same class as the star attraction. However, money tends to solve most problems, especially in boxing, and after the matchmaker emerged from a huddle with the Salem Crescent trainer, Gainford shouted to Junior: "Get some trunks and boxing boots and get weighed in, you're fighting tonight."

Junior jumped at the opportunity and did as he was told. However, when Ben Becker requested his AAU card from Gainford, Gainford dug deep into his bag and produced a card in the name of Ray Robinson (Before being allowed to box on amateur boxing tournaments, it was a stipulation that the boxer had to have an Amateur Athletic Union card). Becker was also an official of the AAU. Ray Robinson was one of Gainford's former fighters who had either finished with boxing or moved somewhere else. Junior, boxing under the assumed name, left the local favourite bemused and confused and won the bout in style, receiving a beautiful watch for being the star of the show. The procedure was that the boxer would then hand the watch back to the promoter and, in return, would receive $8. Leila was overjoyed when her son handed her the money the following day.

This was the birth of a legend.

2.

The Birth of Sugar Ray Robinson

FIGHTING AS Ray Robinson, he went on to take part in 89 amateur fights in which he was victorious in all of them. One of the most notable wins was against an opponent called Johnny Dellasandro in a Jersey City tournament.

Dellasandro was the Diamond Belt featherweight champion and Gainford did not want his man to box this experienced amateur champion because he deemed him too tough. Robinson disagreed and persuaded Gainford by promising that he would get on his toes and box from a distance. Robinson was, by now, a beautiful mover in the ring and he could switch styles to be able to box from a distance or stand close and fire his two-handed combination punches at his unfortunate opponents like a sledge-hammer. On this occasion, he kept his promise and won the close contest.

Dellasandro pleaded for a return bout and Robinson granted it. The second time, it took place in the Jamaica Arena, New York. As the rematch loomed closer Gainford instructed his charge that he was withdrawing him as punishment for missing training. Again, Robinson insisted that he be allowed to fight. After some deliberation, Gainford agreed as he reasoned that if his man got beat it would serve as a useful early lesson about the perils of fighting without discipline and commitment. Instead, the contest revealed a new facet of Robinson's. Initially, it was extremely close for a couple of rounds before Ray took a gamble and decided that instead of sticking to his cultured boxing he would go toe-to-toe. He won by a knockout!

Ray was quickly becoming a huge attraction on the amateur circuit and was boxing regularly, not only in New York but also in upstate Kingston, Watertown, Hartford, and even Canada. He constantly badgered his mother to be allowed to leave school but Leila would not hear of it. Ray enlisted others to help fight his cause and one neighbour casually suggested that she visit Doctor Vincent Nardiello, New York State Boxing's official medical officer, and discuss Ray's request with him.

When she entered his surgery, she outlined Ray's requests and asked his advice. The doctor asked if her son was academically clever and how he was performing at school. Leila admitted that although he was no rocket scientist, she explained that his chances of getting a decent job would surely be enhanced if he remained within education. After patiently listening to his worried mother, the doctor responded, "Well, Mrs. Smith, he doesn't seem to be a great scholar, but he sure is a great young amateur boxer."

She was now working in a laundry, where she operated a sewing machine and lived alone with Ray because his sisters, Marie and Evelyn, were both married and living with their partners. His fighting meant that he would be bringing money home regularly. Additionally, Leila reasoned that his boxing interests would keep him on the straight and narrow and she recognized that Gainford was becoming a much needed father figure to the budding young star, and she felt secure that her boy was being looked after by somebody she felt she could trust. Leila finally relented and Ray was allowed to leave school and concentrate on boxing.

It was not without incident though as the young Robinson was starting to develop his charismatic, single-minded and, at times, exasperating and bombastic personality. For example, on his journeys to the different places for the amateur and bootleg tournaments he scrutinized Gainford meticulously. He saw that big George would converse with the various matchmakers and amateur organizers and was quick to spot that money changed hands, usually into his trainer's. He listened to rumours that Gainford was earning about $300 a week taking his amateur team to various tournaments and so, without telling the rest of the boxing team, Ray spoke to Gainford. Initially, George was gobsmacked at the youngster's cheek and bluntness and told him to mind his own business.

In what would become a trademark characteristic of his career, with Robinson's hard bargaining with members of the boxing establishment, Ray wasn't to be put off and continued his questioning until Gainford eventually cut the youngster into the deal he had on the amateur circuit. He also displayed this strong sense of independence and worth when he later entered the prestigious Golden Gloves competition. He complained to amateur officials about the food allowances, expenses and other items.

The amateur scene saw Robinson continue to gain prestige. After one tournament in Watertown, New York, Ray had looked sensational. After the bout Gainford was guiding the youngster down from the ring when a newspaper reporter, named Jack Chase, buttonholed the trainer and told him he was very impressed with young Robinson. He said, "George, this kid is sure a sweet fighter."

A big smile spread across Gainford's melodious face and, laughing, he replied, "Yes sir, you're spot on. This, here, fighter is sweet alright, as sweet as sugar." Upon hearing this compliment from Gainford, who was not known for being generous in his compliments, Ray felt a warm glow inside and the soubriquet 'Sugar' was added to his name.

To build his experience, he also boxed in several 'bootleg' tournaments. This was a common practice amongst many promising boxers. On one occasion, he travelled to Buffalo to box Jimmy Winters, who was a massive drawing card. The venue was predictably packed solid, with the fans going wild to get inside and see the action. Robinson beat Winters in such a convincing manner that the promoter gave Ray an extra $150.

In 1939, the Salem Crescent team entered the prestigious Golden Gloves tournament. Robinson told his friends and neighbours that he was going to be a champion. It was February 1939, when in front of a large crowd wearing his favourite white satin boxing trunks, white cotton sports socks and black boxing boots and dancing lightly on the balls of his feet, a ritual he would follow throughout the following 25 years as he believed that it kept the rhythm in his body and relaxed him, he started his campaign with a three round decision over Alfredo Guido. A few nights later he beat Patrick Brady in one round before outpointing Frank Arcidiacano over three. These bouts were held at various venues like the 92nd Street YMCA, Columbus Council Hall and the Hippodrome.

After these early rounds he fought the final in Madison Square Garden where he met his close friend Louis 'Spider' Valentine in front of a phenomenally large crowd of 18,231 spectators. Because both Robinson and Valentine were coached by Gainford he declined to go in either corner and it was Harry Wiley who seconded Robinson.

As the bell rang to start the bout the taller Robinson was the aggressor with ferocious two-handed punching and using lightning-fast speed. He looked like the star he thought himself to be! In the second round, he hit 'Spider' with a pulverising right cross which put him down for a count of five. Despite being friends, Ray wanted to add Valentine to his list of knockout victims and so became more wayward in his quest to find it. The sprightly 'Spider' managed to keep out of trouble and last the distance to be able to see his friend crowned as champion. Ray was overwhelmed and later described this as a moment he would always remember. Boxing in the Garden was the highlight of Sugar Ray's amateur career up to this point.

In the Open Eastern Regional Finals a crowd of 9,335 gathered in the Garden to watch action taking place in two rings, which were used for this five-hour marathon championship tournament with 69 contests taking place. Robinson was very impressive in his first two bouts. He used vicious uppercuts to stop Armann Dascenza in one round and fought later the same evening, where he hit Edward Dowell at will but his opponent's durability allowed him to last the distance. He next met Bob Fisher and blasted him out in a round before beating Mario Centi on points. In the Open Inter-City finals, held in Chicago Stadium, a crowd of over 20,000 saw Robinson outpoint

Tony Ancona. After this victory, he walked around Harlem as if he had won the world title. Robinson loved the growing attention and being described as "the jewel in the crown of amateur boxing".

On the 20th April 1940, the Salem Crescent staged an amateur tournament at the Golden Gate. George Gainford was filling all one side of the bill with his own boxers. The newspapers reported: "Featured on the tournament will be the fistic marvel Ray Robinson."

Also on the bill was one of Ray's gym mates, a young heavyweight named Eddie 'Buddy' Moore. Buddy was, according to the experts of the amateur boxing circuit, a certainty to emulate the great Joe Louis and become heavyweight champion of the world. Moore was a light-skinned black boxer who stood at an imposing 6ft 1inch; he looked physically impressive and could box and carried a dig in either hand. He had also been successful in the Golden Gloves. George Gainford, however, was reluctant to push him too far as he knew that he possessed a serious weakness - he couldn't take a punch! He didn't make this public though and Moore gained all the attention and newspaper coverage on this tournament, but whereas Robinson defeated Jimmy Winters, Moore was surprisingly knocked out by a fighter named Cyclone Williams.

Moore was sponsored by a millionaire businessman named Curt Horrmann, who was reputed to have been a top-class athlete at Cornell and was now vice-president of the R.H Brewing Company and an avid sports fan with a particular interest in boxing. He appeared to be in and out of the Salem Crescent gym every day and followed the young boxers wherever they fought. He seemed to spend a great deal of time with Buddy Moore because he was a heavyweight. Horrmann helped the Salem Crescent boxers by buying them equipment and giving them a few dollars after they fought. It had been arranged, however, that he would eventually become Moore's manager when the young heavyweight colt turned professional. Horrmann knew that it was only in the heavyweight division that a young black heavyweight had any hope of earning top money and prestige.

The former professional fighter and actor, Canada Lee, helped out in the Salem Crescent gym and he took a special interest in both Robinson and Moore. Lee wanted the two youngsters to go professional with a manager named Eddie Mead, who managed the great triple champion, Henry Armstrong. Lee urged them to sign a contract with Mr Mead, but Robinson was shocked and refused point blank, despite a cash inducement. Moore, however, accepted the cash and signed with Mead. Buddy started out his pro career with five straight knockouts in his first five bouts and the publicity machine was in over-drive. Everyone in boxing in the New York area was touting him for honours and some reckoned that within two years he would be fighting Joe Louis!

Eddie Mead was happy with his heavyweight signing but got a little carried away with Moore's initial success in the ring; he matched Moore with two fighters who were known as big punchers, Johnny Shkor and Al Hart, who blasted him out in three rounds and two rounds respectively. Although Buddy Moore carried on boxing after these setbacks, he was finished as a potential future champion and in his final five bouts he was knocked out four times, the final time against Charley Norkus in October 1949. He sadly drifted out of boxing.

Although George Gainford coached Robinson from the start, Robinson said in his book, *The Sugar Ray Robinson Story*, that he often trained at Grupps gym, which was situated on 116th Street off Eighth Avenue in New York. "It was here that I became a student of the Noble Art! It was also here that I learned all about the science of boxing. I was taught by the former fighters about balance, the most important aspect of a boxer. Where to hit my opponents in the most vulnerable places, like the temple and his heart," he said.

He also spoke glowingly about famous old-time fighters like Harry Wills, the heavyweight whom it was claimed Jack Dempsey refused to fight because he was so good, and Kid Norfolk, Panama Joe Gans and Solider Jones.

The young Robinson made a positive impact on the old professionals. They liked his physique; he was tall at just under 6ft, and had long thin arms. The way he punched and the way he turned his hips and shoulders into the punch allied with great footwork also impressed them. They enjoyed watching his careful and considered approach to everything he did and he listened to their advice about how to use a mirror for shadow boxing and checking his footwork along with the importance of where his hands should be before he punched.

'Old Soldier' Jones emphasized to him about what a great weapon the left jab was and how to cultivate it. Boxing historians would latterly recall how Jones' advice paid off with interest. "That left hand of Sugar Ray's was harder than most fighters' Sunday punches," said Tommy Bell, the fighter Robinson fought for the world welterweight title in 1946.

Robinson had great faith in Jones and had him in his corner when he turned professional. Jones told him that if he could hit his opponents with the left jab, then he could catch him with the follow through right cross. "The left jab is your offensive side, and your right cross is your defensive," Solider preached to him regularly.

Robinson was also befriended by the former Golden Gloves champion, Cedric Harvey. Harvey was well-respected in Harlem and considered a hero to the neighbourhood youngsters. Robinson praised the former Golden Gloves champion for teaching him how to cut the ring on his opponent, walk his opponent the way he wanted them to go, not where they chose. "If your opponent moves around to his right, you circle the opposite way," Harvey told him.

All these wonderful craftsmen, who were steeped in knowledge of boxing, helped mould him into the phenomenon he was beginning to become.

However, there was a fly in the ointment before 1939 petered out and the 1940s swept in. Ray Robinson was a married man. In the 1930s the Big Band sound was all the rage for youngsters. The favourite 'hit' song was 'Margie'. For quite some time Ray had been besotted by a beautiful looking black girl who lived in an apartment facing his. Her name was Marjorie 'Margie' Joseph. Both his sisters were married and there was only him and his mother in their apartment and Leila was out all day working

One night Ray and some friends attended a dance at a clubhouse on Lenox Avenue. The place was packed solid and the music was brilliant. The young men and women were on the dance floor and eager to display their different dance routines, like the Lindy Hop which was a jitterbug. For weeks Robinson had been sneaking looks at this beautiful young black girl with lovely long legs from the apartmet opposite. Ray would watch her leave for school and he became infatuated with her.

As it happened Marjorie was at the dance. During a break at the dance he plucked up the courage and asked her to dance. She smilingly agreed and the couple took the floor and started jitterbugging, much to the delight of the other dancers who immediately started clapping in rhythm to the music. Robinson was in his element with the attention he and Marjorie were receiving and he started various dance routines and the whoops and hollering from the audience got louder and louder. He was really showing off now and started throwing Marjorie through his legs and over his shoulder. After the dance he walked her home and they became inseparable.

Marjorie's parents worked full time, like Mrs Smith, so the couple spent afternoons together in Marjorie's parent's apartment. After several weeks of courting, going to the cinema, dancing at the Savoy and various other dancing venues, and using George Gainford's car for quiet drives, Marjorie suddenly told Ray she was pregnant. Both started crying. They didn't know what to say or do. When he got home he told his sister Marie what Marjorie had told him. Marie told him they would have to tell their mother. Upon hearing the news Mrs Smith was mortified and deeply upset but decided she and her son must face Marjorie's parents. After a great deal of heated discussion Mrs Smith said that her son would have to marry Marjorie (who was still at school). At this, Mr Joseph sprung to his feet and shouted, "No, no, never!"

Leila, although shaken and upset, explained that the child had to have a name. Illegitimacy was frowned upon in this period. The outcome was that in order to give Marjorie and the baby some respectability and legality, and a name, the couple would have to marry but would never live together. The young couple had no say in the matter. A few days later both families went to City Hall to obtain a marriage license and underwent a quiet ceremony performed in a little church. Afterwards both families went their separate ways. A short while later Marjorie and her family moved to another part of Harlem. On the 25th September 1939 baby Ronald was born. Shortly afterwards the marriage was annulled.

3.

The Beginning of a 25-Year Adventure

VARIOUS MANAGERS, promoters, matchmakers, gangsters and other undesirables converged on New York City for the 1940 Golden Gloves Tournament, held in Madison Square Garden.

Robinson's club, the Salem Crescent, entered 50 boxers and the professional scouts hovered around them, looking to sign up the young ambitious boxers on view in these prestigious championships. All of them, however, had their eyes fixed on one particular youngster, boxing at lightweight, who was considered to be the prize catch, Sugar Ray Robinson.

What most of these suitors were unaware of was that plans for Sugar Ray's professional career had already been drawn up long before this tournament.

Ray's tournament had begun in January when he flattened Woodrow Tolliver in two before receiving a bye. After this, Michael Solicito was stopped in the second, closely followed by William Wolfe, who went out in the same round. Bellesandro Carubia was stopped by TKO in the third round in the New York Coliseum, with a crowd of 5,700 watching. The New York Times referred to him the following day as "a miniature Joe Louis". He then returned back to his favourite venue, Madison Square Garden, where Andrew Nonella was dispatched in the opening round. In this bout, Robinson displayed vicious punching combinations and hit Nonella with a right cross, which dropped him like a sack of coal. On this evening, Sugar helped his club to win the keenly contested club prize.

In the open Eastern Regional section, he took part in a further four bouts. He looked impressive beating Joe Vidulich in the first round and following it up with another opening round stoppage of Howard Hettrich. Steve Kukol, from Syracuse, did better and lasted the distance but lost on points. He then needed only one minute and forty-one seconds to dispose of Jimmy Butler.

In the Open Inter-City section, staged once again in Madison Square Garden with 18,388 spectators present, he stopped Tony Ancona in the third round. This was a sign of Ray's progress as Ancona had lasted the distance with him the previous year. On this occasion however, Robinson boxed like a seasoned veteran and made mincemeat of Ancona. This was after he had also visited the canvas after a brutal body shot had caught him by surprise. He then gained a points decision over Frank 'Smokey' Robinson before demolishing Joseph Smalls in a single round. In his final contest, he beat a white lightweight from Savannah in Georgia. After this contest, Robinson finally turned professional with Curt Hormann as his manager.

Sugar Ray would have loved to have gone to an Olympic Games but because of World War Two, the games were scrapped. In 89 registered amateur bouts, he won them all with 69 inside the distance and 44 of them in the first round. In a total of 125 registered and unregistered contests, he also emerged with a 100% record.

Gainford was approached by lots of managers, including Mike Jacobs, who all enquired about signing Robinson. Gainford envisaged a deal along the same lines as Joe Louis had accepted when he turned professional. As well as having the power to veto all future opponents, according to Robinson, Gainford agreed that Horrmann would be entitled to 33% as the official manager while he would receive a mere 10% as trainer.

It was for Horrmann's financial clout that Gainford included the businessman. He had seen that all of the elite fighters had the backing of moneyed people. They needed them in order to fund and organise training camps, sparring partners and hotel bills. "He could produce a hundred-dollar bill from his pocket faster than any other man I knew," Gainford told the young fighter. Horrmann also had the right connections with the people who counted in boxing; he personally knew the Madison Square Garden officials.

Because of Robinson's burgeoning reputation from his Golden Gloves victories, the news of his switch to the paid ranks received reams of newspaper publicity. Esteemed journalists like Walter Winchell, Danton Walker, Ed Sullivan and Earl Wilson gave mention of the talents of the young Robinson.

He was booked to take part in a four round professional debut at Madison Square Garden on the 4th October 1940. The main event featured one of Robinson's schoolboy idols, Henry Armstrong, who was defending his welterweight crown against the tough, rough, dangerous Fritzie Zivic.

Robinson began his journey that would allow him, as a double Golden Gloves champion, to join a select band of champions who turned professional and went on to win world honours. The great Barney Ross became the first and others included Joe Louis, Gus Lesnevich, Tony Zale and Harold Dade to name a few.

Robinson's first opponent was Joe Echeverria. Little is known of Echevarria, but he was a tough Puerto Rican who had settled in New York and had his first pro' fight in September 1939 before fighting a further 22 times before he faced Sugar Ray. He had won only twice with four draws and 15 losses. His opponents had included world-rated fighters like Lulu Costantino and Terry Young and he was generally perceived as a tough fighter who had never been stopped.

When Robinson entered the dressing room he began to look around for Echevarria. "This is the pros now," reminded Gainford. "This isn't like the amateurs where all the fighters get changed together."

Sugar Ray was wearing what would become his ring attire throughout his career, the white satin trunks, white cotton sports socks and black boxing boots. When he received the call to action he started jigging his shoulders and throwing punches into the air as Gainford and Wiley followed him dutifully. All the way down the aisles to the ring he was dancing on the balls of his feet. This was a ritual which he would adhere to in every fight; he claimed that it helped him relax and get the rhythm into his body.

He flattened Echeverria in two rounds and he proved himself to be an extremely astute operator. "My rhythm sets the pace of my fights," said Robinson afterwards, "If it does, then I can penetrate my opponent's rhythm. I can then make him fight my fight, and that's what boxing is all about."

Curt Horrmann gave the youngster the full $150 purse and paid Gainford out of his own pocket. Instead of then going out on the town to celebrate his first professional victory, he showered and changed and joined his mother and sisters to watch Armstrong fight Zivic.

Robinson wanted to study the styles and moves of the world class fighters and he watched Armstrong suffer a bad beating at the hands of Zivic, who was notorious for his rough and fouling tactics. He worked poor Armstrong over good and proper during the full 15 rounds and Ray cried as he watched his idol being demolished. In the taxi on the way home Sugar told his mother that he wanted to fight Fritzie Zivic. His mother was shocked and told him he mustn't even dream of fighting that man. But his sister Marie told him she thought he could beat Zivic any time. Mrs Smith lost her temper and yelled at Marie, "Don't you dare encourage Junior to fight Zivic. You're brother is only a boy."

In later years Robinson claimed that he had sneaked into Armstrong's dressing room and when Henry walked in after the fight, he flopped on the table and Robinson walked over to him and whispered, "Don't you worry none, champ, I'll get that guy for you. I'll really get him." Armstrong smiled and looked at the tall skinny kid. He thought the kid was brash but thanked him as he made his way outside.

One of the ringsiders at Sugar Ray's first pro contest was Nathaniel S. Fleischer, known simply as Nat. He had founded 'The Ring' magazine in 1922, which became known as 'the bible of boxing'. He continued to publish it until his death in 1972.

In 1883, when only 12 years old, Fleischer had seen his first professional fight when 'Terrible' Terry McGovern annihilated the British champion, Pedlar Palmer, to win the vacant world bantamweight title in one round. By 1904, Nat had become a correspondent for the Morning and Sunday World and New York Press. Fleischer would go on to sit ringside at the majority of Sugar Ray's fights. Although he was a great admirer of the Harlem star, he would occasionally be critical of him but in this first pro' encounter, he recorded that he thought Ray had handled himself well.

Four days later, the Robinson team travelled down to Savannah, Georgia to fight their toughest black fighter, Silent Stafford. Seven moths beforehand, Stafford had lost a very unpopular points decision to Beau Jack, who would eventually become the world lightweight champion. Ray won the bout by the second round when he connected with a terrific left hook to the jaw and dropped Stafford before the referee, Joe Magee, called a halt.

Twelve days later, he fought Mitsos Grispos in New York and beat him on points over six rounds. The watching boxing writers all had expressed an interest in seeing whether he could take a punch on the chin and in the 5th round they received an answer. The savage-punching Grispos caught him flush and he went down heavily. He took his time to rise but did so and boxed his way to victory. His courage was duly noted.

Less than three weeks later, in Philadelphia, he was matched with Baltimore's Bobby Woods, whom he flattened inside the first round. The Philadelphia fans enjoyed Robinson's style and within the month, he returned there to stop Norment Quarles in four pulsating rounds.

Quarles originated from North Carolina and was five years older than Robinson. He was a vastly more experienced campaigner, who had recorded over 100 fights, including matches against world champions Bob Montgomery, Chalky Wright and Lou Ambers. Despite this advantage of experience, he was no match for the rampant fistic star and the referee, Leo Houck, counted him out.

The pace of Robinson's education was relentless. Four days later, he was back in Madison Square Garden to meet Brooklyn's experienced Oliver White, who had a record of 34 wins, 10 losses and 6 draws. Robinson had him on the canvas three times in the third round before the referee showed mercy and stopped the fight.

Robinson's reputation was growing and the newspapers started to feature him prominently. They praised his speed, skill and his deadly anticipation, which seemed to give him a clear advantage over most fighters. They drooled over the fact that he was light on his feet and quick in his thinking. In short, they highlighted that Robinson was a joy to watch and a real crowd-pleaser who was starting to create a ripple of excitement amongst the cynical and hard-bitten press pack.

This all fuelled his own self confidence and Gainford, whom Robinson started to call 'The Emperor', and Harry Wiley, a small, rotund and fleshy-faced man were in the gym every day with him working on his development. At times they would have their own bust-ups and all of the boxers would enjoy their antics, made more amusing by their physical contrasts as Gainford was a huge mountain of a man whilst Wiley was small and stocky; they were like chalk and cheese.

At the same time, Horrmann was developing his connections with a wily old promoter named Herman 'Muggsy' Taylor, who was based in Philadelphia. This connection ensured that Ray would fight regularly on Taylor's promotions in places like Philadelphia, Brooklyn, Detroit, Atlantic City and Washington. He knocked out 17 of his first 20 opponents and his earning power was subsequently rising too.

In his first two fights for Taylor, he fought Bobby Woods and Norment Quarles. Most notably was his match up with Quarles, from North Carolina, who was rated at number six in the lightweight division by The Ring magazine's 1938 ratings; he had fought 102 times before meeting Robinson. Among the opponents he had faced were Bob Montgomery, whom he held to a draw, Chalky Wright and Lou Ambers. This experience was not enough to prevent him being stopped by the Harlem youngster in four brutal rounds, when referee Leo Houck stepped in to save him from a certain knockout.

After these two victories he became a big favourite on many of Taylor's promotions. Taylor was a real 'hands-on' promoter and had learnt about the trade by doing almost every job that a non-combatant needed to do in order to stage boxing promotions, starting with his first ever job of sweeping the floors of a his local Philadelphia arena. During his 79 years involvement in the sport, he was involved with Jack Dempsey, Billy Conn, Willie Pep, Ike Williams, Harry Grebb, Sam Langford, Joe Frazier and Mickey Walker to name a few. Robinson came to trust the vastly experienced promoter. He ended 1940 by facing Oliver White from Brooklyn on the undercard of Ken Overlin's meeting Steve Belloise for the world middleweight title. In a the third of a scheduled four rounder, Sugar Ray twice decked his foe for counts of nine, and when White was dropped for the third time the fight ended. Newspapers described him as "a powder keg of energy and finesse, instantly ignited by a hurricane force of commitment once the opportunity presented itself".

4.

Beating the Clutcher

ON THE 4TH January, 1941, Robinson heralded the New Year by battering Los Angeles' Henry LaBarba within 40 seconds of the first round. Nine days later he was matched with Frankie Wallace in Philadelphia. Wallace, whose real name was Frankie Angelora, was born in Clasacolanda, Compobasso, in Italy, before settling in America. He was a teak-tough, experienced veteran who had met illustrious opponents such as Tony Canzoneri, Pete Scalzo, Lou Ambers, Tippy Larkin, England's Jackie 'Kid' Berg and Freddie Miller. Coming into his fight he had fought 96 times and was regarded by boxing insiders as representing a step up in class for Robinson. He bridged it with ease as Matt Adgie, the referee, witnessed enough of the slaughter to halt the fight within two minutes and ten seconds of the opening bell.

Three weeks later he was active once again on the undercard of the Joe Louis confrontation with Red Burman heavyweight title clash in Madison Square Garden. His opponent was the 78-fight veteran, George Zengaras.

In preparation for the contest, Robinson trained with his friend Louis in the champion's training camp at Greenwood Lake, bordering New York and New Jersey. The beautiful, idyllic setting amongst pine trees and long, winding roads was ideally suited for roadwork. When he arrived, Louis's trainer, Jack Blackburn, outlined the rules and regulations of the camp. Blackburn, a former fighter who cut a tall, imposing figure and possessed a long, jagged scar along his left cheek and had deep, piercing eyes, explained that he would not tolerate any fooling about from the young prospect.

One day, a huge crowd had assembled to watch Louis sparring. Robinson was on the speed ball. He felt neglected and decided to try and attract the crowd's attention and so put on an act of impressive, fast punching which caused many of the crowd to turn and pay attention to him. Later that same evening, Blackburn pulled Sugar to one side. "Don't you ever do that again," he said, in no uncertain terms, "you are here to get ready for your fight. You have got to be ready for the night of your fight, not peaking before or after it. Do you understand?" Robinson nodded his head; he understood. There was no way he was going to argue with Mr Blackburn. He brought his preparations to a perfect end by winning a clear six round points verdict over Zengaras.

Shortly after this match up, he maintained his busy schedule with a first round stoppage over Benny Cartagena in the Ridgewood Grove, Brooklyn, and a six round points victory over the 5ft 8 Detroit fighter Bobby McIntire in Madison Square Garden before returning to his hometown of Detroit. The local press responded kindly and heralded him as the local boy making good in New York. He didn't disappoint ringside spectator Joe Louis and the partisan ringside crowd by stopping Gene Spencer in five. Spencer, a Chicago battler, was experienced but had no answer to the quick-fisted bombardment Robinson hit him with.

Afterwards he met his father again, who was keen to take him around his old neighbourhood and reacquaint him with old friends and neighbours. When he got back home to Harlem, this news, along with the knowledge that he had given his father money, left his mother upset and angry. She spent a long evening recounting the occasions when she and the three children had been left with nothing by their errant father. She counselled him not to repeat it.

The pace of his education inside the ring continued at a frenetic rate. He had two fights against Jimmy Tygh in Philadelphia. Tygh was a local boy and a big favourite with the hometown fans because he fought like a wounded tiger. He was a sturdy 5ft 7 and, like Robinson, was a lightweight. Jimmy's record of 46 fights with 31 wins, 10 defeats and five draws was regarded as representing another stern test. In their first contest, Jimmy gave a good account of himself and caused his fans to roar themselves hoarse for him before being counted out in the eighth round. Calls for a second meeting were such that it was arranged for five weeks later. This time, Robinson demonstrated his capacity for learning and demolished him in the first round by using extraordinary speed of hand and foot, aligned with perfect timing and control and thundering combinations. Tygh, sickened from the two Robinson beatings, only had a further seven bouts in his career.

There was increasing talk in the newspapers about Ray being matched against the world lightweight champion, Lew Jenkins. Gainford, however, moved quickly to dispel this thought from his starry-eyed charge, reminding him that he had only fought 14 times as a professional. He reassured him that his time would come. First, however, he had to deal with Charley Burns from Johnstown in Pa, his next opponent in a fight staged in the Waltz Dream Arena in Atlantic City. A few weeks previous to meeting Sugar Ray, Burns had been knocked out in a single round by Mike Kaplan and must have been suffering from deja-vu as he suffered the same fate again as Sugar Ray ripped him apart before knocking him out. This loss persuaded Burns to retire immediately.

Joe Ghnouly was next to face Robinson in the Vline Arena in Washington. Joe had had 110 bouts and had been stopped by Henry Armstrong when challenging for Armstrong's world welterweight title fifteen months earlier.

Robinson battered him to a pulp in three one-sided rounds. A few days later, he followed up his win with by stopping Brooklyn's Vic Troise in the opening round by smashing him to the canvas with a whiplash left hook at the Ridgewood Grove Arena in Brooklyn. Referee Eddie Joseph showed mercy for this game but out-classed opponent.

The calls from the press to test the prospect grew louder, but Gainford insisted on a further three contests before he was prepared to test him against world class opposition. Nick Castiglione, Mike Evans and Pete Lello were the opponents and he cut through the three of them like a knife through butter. He demolished Castiglione in one minute and 21 seconds of the first round before chalking up his eighth consecutive stoppage victory in Philadelphia, by stopping Evans within 52 seconds of the second round at Shibe Park (know later as the Connie Mack Stadium) in Philadelphia. Evans kept backing away from Robinson's dynamite-laden fists in the opening round, but in the second Sugar Ray nailed his elusive foe with a wicked left hook that brought a sudden end to the bout. Evans fell on his back, got to one knee at nine, and then finally fell backwards again. Finally, he annihilated Lello from Gary, Indiana, but who fought out of Chicago, in a one-sided bout. Lello was an experienced campaigner. This fight was staged in the Polo Grounds in New York. Lello had fought for the world lightweight crown against Lew Jenkins a few months previously; he had previously stopped Jenkins in 1939. He had drawn with Sammy Angott and his pedigree was excellent. Robinson annihilated him, decking him three times before referee Arthur Donovan halted the bout.

21st July 1941 was the date earmarked as the litmus test of whether his first 20 victories were an indication of ensuing greatness. He was required to face the World National Boxing Association lightweight champion, Sammy Angott, widely regarded as one of the most experienced and cagiest fighters around, with 82 pro fights under his belt before facing the young Robinson. Angott, who stood a solid 5ft 8, was nicknamed 'The Clutch' because his boxing style occasionally resembled an octopus as his opponents felt like he was throwing punches with eight hands. He wasn't a respected 'big' puncher in the traditional sense, but one whose style threatened to make Robinson look bad. The venue was Shibe Park, the old baseball park in Philadelphia.

Angott was confident and told the press that he would put "this new wonder boy firmly in his place." He was not so confident, however, that he would risk his world title belt and insisted that the match was made a couple of pounds above the lightweight limit.

Angott - his real name was Samuel Engotti - was from Italian stock. He had his first professional bout in 1935 at the age of 20 and had beaten Davey Day five years later to win the vacant world title. In December 1941, he gained world-wide recognition by outpointing Lew Jenkins before becoming the first boxer to beat the sensational Willie Pep in 1943. Later that same year, he won the NABC world lightweight crown when he outpointed Luther 'Slugger' White. He would eventually lose this title in March 1944, when he was outpointed over 15 rounds to Juan Zurita. However, before meeting Robinson, he had fought 82 times, winning 64, drawing five and losing 13.

On the morning of the contest Robinson, with a couple of days growth of beard on his face, phoned his mother's supervisor at the laundry where she still worked and asked to speak to the owner. When he answered the phone Robinson asked if he would pass on the request for his mother to pray for him. The owner readily agreed before Robinson followed this by stating that "if I win tonight, she won't be coming back to work in your laundry again."

The growth of beard was a ritual he adhered to before he fought. Old Soldier Jones had told him that not shaving a few days before he fought toughened his skin. He also had another ritual which he observed on the morning of his fight, by having a light breakfast of perhaps toast with tea or coffee. Then of course the weigh-in, which in those days was usually performed on the afternoon of the contest. After that he would eat a steak and salad. In his dressing room he would discus his strategy with Gainford and other team members. He would then loosen up by stretching and shadow boxing. Then he would kneel and pray, he always prayed. He would then commence putting on his white woollen socks, protector, his Everlast white shorts and boxing boots, which had been laid out immaculately by Harry Wiley. Then he would receive his usual massage from George Gainford, and then Gainford would bandage and tape his fists. There would be total concentration from him; totally one hundred percent focus on the fight ahead.

When he entered the ring Robinson had to wait until the master of ceremonies had made the lengthy introductions. He was unaccustomed to this practice as his earlier fights had involved a quick introduction and the referee swiftly issuing the instructions before getting down to business. This unexpected wait interrupted his rhythm, and when the fight finally got underway Angott began by living up to his nickname and held and disrupted its flow. It took Sugar Ray the whole of the first round to fathom out the champion's unique style and to formulate his plan of action. He thought he had mastered it in the second round, when a whiplash right cross hit Angott flush on the jaw and put him down. The world champion looked out for the count but later recalled that the noise of the official timekeeper's hammer banging on the canvas had brought him to his senses. He scrambled to his feet before the referee was able to call a halt. This breakthrough allowed Robinson's belief to blossom and the respected champion took a unanimous beating on points.

The following day Sugar Ray picked up his share of the career best $6,000 purse and proudly walked into the laundry where his mother worked. He instructed her to put her coat on, get her bag and come home with him because he was officially retiring her from work. "Mama," he declared, "you won't have to work anywhere else ever again." He also promised that she would not have to worry about paying the rent on their new four-room apartment at 940 Saint Nicholas Avenue, which he rented for $60 a month. He treated his mother to brand new furniture and also rewarded himself with his first ever car, a blue Buick convertible.

His victory drew reams of press publicity, with most sportswriters now opining that he had elevated himself into the upper echelons of boxing. His good looks, charismatic personality and captivating smile also made him a favourite with women, which he was quick to exploit.

A few days after the fight with Angott, Robinson and his friends visited the Lindo Pool in Harlem. This was a popular meeting place, especially during the summer months, for most Harlem youngsters. Sat on a deckchair, relaxing after a swim, he saw Edna Mae Holly. He was immediately smitten and tried to attract her attention by talking loudly. She ignored his crude attempts and was stood near the pool when Robinson walked up behind her and pushed her into the pool before displaying an uncharacteristic reticence and disappearing. He later made enquiries and found out that she worked as a dancer at the Mimo Club, and so he became a regular visitor. He then got a friend to introduce him and he told her that he was the culprit who pushed her into the pool and from these shy beginnings a deep relationship was quickly formed.

Edna Mae was born in Miami, Florida and had attended the Bethune-Cookman College in Dayton Beach, Florida. Her great-grandfather was the Reverend James Theodore Holly, a minister who had become the first black man to be consecrated an Episcopal Bishop. Edna had learned to dance as a child and her parents had high hopes that she would pursue a career on the concert stage. Both of her parents died when Edna Mae was young and so she went to live with her guardian, an auntie named Blanche, in New York. Later, she pursued her dancing career in a number of the city's legendary nightclubs, including the famed Cotton Club, where she was renowned for dancing on the drums. In fact, when Francis Ford Coppolla was making his 1984 film based on the club, Edna was credited as the film's official historian.

Back in the world of boxing, political machinations were being played out. After his victory against Angott, Robinson should have been the automatic choice to box for the world lightweight championship. However, six months after his resounding defeat, Angott fought Lew Jenkins for the undisputed world lightweight crown and and won a points decision. Robinson was aggrieved and felt cheated that he had not being afforded the opportunity of fighting for his first world title. Thomas Myler, the biographer of Robinson, suggested that "there was little doubt about the existence of a conspiracy against Robinson for many years." Myler claims that the famed promoter Mike Jacobs had conspired to keep Robinson from fighting for the world welterweight championship. As the director of the Twentieth Century Sporting Club, he hosted a secret meeting of his organization and informed them that they "couldn't let Sugar Ray become world champion because he would stifle the welterweight division and would demolish all the contenders." He explained that "it's much more profitable for us to keep two or three guys fighting for the title, and drawing good gates" rather than having one man dominate the division. Robinson was unaware of the meeting but sensed that Jacobs was doing his best to shut him out and had trouble trusting him; he would refuse to ever sign an exclusive contract with him.

Within a month of beating Angott, Robinson returned to the ring where he was matched against Carl 'Red' Guggino, a hard-punching fighter from Florida, who possessed a murderous left hook which had dispatched several opponents. The fight was staged in the Queensbury Arena in Long Island City. Ray, buoyed by the Angott win, was patient and content to box his way through the first two rounds and evaluate his opponent before stopping him in the third. It was a flurry of lefts and rights which dropped Guggino for a count of nine before he resumed and had Robinson drive him into a neutral corner and drape him over the ropes in a sitting position, which prompted the referee, Arthur Donovan, to step in and stop it. The pace of his development was unrelenting and just two days later he was in the Atlantic City Convention Hall to fight Maurice Arnault. It was over within two minutes of the opening round. After these two victories the boxing officianados were starting to refer to Sugar Ray as 'Great'. And Ray savoured the word!

Because of his burgeoning reputation, Mike Jacobs offered Curt Horrmann a top of the bill fight for Robinson at Madison Square Garden. His opponent was fellow New Yorker, Maxie Shapiro. Up to this point in his career, Robinson had only fought on nine occasions in his home city of New York. 'Why?' Sports writers were asking. They found this very strange and mentioned it in their columns. They also mentioned the fact that because 'Uncle' Mike (as Jacobs was known) was Joe Louis's promoter and Louis and Sugar Ray were close friends, he would have first call on Robinson's services. This, however, was not the case. "Robinson was a sharp-witted guy," said Pete Hamill a brilliant journalist. "Most of Robinson's early fights were outside of New York because Sugar Ray was always arguing with Mike Jacobs. He insisted on being independent. He thought that as it was he who was taking the punches, he wanted the right money. He believed that at this stage of his career that he was special. And would not be dictated to by Jacobs, hence he drove a hard bargain."

Another prominent journalist was Jack Newfield. His opinion was: "If someone asked God to mould the perfect boxer, he would have chosen Sugar

Ray Robinson. This, after all, was a boxer intelligent enough to have become a successful businessman while still in his prime as a fighter. He often made outspoken comments about the money side of boxing, things that upset certain powerful people which didn't endear him to the hierarchy, and this was why he fought outside of New York."

Mike Jacobs and his Twentieth Century Sorting Club associates had been monitoring Ray's progress and eagerly signed the deal for Robinson to top their bill in the Garden. When Sugar Ray saw his name in bright red letters splashed across the yellow and black posters which were plastered all over the city, he was ecstatic. He would regularly take a detour past the Garden in his car just to see his picture and name on the billboards. The newspaper journalists were accustomed to interviewing fighters who were very shy, awkward or aggressive in their manner. Sugar Ray, however, was fluent and would happily talk on a number of subjects outside of boxing. His intelligence, good manners, soft voice and the respectful way in which he conducted himself, such as refusing to denigrate his opponents, was a welcome change.

The majority of reporters suggested that Maxie Shapiro would represent Robinson's sternest test to date and that topping the bill would reveal a lot about his temperament. Maxie was a clever fighter who, at one purple patch in his career, had wracked up 37 victories in a row. He was a contender for the world lightweight title and had never been knocked out during his five defeats.

When they faced each other in the centre of the ring, Robinson stood head and shoulders over the squat, round-shouldered 5ft 7 Shapiro and he used this to his advantage. The early action ebbed and flowed with Shapiro mixing it up and attempting to rough up the younger man, even staggering him with a booming overhand right cross. In the second, Robinson's response was brutal. He twice had him through the ropes for counts. In the third, he wasted little time and delivered a stunning right cross/left hook combination to floor Shapiro for a nine count; as he clambered unsteadily back to his feet, Robinson unleashed a dynamic two-fisted body attack to return back to the canvas for another count. Arthur Donovan instructed them to continue and Sugar continued firing a steady stream of body punches which rendered Shapiro helpless. What had been suggested as his toughest test proved little more than a brisk workout for the Harlem lad.

Shapiro later suggested that he should never have fought Sugar Ray. "It was no contest," he said. "He was too tall and fast, and a great puncher, a great boxer and he was too much for me. I had not checked his record. If I had, I would have told my manager that I didn't want him." He admitted that the lure of headlining a Madison Square Garden bill was his deciding factor. "The purse wasn't much, but it was an opportunity. I was told if I beat Robinson, I would fight for the world title. And every fighter wants to fight in the Garden."

Six days later he fought the undefeated 22-year old Marty Servo, in the Philadelphia Convention Arena. Could you imagine the outcry if present day fighters were expected to top two major tournaments less than a week apart? Firstly, the fighters would refuse and, secondly, it would not be allowed under current day regulations. Sugar Ray did it. Marty's real name was Mario Sevarino and he was related to the former world lightweight champion, Lou Ambers. He was managed by the astute Al 'The Vest' Weill and trained by Charley Goldman, who would later manage and train the world heavyweight king, Rocky Marciano. Marty had been an outstanding amateur boxer and won the 1937 Golden Gloves featherweight title. He had also won the Diamond Belt Championship. In 95 amateur bouts he had been successful 91 times, winning 63 inside the distance. His best professional victory was achieved in August 1939 when he defeated George Salamone. He wasn't considered as a knockout puncher but his relentlessly aggressive style thrilled the crowd.

After his impressive victory over Shapiro it was widely expected that the taller Robinson would flatten Servo, but he never even came close to stopping him. Sam Taub was doing the blow-by-blow radio commentary with Jack Frazier summarizing the action. Both men acknowledged Robinson's growing public following and commented that, "on the main floor the crowd are standing two-deep in the back aisles."

Promoter Herman Taylor was overjoyed at the turnout of fans. "This is a magnificent spectacle," he said with a beaming smile. "There isn't a vacant seat…and down there on the main floor they are standing two-deep in the back aisles."

The meeting was a fast-paced and relatively even confrontation where both fighters showed their respect by keeping it clean and avoiding any malicious or underhand tactics. Servo, from proud Italian stock, was unbeaten in 45 pro contests and proceeded to give Robinson problems by coming in low and fighting out of a crouch. Ray tried using uppercuts but his opponent countered this tactic by crossing his right hand underneath his chin and making the youngster work hard. It was in the interval preceding the eighth round when Frazier told his listeners that "Sugar Ray had fathomed Servo's style." Frazier was correct and spoke in glowing terms about his ability to move through the gears, but he still was unable to find a killer punch and travelled the full ten rounds to gain his hard-fought victory. At the conclusion of the bout the 10,000 spectators gave both fighters a noisy ovation, but when the decision of the judges was announced they loudly booed and jeered as Robinson was declared the winner.

Servo's career after this defeat took an interesting route. Eight months later, he was again beaten over ten rounds in a rematch with Robinson. After this second loss, he spent three years on combat duty with the Coast Guard before becoming the world welterweight champion when he fought and knocked out the holder Freddie Cochrane in 1946. He was subsequently battered to a second round defeat to the heavy-punching middleweight Rocky Graziano and suffered irreparable damage to his nose which forced him into retirement. He later made a comeback and was flattened in the first round. He immediately hung up his gloves but suffered ill health and died in 1969.

In Sugar Ray's next fight, he was mooted to be facing the world welterweight champion Freddie Cochrane over ten rounds in a non-title fight to be staged at Madison Square Garden on Halloween. Robinson returned to the venue where he had joined Joe Louis, in Greenwood Lake, New York. During the long evenings in camp, he was forever phoning and sweet-talking Edna Mae and could be heard serenading her and enjoying the feeling of falling in love. George Gainford was niggled and never missed an opportunity to remind him what they were in camp for. Despite this, he was impressed by his willingness to train diligently.

One afternoon after training Robinson was upstairs enjoying a nap when he was woken by the sound of raised voices. He could hear George Gainford and Curt Horrmann arguing. Horrmann had driven from New York to tell Gainford that Freddie Cochrane was unable to box due to an injury sustained in training. Gainford was disappointed and Horrmann attempted to pacify him by explaining quietly that, "I've been offered another fight. They've offered me Fritzie Zivic." Gainford shook his head and was adamant in his insistence that under no condition would he allow his charge to take the Zivic fight. When Ray heard his manager suggest that he could negotiate a purse of $10,000, he ran down the stairs, nearly falling head over heels. He pleaded with his trainer to agree to this change of opponent, and after a couple of hours of heated and fluctuating arguments, Gainford finally conceded. Just a year since he had had his first professional fight, he was due to avenge an old friend and keep a promise he had made. "I'll get revenge for what Zivic did to Henry Armstrong," he told Gainford.

During this period 1941 to 1945, Sugar Ray established a record of being ranked as the number one contender for the world welterweight championship for the longest time by the prestigious The Ring magazine. This was responsible for the phrase 'uncrowned champion' becoming part of boxing's lexicon.

5.

Sugar Ray vs.
The Croatian Comet

THE SPORTWRITERS claimed that the young Robinson would be taught a lesson when he faced oppoments of the calibre of Sammy Angott, Maxie Shapiro and Marty Servo to name but three. But in his fight with Fritzie Zivic they reconed he had taken on more than he could handle at this stage of his fledging career and he was in for a really tough lesson. Fritzie Zivic, known as 'The Croat Comet', was the youngest of five brothers who all boxed. His older brothers, Pete and Jack, had represented America in the 1920 Olympic Games before Fritzie commenced his professional career in 1931. He took the world welterweight title from Henry Armstrong (on the night Sugar Ray made his pro debut) and gave him a return where he stopped him in 12 brutal rounds. He had lost his world title to Freddie Cochrane on a questionable decision and he was frustrated by Cochrane's insistence on ignoring him and choosing to box non-title fights instead. Zivic was still rated as the number one contender whilst Robinson was at number six. Zivic believed that the best way to get Cochrane back in the ring with him for the title was to hammer Robinson and force the world champion to grant him a return, and so he pasted photographs of Sugar Ray on the walls of his gym and laughed at the prospect of inflicting damage on his handsome features. While speaking to Mike Jacobs he suddenly shouted: "You're making a big mistake in matching me with this kid. Bring him on; I'll ruin him." He told the press that "He couldn't wait to bust 'this pretty kid' up."

In the dressing-room beforehand, Gainford was uncharacteristically nervous, in contrast to Sugar Ray who was ice-cool. This was a fight he cherished Over 23,266 excited fans packed inside the Garden, which was only 40 less than the previous record attendance and included the Robinson clan, who sat nervously alongside Edna Mae. The bookmakers favoured Zivic, who had a six pound advantage, at 8-5 and most pundits believed that that Sugar Ray's advantage would be to remain at long range because once Zivic got inside he had the ability to pulverize him with his body punches.

The tension and expectancy of a big occasion could be felt all around the Garden. The atmosphere was electric, red hot, reminiscent of a world championship match. As soon as the bell sounded Zivic moved quickly from his corner, pursuing Robinson and catching him with solid walloping shots to his lean body. Gainford shook his head and cringed. Ray, however, shook off the effects, got up on his toes and his masterful dancing feet began working overtime. Zivic tried every trick which he had acquired during his long career but was shocked to find Robinson prepared to give it back; Zivic tried counter-punching, Robinson did the same; he attempted a head butt and got one back; when they fought inside Zivic would pull Ray's head down and attempt to thumb him in either eye, Robinson copied him. This was Sugar Ray Robinson at his scientific best. The pace he set from the first bell was furious and the older man was blowing and looking exhausted but never indicating he would shrink from his task. Every round had been exciting and nail-biting. This lived up to expectations and was a truly memorable contest. The experts had been proven wrong! The judges, Bob Cunningham and Bill Healey, both joined referee Arthur Susskind in voting Robinson as the unanimous winner over ten enthralling rounds. Nat Fleischer, editor of The Ring magazine, commented that Robinson displayed "confidence and was never perplexed or feared by the roughhouse tactics of his vastly more experienced opponent. He proved that he was far from being a 'flash in the pan' but possesses every asset of a great champion."

Promoter Mike Jacobs was dancing with delight at the turnout of fans and said a return bout was called for. Zivic showed dignity in defeat and sat in his dressing room, bruised and battered, but offered praise for his conqueror, suggesting that "he's a great young fighter." He echoed Jacobs in suggesting that he would have won "if the fight had been over 15 rounds. I would love to fight him again." He was of the opinion that Robinson would defeat Freddie Cochrane quite easily if they ever fought each other. Robinson said that he wanted to fight for the world title but felt confident enough to voice his frustration that he was being held back and pointedly blamed Cochrane's management and Mike Jacobs as being responsible.

****

After the frenetic pace of his ring education, there was now a two month rest for Sugar Ray before he was due to fight again. He spent all of his spare time with Edna Mae. They made an unlikely pair of lovebirds; the graceful dancer who possessed a College education and her flashy pugilistic partner. She reflected that "he was just so different from anything I'd ever known or experienced." They would go dancing in the city's night clubs and the besotted Ray would shower Edna with expensive gifts such as jewellery and mink coats. He loved to hear of her family background, which boasted of doctors and lawyers and also contained a distant family link to the film star Sidney Poitier.

Her Aunt Blanche, who had become her guardian after the death of her mother through TB when Edna Mae was only three years old, shared Leila Robinson's dissatisfaction with the relationship because both women believed that their children could better themselves by courting someone more professional than a mere prize fighter and nightclub dancer.

During this period, contracts were signed for the rematch with Zivic on 16th January. It was again staged on a Mike Jacobs promotion at Madison Square Garden and it quickly attracted plenty of public interest, guaranteeing 16,000 fans would attend. Jacobs was rubbing his hands with glee and he shared his views that Ray was "one of the special ones of the ring who crowds would pay dearly to watch in action."

However, before the fight took place Herman Taylor announced he had brought an injunction to halt the Robinson v Zivic bout on the grounds that Sugar Ray must first fulfil his contractual duties to meet Marty Servo in Philadelphia. Taylor claimed that Robinson had agreed to box Servo on his promotion on 10th November 1941. "The fight was postponed twice before Robinson then repudiated the agreement and signed with Mike Jacobs for the Zivic fight," he told the press. He stated that he was determined Robinson would honour his contract and box in Philadelphia. "Once Robinson faces Servo, he is then free to fight anywhere he pleases. But he must first fight here." The Pennsylvania State Boxing Commission followed up by barring Sugar Ray from boxing in their State until he fulfilled his contract obligations.

In the two months since they last fought, amazingly Zivic had crammed in a further three bouts, winning two and drawing the other one. The draw was with a highly regarded young Detroit welterweight named Young Kid McCoy, whose real name was Adam Pianga. Mike Jacobs had staged this fight in Madison Square Garden and rumours abounded that the promoter was hoping McCoy would emerge victorious so he could match the blond-haired McCoy with Robinson for Freddie Cochrane's world title. However, this conjecture was to prove futile as a small crowd of 9,371 watched a fast, exciting fight judged as a draw, despite most newspapers having McCoy as the winner. After this battle Zivic outlined his determination to avenge his loss to Robinson. He successfully lobbied to get his wish granted that the fight would be two rounds longer than their first; a 12 rounder. He also suggested that Robinson would try and withdraw from the fight, sensing the beating he would take.

If this was true Robinson didn't betray his emotions and show any signs of tension or worry in the fight. He was far more aggressive in his attitude and moved sprightly around the ring, employing his trusty left jab to good effect. Zivic was confident because he believed the extra two rounds would help him more than it would the younger Robinson. Quietly though, Sugar Ray had no intension of having to travel 12 rounds. As the rounds flew by, both fighters were hitting with precision and power.

Despite his pre-fight boast, Zivic had been comprehensively battered throughout the eight previous rounds and Robinson was connecting with volumes of combination punches which brought sustained applause from the fans who appreciated such science. Fritzie managed to hurt Ray with a ferocious body punch which saw Robinson's gumshield fly out of his mouth, but the youngster refused to show he had been hurt and fought back like a fury and surprised his vastly more experienced foe. Within seconds of taking the Pittsburgher's tremendous solar plexus punch, Robinson unleashed an explosive right hand which almost separated the tough Pittsburgh fighter's head from his neck as it landed on his jaw and sent the former world champion face first to the canvas in his own corner. He managed to rally and got back onto his shaky feet before referee Arthur Donovan's count reached nine after resting on one knee through half the count and keeping his face covered in resin powder. Donovan wiped the resin from his face and allowed the contest to continue.

As he stood erect, Zivic was faced with a terrifying tornado as Robinson went wild in his eagerness to flatten his opponent and so missed his opportunity of finishing the fight. Gainford managed to calm him down in between rounds. And so in the tenth round, there was no respite for one of boxing's genuine hard, brutal fighters. Robinson showed true greatness. He smashed home another fearful right cross, which found Fritzie's ample jaw…Crack! The impact of Ray's leather glove exploding could be heard around the ring. It had the press corps wincing and screwing up their faces with the thought of such power. Referee Donovan didn't bother with a count, it was unnecessary; he wisely stepped forward and rescued the courageous fighter and helped Zivic back to the safety of his own corner. Amazingly, Luke Carney, Zivic's manager, attempted a ludicrous protest that the fight should not have been stopped. This was an outrageous and futile protest. He was criticising a compassionate referee who saved his man from perhaps fatal damage.

James P. Dawson, writing in The New York Times, suggested that "Ray Robinson, Harlem's spectacular contender for the world welterweight title, wrote the most brilliant chapter in a sparkling career when he knocked out Fritzie Zivic in the tenth round. At the same time, Robinson brought an end to one of the most amazing ring careers a boxer as ever known. In subjecting the veteran to the worst drubbing he has ever suffered, Robinson gained the distinction of stopping Zivic for only the second time in his ten-year career encompassing 150 fights." He continued: "The Harlem youngster was good as a lightweight, but was never better than last night. In crushing Zivic, Robinson beat one of the strongest, craftiest, gamest fighters in the business."

This second victory over Zivic made Sugar Ray an even bigger attraction than ever. Gainford didn't inform him, but soon afterwards during a training session, three notorious Broadway gangsters visited his training camp and approached the veteran trainer and offered to pay him $25,000 if they were 'cut in to Robinson's contract'. The big trainer stood his ground and politely explained it was just not possible. Undeterred, they doubled their offer to $50,000. Gainford explained that Robinson wanted no part of criminal activities and his sincere manner seemed to be appreciated by them and they went away and never returned. It was an important moment in establishing Robinson's career-long reputation as someone who could not be bought.

After the Zivic fight there was another celebration party in the Hotel Theresa. Ray saw this as an opportunity to further cement his affections for Edna Mae and to ease the friction with his mother, he deliberately sat Edna Mae next to her and his two sisters and also formerly introduced his new girlfriend to all his friends and to George Gainford and Curt Horrmann. From that night on they were with each other as often as possible.

One of Sugar Ray's proudest moments was around this time when he was able to purchase his first house, a ten-bedroomed, two garage property for his mother based on 238th Street in the West Bronx. It cost him $8500 and he spent an additional $3000 on alterations. When his mother saw it she was overjoyed and wept tears of joy. She told everyone she met how proud she was of her son and how much she was pleased with the house. Within weeks, she had the house to her own immaculate tastes, including twenty-three photographs of Ray placed all over the house. Ray enjoyed recalling the occasions when they had all lived in West 114th Street in Harlem and had been dispossessed because his mother did not have the requisite $28 monthly rent. His mother was crying uncontrollably and he told his mother that if she could afford to pay for him to take drumming lessons, he would make a great deal of money and he would buy her a house of her own. He also recalled the time when he had just turned professional and he bought his mother the first new furniture she ever had. Sugar, George Gainford and his sister Marie went to a store and bought two bedroom sets, a parlour set and a kitchen set. None of them uttered a word to the matriarch about the purchase and so when she opened the door, when she set eyes on the new furniture, she broke down and cried.

The Sugar Ray roadshow continued as he faced Montreal's Maxie Berger at Madison Square Garden again. At one time, Maxie was the World Junior welterweight champion and Canadian lightweight champion before he moved to the Bronx to enhance his fighting career. He was a sturdy, tough 5ft 8 welterweight trained by the famous Whitey Bimstein. He had fought 98 times before facing Robinson over the scheduled 12 round course.

The 12,464 crowd had only just settled down for what they thought was going to be an interesting bout when early in the second round Sugar Ray opened up with rapid-fire two-handed punches complemented with a left hook that dropped Berger for six. When he rose he ran into a blizzard of unerringly accurate punches before Robinson finally unleashed a short left hook to the jaw which dropped his opponent onto all fours for a count of three. When he regained his feet, referee Frank Fullam clasped his hands around him and called a halt after one minute and 43 seconds of the session to the anguished protests of Berger's corner. Berger had never been stopped before and was visibly upset, but he was a well beaten fighter.

The newspapers speculated that Robinson was scheduled to have fought Freddie 'Red' Cochrane for his world title but the champion could not obtain the necessary leave from his duties in the navy training base in Newport, Rhode Island. Those members of the press who were present were of the considered opinion that even if it had been Cochrane in the ring instead of Berger the outcome would have been the same. A donation from the tournament was made to the National Foundation for Infantile Paralysis.

A month later, Robinson appeared at the Garden again when he fought Norman Rubio from Albany, New York. For the first six rounds Rubio gave a good account of himself and the 11,274 spectators gave him plenty of encouragement. But suddenly everything changed dramatically in the seventh, when Ray connected with a blinding two-handed attack which put Rubio down. He clambered to his feet just as the bell ended the round. During the rest period, the referee Arthur Donovan visited Rubio's corner and stopped the fight. There was a misunderstanding as to the ending of the fight which was incorrectly included on the record books. Donovan stated that he stopped it in the seventh but the technical ending of the fight was classed as coming in the eighth round. Bill Brown from the Athletic Commission argued, "How can you call it a seventh round knockout when the man was on his feet when the round ended? The official ending was a technical knockout in the eighth round."

Less than a month later Sugar Ray was back in Detroit where he was opposed by Harvey Dubs. Over 8,500 fans paid to watch their hero completely butcher Dubs, who hailed from Canada. The Canadian clouter tried valiantly but Robinson slaughtered him in six rounds. In the second Ray decked his opponent three times with the crowd screaming themselves hoarse. In the following round the game Dubs was down for a count of 9, then in the fifth he took a further two counts of 9 before referee Elmer McClelland sensibly halted the one-sided annihilation in the sixth round.

Less than a fortnight later Sugar Ray breezed into Minneapolis to appear in a triple header at the Minneapolis Armoury to face Dick Banner, a tough black fighter from Atlanta. Ray arrived in the city after attending the Chicago funeral of Jack Blackburn, the great trainer who had tutored Joe Louis. Robinson had thought a great deal of Blackburn and had often stated that he had learned a tremendous amount from the great teacher. He had been determined to attend and pay his respects as well as being a support for Louis, who was inconsolable and taking his mentor's death badly.

Also on the same Minneapolis bill was a future Robinson opponent, 'Cowboy' Ruben Shank, who was getting rave publicity for his exciting fighting style, and the fighter whom the press were comparing Robinson with, Charley Burley. Burley had located his fighting base in Minneapolis under promoter Tommy O'Loughlin. At the hotel, Sugar Ray was in a light-hearted mood and was speaking about baseball and the Detroit Tigers but the local newspaper reporters were keen to discus his upcoming fight and whether he intended to fight Burley at a future date. He charmed the local sportswriters with his wit and intelligent conversation and gracefulness. He even gave a little demonstration of his tap dancing skills. Frank Diamond, from the Minneapolis Morning Tribune, was intrigued by the tall, sleek Robinson and observed that "he is built like a sleek torpedo boat, doesn't have a mark on his handsome face, and looks like he couldn't punch his way out of a soap bubble." Another reporter suggested that "Ray Robinson is being spoken of...as the best welterweight since the original Joe Walcott."

Ray was keen to pay his respects to his opponent and told the press that he knew how tough Banner was because he had won the Golden Gloves the year before he had achieved that honour himself. "I have great respect for him, and I assure you I'm not taking him for granted," he said. Burley was boxing Sammy Wilson, and Shank was facing Bobby Berger. Dick Cullum of the Minneapolis Daily Times said the three fights shouldn't last long and told the fans to watch all three fighters closely. He said that he felt certain that Robinson and Burley would fight each other, but didn't know when. He thought local promoter Tommy O'Loughlin was hoping to promote the fight in Minneapolis, but suggested Mike Jacobs would most likely sign this fight.

There was about 5,000 seated in the Armoury and they got exactly what they paid for - action and excitement from two special fighters in Robinson and Burley. Ruben Shank easily beat Bobby Berger and secured a fight against Fritzie Zivic. Burley weighed in at 153lbs and Robinson tipped the scales at 146lbs. Sugar Ray flattened Banner in two rounds and looked sensational. From the moment he moved from his corner his left jabbing was a sight to behold, and his dazzling footwork brought gasps of admiration from the crowd. The spectators were being treated to a superb exhibition of boxing at its very best. Within the first thirty seconds of boxing he had everyone convinced they were watching a master at work. At the end of the first round Banner made the fatal mistake of punching Robinson twice after the bell. Dick was angered by having to take the pasting he took in the opening three minutes but Sugar Ray was furious and decided the ultimate conclusion would be hurried. As the second round began it was quite obvious Robinson was still angry at Banner's unsportsmanlike conduct and he attacked him, viscously raining two-handed punches with lightning fast speed. A straight right cross connected on Dick's jaw, followed by a volley of punches that flattened the Georgian fighter.

With both Robinson and Burley winning their respective battles impressively, the press was not slow to make their comparisons as to who was the better boxer. "Sugar Ray Robinson made a spontaneous impression last night when he knocked out Dick Banner in two rounds. He might have done it quicker but gave the fans a show with the magical left jab in the first round before laying in the right hand crusher in the second. In that brief period Robinson showed speed, boxing skill, the finest left hand in boxing today and a knockout punch. In fact he showed everything of which champions are made," wrote Dick Cullum of the Daily Times. He also spoke on behalf of the boxing public, claiming that the fans demanded a Robinson vs. Burley match. He continued: "The 20-year-old prodigy continued his tap dancing and combined it with some wicked left handed punching to give everyone but Banner a thrill. Snaking left jabs smacked against Banner's face throughout the entire opening round as his opponent kept the willing but defenceless Banner in constant distress. Neither man heard the bell's chimes as they swung it out until separated. Encouraged by his ability to survive the opener, Banner rushed at Robinson at the start of the second only to walk straight into a long right uppercut that brought darkness crashing in on him within 32 seconds."

Charles Johnson of the Star Journal said: "Because Banner made the mistake of arousing Robinson's ire, he didn't last long. Sugar Ray didn't hang around the Amory last night as long as Minneapolis boxing fans had hoped. But in his brief appearance, Sugar more than fulfilled all the reams of complimentary comments that have been written about him. Once inside the ring he's all business and certainly a devastaing fighter. It will be a long time before Minneapolis fight fans will see as much rapid-fire punching jammed into two bristling rounds as they witnessed last night. Robinson is one of the smoothest fighting machines that has ever been seen in these parts for a long time."

Burley won his battle in the same round and this encouraged the debate for weeks afterwards about who was the better man and about which one would emerge victorious if Robinson and Burley ever boxed each other. There were further reports in the press that after Robinson had demolished Banner and returned to his dressing room, Curt Horrmann turned to him and said, "Ray, tonight we found out what we wanted to know. You are a better fighter than Burley, and he's a great fighter." The promoter Tommy O' Loughlin was reported to have called into Robinson's room and talked about making the Robinson-Burley fight. Horrmann told him they would return to Minneapolis to fight Charley, but it would cost him a lot of dollars. Horrmann didn't believe that this fight would be a big draw in New York. He also insisted that Burley would have to make the welterweight poundage before he would consider such a fight. For O'Loughlin, however, a more immediate priority was to pacify Burley, who had exploded in a rage of fury after discovering that Robinson had received a bigger purse than him.

George Barton, sports editor of the Minneapolis Tribune and regarded as one of the greatest American sportswriters, turned his attention towards the proposed match up and said that the distinction between Robinson and Burley was insignificant. He had been at a number of fights involving both men and was well placed to assess the respective merits of Ray Robinson and Charley Burley. Barton, a former fighter and referee, was of the opinion that "despite the fact that Burley is a classy combination of a boxer and puncher, Robinson stole the show from him with the flashiest exhibition of skill and speed seen in a Twin Cities ring since Mike Gibbons and Jock Malone were at their peak. The best description of Robinson is to call him Black Lightning. He is fast as a streak with fists and feet, a perfect master of ring technique and all the punches in the boxing book. Watching Robinson is like watching an expert fencer stabbing a bag filled with sawdust with his foil. When Sugar Ray opens up he hits his opponent everywhere except on the soles of his feet."

The Star Journal columnist Charles Johnson also added to the debate and said Robinson was fancier, flashier, hit faster and boxed better than Burley but reckoned that Burley hit harder and appeared more durable. He was of the opinion that Robinson would beat Burley on points in a ten round contest, but over the 15 round distance Burley would win.

Despite the frenzied debate which continued, these two wonderful fighters would never box each other. Many people speculated that Robinson was scared of fighting Burley but the facts do not support this. Several promoters did try and match them but simply could not afford to pay the two fighters what they were both worth. In his later years Burley, speaking about a possible fight with Robinson, said that Sugar Ray would have been in trouble if they had fought each other. He added to this view many years later after the death of Robinson by suggesting that Robinson had ducked him because George Gainford had told him. He was, however, also aware of boxing politics' role in keeping them apart. "There wouldn't be big money in us fighting each other because we would have knocked each other out. They were not going to give two blacks a chance like that in the same era. He was a great talent though. When God said to both of us, 'Which one of you wants to be Sugar Ray?' I guess I didn't raise my hand fast enough."

It is still a debate which splits many boxing historians today. Nigel Collins, one time editor of The Ring magazine, suggested that "both were great fighters but Sugar Ray had that little bit extra, the charisma that let him take that personality beyond the ring. Charley Burley didn't have that going for him. Still you had two great fighters and so who would get a decisive break? You would have to give the break to Sugar Ray because he had the charisma that Burley lacked."

Howard Rainey, a respected UK trainer, had the opportunity to question the great American trainer Eddie Futch about who was the best fighter he had ever seen. "Charley Burley," Futch quickly replied. He recounted that Sugar Ray would never fight Burley, under any circumstances, after Burley had flattened Robinson in a sparring session. This incident has never been documented beyond Futch's recollection but still serves to highlight the merits of both greats and how they can still split boxing fans to this day.

In May, Robinson boxed a ten round return bout with Marty Servo in front of over 15,000 wildly cheering spectators in Madison Square Garden. Servo was now serving in the Coast Guard and was still very popular with the crowd. It was another tough contest and Servo's body punching troubled Robinson at times. He was extended to the limit, although he forced Marty to lead and countered beautifully. The fight was a thriller from start to finish and the crowd cheered lustily. At the final bell, the spectators were split and this was mirrored by referee Billy Cavanagh voting for Servo, but both judges, Tom Curley and Bill Healy, decided in favour of Sugar Ray. After the fight, Servo added to his popularity by donating ten percent of his purse to the United States Coast Guard relief fund.

Just over two months later, Robinson moved on from the Servo encounter and was back again in Madison Square Garden and his next contest, which was another return engagement, with Sammy Angott, in front of 12,073 fans. Angott confidently told the press before the fight that whenever he lost, he always squared accounts in his return fights, but he never looked capable of doing that in this ten rounder. Robinson ripped home punches from all angles and scored repeatedly with his famous bolo punch. In the eighth round, Angott was on the verge of being knocked out for the first time in his career. Robinson threw three left hooks which whizzed onto Angott's jaw, and as he fell, he grabbed Robinson and pulled him down with him. He managed to get up at the count of eight but there was no doubt about the outcome as it was Robinson by a very comfortable margin. Sammy's title was not at stake as the match had been agreed at over the specified weight limit.

In his next fight Robinson met one of the most colourful characters he would meet in his career, a bronco-busting cowboy from Fort Morgan, Colorado named 'Cowboy' Reuben Shank, who had accumulated a highly successful amateur record. The publicity machine surrounding him built Shank up and New York fight fans were anxious to see him in action. Reporters from California, who had watched him rack up wins in 20 of his 21 contests, predicted that the Cowboy's aggressiveness, speed, stamina and powerful body punching would provide Ray with one of the busiest evenings he would ever have. The quick-talking cowboy added intrigue by telling reporters that he intended to add Robinson's names to his gun belt and urged the fans to get to their seats early or they would miss a shock.

His victories over Henry Armstrong, Fritzie Zivic and Artie Levine, along with his recent fifth round knockout over the highly regarded Phil Norman, indicated that Shank deserved to be listened to and 10,437 spectators turned up in Madison Square Garden to see if Shank could live up to the promise. With the contest only a few seconds old it became quite apparent that Shank was tailor made for Robinson's own brand of mayhem. The first round was even and, although Shank caught Sugar with a right to the jaw and hurt him forcing him backwards on his heels, he managed to complete the round without further incident. In the second, the two fighters went toe-to-toe and this was where the Cowboy made his fatal mistake. Robinson hit him with a solid right to the jaw and he went down for a count of nine before another right cross put Shank on all fours for the same count until another right returned Shank back to the canvas where Referee Bill Cavanagh counted him out.

In August Sugar Ray decided to end his association with his manager Curt Horrmann. The newspaper reporters were critical and suggested that it was a despicable thing he had done to the mild-mannered businessman. The relationship had been a rollercoaster ride. In the beginning everything was roses in the relationship but had quickly begun to turn sour. Robinson's ego clashed with the shrewd businessman's desire to manage according to his own plans. Although he was taking his 33% manager's entitlement, he was an enthusiastic sportsman and the money was of secondary importance to him. After Robinson knocked out Shank the partnership came to an abrupt end because Robinson wanted to test himself against the top ten fighters and earn the big money which these fights would generate, whereas Horrmann was more cautious and didn't want to rush his young prospect.

The final straw came when a Chicago promoter sent George Gainford a telegram offering $10,000 for Ray to box Tony Motisi in Chicago. Horrmann, after Robinson's last three fights in Madison Square Garden, had become close with Mike Jacobs and he told Robinson that he couldn't accept the fight with Motisi for a different promoter. He also explained that in future he wanted Ray to fight only under Mike Jacobs jurisdiction on his promotions. This incensed Robinson because he had a deep mistrust of Jacobs and blamed him for his failure to fight for a world title. Robinson told Horrmann that he would fight for whoever offered him the most money and a big argument ensued.

Robinson put his mistrust aside to go and see Mike Jacobs in his office and borrowed $10,000 from him, which he used to offer to Horrmann to buy out his contract. Gainford confirmed that Robinson paid Jacobs back.

Robinson felt justified after the split when he discovered that his manager had let other promoters use him on their promotions cheaply. If a promoter spoke to Horrmann and wanted to feature Sugar Ray on their promotions, the manager would outline the purse money required. If the promoter said he could not afford what was being asked for, rather than end negotiations, Horrmann would frequently agree with what the promoter offered and would then make up the rest of Robinson's fee out of his own pocket. Despite this being commendable and dignified it angered the fighter. Many years later, Robinson claimed that Horrmann's sister had told him that his family had thought that he was spending too much time looking after the fighter's affairs and neglecting the family business.

In a sports magazine article in 1951, Robinson gave another version of his split from Horrmann. He said that perhaps the Horrmann family didn't like the idea of him being a fight manager and mingling with some of the unsavoury individuals connected with the fight business. Sugar Ray said that after meeting Horrmann's sister, he explained to her: "If Curt couldn't continue managing me, George and I would go it alone and we wouldn't engage another manager. And, if Curt ever wanted to come back that would be okay with us." He then said he paid Horrmann the $10,000 to repay him for everything the businessman had done for him. He ended by saying: "Curt's dead now." Apparently he died of a heart attack whilst getting out of a taxi cab. Many vindictive reporters said it was more likely his dealings with Robinson brought on his heart attack….Who knows? What was crystal clear was that from now until the end of his career Sugar Ray Robinson would never let anyone manipulate him when it came to negotiating how much he thought he deserved for any fight.

Gainford also received a shock. He had assumed that following Horrmann's exit, he would naturally become the manager and subsequently collect a higher percentage. Ray sat him down and informed him that from now on he would manage his own affairs but continue to keep George as his trainer on the 10% which they had agreed when he first turned professional. Gainford felt bitterly let down and disappointed but resolved not to argue but carry on as before. They turned their minds towards the challenge posed by Tony Motisi in Chicago.

They were booked into the city's Grand Hotel and one afternoon while sat reading a paper, the phone rang for Gainford. Three men were waiting to meet him in the lobby. He told the operator to send them up to his room and was surprised when the strangers walked in wearing overcoats despite the sweltering August heat. He told them to take off their coats and offered them a cold beer. He got the shock of his life when one of the men had a gun in a shoulder holster. They were there to discover what Robinson was going to do in his fight against Motisi. Gainford pleaded ignorance and explained that Robinson always tried to get his fights finished as quickly as possible. The men looked at each other with a wry amusement before one of them said that he would like Robinson to 'carry' Motisi and would be well compensated in return. He went on to explain that a great deal of money had been wagered on Motisi lasting the full ten rounds. Gainford listened intently before explaining that he couldn't discuss these sorts of offers because both he and Robinson risked losing their licenses. He then politely showed them the door.

The fight was held in the open air at Comiskey Park, the home of the White Sox baseball team. The weather was awful and the pouring rain drenched the 8,666 spectators. Hometown boy Motisi was a muscular welterweight who came with a puncher's reputation. He had beaten the well regarded contender Willie Joyce and had also taken the scalp of Fritzie Zivic in order to gain this fight.

From the start Robinson was into his rhythm and he bewildered Motisi with his speedy left jab, his poise and combination punching. Within the opening seconds, he whipped over an awesome left hook which hit Motisi on the chin and dropped him like a lead weight. As the count was being recorded he tried valiantly to regain his feet but was too dazed and slipped back on the canvas and was counted out. The fight was over in an amazing two minutes and forty one seconds of the opening round; even more impressive was that it was his second knockout in less than a week, having flattened Shank a few days before. Joe Louis, who was sat at ringside, joined Ray at the evening's celebration party.

Nat Lewis, the experienced Chicago boxing manager known as 'The Bald Eagle', watched the demolition and told the Chicago press pack that Robinson was the finest welterweight he had seen in over forty years of watching the sport. He explained that ever since Robinson had turned professional, he had witnessed him box all kinds of fighters and seen him improve with every match. He did coat his lavish praise with a warning. He suggested that once Robinson entered the armed services, this might have a detrimental effect on him in the future. "Army food and discipline takes a great deal out of a fighter," he said.

In September, Sugar Ray found himself in hot water again. The Massachusetts State Boxing Commission suspended him for failing to report for a proposed contest in Boston against the city's George Martin. The suspension would remain effective until he fulfilled the contract or managed to secure a release. Robinson had claimed that he could not go through with the bout because he was suffering with a heavy cold. It was not until December 1944 that he did eventually box Martin in the city.

Sugar Ray continued to increase his own education outside the ring and regularly visited Mike Jacobs in his office along with Joe Louis. He would study the promoter meticulously, especially when he talked about money. He knew that Jacobs was a cunning man who regularly double-crossed fighters. He wore ill-fitting false teeth which would comically clatter and fall down from his gums when he was arguing or getting excited. His appearance belied a shrewd operator. Robinson would listen intently to the conniving way which Jacobs dealt with managers and how he discussed purse money. He noted Jacobs' habit of crying poverty about why he could only pay a certain amount of money to certain fighters, which piqued Ray's sense of justice that a promoter should be allowed to make more money than the main attraction - the fighter. As time wore on, Robinson considered Jacobs and his associates as sarcastic, malicious, cynical, and contemptible.

6.

The Rivalry with the Bronx Bull

ON THE 2ND August 1942, Robinson engaged in the first of a six fight series of wars against a fighter who would go on to secure the status of a living legend, renowned for being one of the roughest, toughest fighters in the history of boxing; The Bronx Bull, Jake LaMotta. Robinson was matched with the young middleweight in Madison Square Garden. Mike Jacobs knew that he had another sell-out crowd with this confrontation and he was to be proven right. Within a short while of the fight being announced, fans clamoured for tickets to ensure that the Garden was completely sold-out.

Born Giacobe LaMotta in October 1921 in New York he had turned professional at the age of 18. Before facing Robinson, he had fought 31 times, securing 26 wins accruing four losses and one draw. His looks were not deceptive; he looked exactly what he was - the roughest, toughest and crudest fighter to set foot in a boxing ring; he had a fear of nobody. He possessed a face which was big and round with an impressively flattened nose sitting atop big broad shoulders and a squat body.

Many considered that it was a suicidal match for Robinson to take at this stage of his career because he was focused on pursuing the world title at welterweight while LaMotta was heading for the world middleweight crown. The Bronx Bull respected no-one and his unchanging approach, which consisted of burying his chin onto his chest and firing punches from every conceivable angle without regard for where they landed, was difficult to combat. He talked tough, looked tough, and he was tough!

In training for this fight Gainford deliberated how his man should go about defeating LaMotta. He used the metaphor that this was going to be a fight between a matador and a bull. "You," he told Ray, "are the matador, LaMotta is the Bull. Don't try and fight his fight," he instructed "if you do, then the Bull will win. You possess class and brains and so use them." Sound advice as LaMotta considerably outweighed his opponent.

The match was exactly what the crowd had anticipated; a great fight! Firstly one would establish his authority and then the other would dominate.

They each rocked the other with solid punches but both refused to yield or fall. Robinson tried to remain up on his toes and pop out his immaculate left jab to claim the decision, but he found out, like many of LaMotta's opponents, that he was a teak tough competitor. He insisted on making it increasingly physically hard and attempted to erode Robinson's skills. For the lucky spectators it was regarded as a wonderfully entertaining contest and there was little disagreement when all three officials voted for Robinson. Referee Frank Fullam and two judges, Joe Agnello and Bill Healy, all concurred that by beating the Bronx Bull, the increasingly maturing Sugar Ray had given one of the best boxing exhibitions of his career.

Immediately after the fight, Ray and his sweetheart Edna Mae spent all of their time together. There began to be increasing amounts of gossip and rumours circling around his private life. After his burgeoning relationship was discovered some journalists began to ask questions about the beauty on his arm. Anything concerning Robinson was big news in the various newspapers. Sportswriters wrote about fights, his negotiations, why he would pull out of scheduled fights on a whim. They also impinged on his private life as well. There were unsubstantiated rumours that she had a brief affair with Joe Louis and that she had been married before. Robinson was insanely jealous and these stories drove him to distraction. He resolved not to forget this kind of talk and many people close to him believed that these innuendoes would later cause friction between him and Edna Mae.

Seventeen days after the gruelling LaMotta fight, Robinson was back in the ring in Philadelphia. His opponent was New York's Izzy Jannazzo, renown for his durability and who carried a record of over 100 fights. In November 1936 he had lost a close 15 round decision in his tilt at Barney Ross' world welterweight title before he won the Maryland version of the world welterweight title in April 1941, beating Jimmy Letto. He was no respecter of reputations and was determined to beat the Harlem star. Over 10,000 people jammed into the arena for the confrontation, which proved to be an entertaining spectacle. The ring-wise veteran survived being knocked out in the first, third, fourth and ninth rounds and at the end of the bout proclaimed himself pleased to have taken "Sugar Ray's Sunday punches". Such was his delight at surviving the full distance, he performed a cartwheel in the ring. The referee, Irving Kutcher, shook his hand for showing such bravery and resilience.

Following this match up, Vic Dellicurti became Ray's next victim. The East Harlem fighter was chosen because he had recently gone the full distance with LaMotta and would appeal to the patriotic New York crowd because this was his last fight before joining the Army. Robinson easily won every round without ever facing serious danger in front of another bumper 10,349 crowd in Madison Square Garden. All three officials, referee Frank Fullam and Judges Charlie Draycott and Bill Healy, voted him a unanimous winner

During December, he was scheduled to meet Al Nettlow in Philadelphia. He booked into the Douglas Hotel, which was near to promoter Herman Taylor's office. Whilst Gainford popped into the promoter's office to settle the final arrangements, Robinson waited outside the restaurant owned by the former fighter Lew Tendler. While he was idling and taking in the view, he noticed a man in a grey suit motioning to him. He wandered over and was introduced to the notorious ganglord Frank 'Blinky' Palermo, who greeted him with a huge welcoming smile and an eager handshake.

After exchanging pleasantries, Palermo asked in his trademark gruff voice, "Is everything set?" Robinson, oblivious to the sinister undertones, asked what he meant. According to Robinson's later recollections, the gangster told him that he had held a meeting with George Gainford and when he saw that Robinson was still none the wiser, he suddenly became agitated and told Robinson that it would be explained to him later and he then walked away briskly. Once back in the hotel, Robinson confronted Gainford to uncover what was going on with Palermo. Gainford explained that he had been informed that it would not be a good idea if Robinson were to knock out Al Nettlow when they fought. He explained that because Ray was dispatching so many opponents, it was becoming increasingly difficult to get fights. Robinson was fuming and had a heated argument with his trainer.

Ray carried his anger with him into the ring and hammered his hapless opponent in three devastating rounds. The large Convention Hall crowd were treated to a spiteful Sugar Ray performance. He battered the chief boatswain's mate from the Navy's Jacksonville, Florida base from pillar to post with such brutality that his manager Al Weill implored referee Matt Adgie to stop the fight. "He didn't have a chance," protested Weil.

Back in the dressing-room Gainford was sweating profusely and a bag of nerves. Robinson claimed that the trainer had assured Palermo that he would get him to carry Nettlow for the full ten rounds. Later that same night, Robinson met Palermo and excused himself and explained that it had been an accident that he kayoed Nettlow. 'Blinky' smiled and said there was nothing they could do about it and so to forget about it. After his retirement, Robinson claimed that he had agreed to carry some opponents in warm-up fights, but if he sensed that the paying fans were not satisfied he would then go all out for a stoppage or knockout.

This revelation should not be a huge surprise. Powerful underworld forces have always been on the periphery of the business of boxing and their prevalence and influence coincided with the sport's peak during this era. The boxing authorities, law enforcement agencies and boxing commissions should have been at the forefront of helping and advising young impressionable boxers about the racketeers and mobsters but chose instead to turn a blind eye. It speaks volumes that despite all this racketeering that was rife in boxing, especially in America, Sugar Ray Robinson left the sport largely untainted by these associations and with his honesty, dignity and self-respect intact.

Betting on fights has always been a part of boxing, especially around the ringside. For instance, a fighter like Sugar Ray Robinson would of course be favoured to beat an opponent of the calibre of Al Nettlow. So betting would take place not on the result, which would be considered a foregone conclusion to gamblers, but on how many rounds the fight would last. Reptiles like Carbo, Palermo and their ilk would get certain fighters to 'carry' their opponent the full distance.

****

At the end of 1942, The Ring Magazine honoured Robinson by naming him Fighter of the Year for 1942. He was overjoyed to attend the ceremony, which took place in a brewery, and proudly accepted a medal for his achievement. During this period, boxing was heavily saturated with a proliferation of talented fighters through from the featherweight to the heavyweight divisions, especially in America. There were only eight recognised world champions and the social conditions for most of these fighters were hard. Additionally, racial segregation made it even harder for black fighters. In order to get to the top of the boxing ladder, it was accepted that you had to fight the best around. There was no dodging or side-stepping difficult opponents. You fought the best to get the opportunity to fight for a world championship, and so it took a special breed of boxer to rise, like a phoenix, to become a world champion. This acknowledgment of his potential from the influential trade magazine meant such a lot to Ray and to George Gainford.

1943 would be one of Sugar Ray's leaner fighting years. He would only box six times. The 5th February was a freezing cold night and the icy wind was howling, it was suited more for polar bears and the fans were bundled up for protection against the blistering cold weather. Inside the Olympia Stadium in Detroit, Robinson was booked to fight a return with The Bronx Bull, Jake LaMotta, and the atmosphere was red-hot in anticipation of a great fight to start the new campaign. This attraction was another sell-out and the promoters publicity machine worked overtime to ensure an overflowing turnout of 18,930 with hundreds locked out in the cold outside.

Ray, however, was starting to believe in his own seeming invincibility and started to give undue credence to the hype and publicity which was starting to swell up around him and, along with his growing obsession with Edna Mae, meant that he had started to miss training sessions and frequenting night clubs until the small hours of the morning. Even Leila started to notice her son's complacent attitude to training and warned him constantly, but saw that her warnings were having no effect on his increasingly wayward behaviour and so resorted to begging him to pull out of the fight. "LaMotta ain't no play thing. You gotta train hard for this man," she tearfully told her son, but he took no notice of this well-intended advice, choosing to believe that he was, indeed, a 'wonder boxer'. Leila was so concerned that she refused to attend the fight; one of the few occasions she did not attend one of her son's fights.

He was giving away another large chunk of weight, 16 pounds, and LaMotta was eager to get into the ring first, where some of Robinson's fans rushed to his corner to heckle him. Jake didn't bother to respond but he just stared down at them with a glare colder than the weather outside. All eyes were on the Bull, who was rubbing his black boxing shoes in the resin box placed near his corner. His all-black satin trunks glistened in the light and made him look a menacing prospect. Suddenly, a loud roar rose up from the back of the stadium and quickly spread throughout the Olympia when Sugar Ray emerged from his dressing room. When he waved to the crowd, they responded with an ear-splitting cheer which grew louder when he entered the ring and danced around, throwing punches at his imaginary opponent. He then stopped dancing and moved to his corner and allowed George Gainford to remove his robe, which prompted shrieks around ringside from both men and women. There wasn't an ounce of fat on him, his powerfully muscled back, sinewy arms and long, lithe legs revealed that he could punch. When LaMotta discarded his robe, the gasps of admiration turned to stifled laughter because he looked like the middleweight's answer to 'Two-Ton' Tony Galento. His squat, barrel-like body made him look three feet, not the actual three inches, shorter than Robinson. His 67 inch reach looked incapable of getting to Ray, whose reach was an impressive 73 inches. When they met in the ring's centre, LaMotta quietly muttered, "Tonight's my night." "That's what you think," Robinson calmly replied.

For the first seven rounds Robinson boxed smartly and racked up a slim lead. In round eight, he almost came a cropper. LaMotta, bulling his way forward, hit Ray with a hefty wallop smack on his belly button. Robinson tumbled through the ropes, hurt and winded. He clambered back into the ring before the referee, Sam Hennessy, reached the count of ten. Sensing the balance shifting back into his favour, the Bronx Bull gored him and took the ten round points decision. Sam Hennessy had it close 5-4-1 for the Bronx Bull.

After the fight, Robinson was severely dejected. He had lost his unbeaten record as both an amateur and professional and in the process had learned a very valuable lesson, never to enter the ring for a competitive fight unless he was in supreme shape. Unfortunately this encounter meant the start of a career-long bad name and reputation within the boxing world for a lack of preparation and for cancelling fights at the last minute. In the aftermath of the defeat he stated that in the future he wouldn't fight unless he was 100% fit and sharp. "No boxing commission will call you a hero for fighting when you are not ready," he said, but this unreliability would cause him to become unpopular with some fans and a number of boxing officials and journalists.

Two weeks after his first defeat, Robinson climbed back into the ring despite George Gainford's concerns that he could not have recovered, either physically or emotionally, from the physical man-handling he had received from LaMotta. His opponent in Madison Square Garden was 'California' Jackie Wilson, a former Golden Gloves champion and a member of the US Olympic Boxing Team. He used the name 'California' because there was another Jackie Wilson fighting at the same time.

The fight caused a number of problems before the two men actually met because both boxers were black. During this period it was not considered the done thing to match two black fighters in a main event because promoters feared that they would not draw a big enough audience. Mike Jacobs was concerned and phoned a few reporters to seek their opinion on the fight and he received a favourable response and so allowed the fight to proceed. Contrary to the perceived wisdom, 16,336 fans crammed into Madison Square Garden to watch how Ray would respond to his first setback. The response was swift. In the fourth round, he decked Wilson, who was a serving solider and had been promoted to a sergeant, for a nine count before he ran out a clear points winner. He told reporters that he had not wanted to go all out against Wilson because he had already agreed to fight a return with Jake LaMotta in Detroit again. He used 'California' Jackie Wilson more as a sparring partner to prepare for the tougher opposition he was due to meet a few days later in Detroit's Olympia Stadium.

As he jigged in his corner, his torso glistening brightly under the hot arc lights, Ray felt confident, extremely confident.15,149 excited fans packed in to watch the latest instalment of this all-action thriller, and as the bell rang it was quite obvious that Sugar Ray was intent on revenge. He dominated enough and boxed superbly to beat LaMotta on points to take a 2-1 lead in their contests. In gaining his revenge, he had employed an almost faultless strategy. He used his left jab to perfection and, as LaMotta continued rushing forward to throw body punches, he was repeatedly hit by Robinson's looping right uppercut which caused him no end of discomfort. Robinson was still forced to ensure a few anxious moments as he walked into a power-packed left hook in the seventh round to take a count of eight. This victory, however, allowed him to feel considerably better because he had regained his pride.

In April, he journeyed to Boston Garden and stopped the local fighter Ferdinand Cabral, who boxed under the name of Freddie Cabral, and he finished him in two minutes and 20 seconds of the first round when referee Jack Watson counted him out. The following day was significant for Ray as he was required to report for Army service. Mike Jacobs had alerted Robinson a few weeks beforehand that he was going to be called up to do his military service and the news surprised and annoyed Ray. He demanded to know how Jacobs was aware and the wily promoter gnashed down on his false teeth, smiled and removed the cigar from his mouth. "I just know," he laughed.

7.

You're In The Army Now

THE 27TH FEBRUARY 1943 was the day when Sugar Ray Robinson became formally known as Private Walker Smith Junior of the United States Army's armed services unit. Between the dates of 27th February 1943 until his discharge on the 3rd June 1944, the 15 months and 4 days service is surrounded in mystery and intrigue. During these dates, he still appeared in three professional fights, for which he received over $20,000 from one fight alone while still receiving his meagre monthly army allowance. Oddly enough, Ray himself rather glossed over his army career in his book.

He was officially declared fit for duty after undergoing his comprehensive medical and was then assigned to the Fort Dix base in New Jersey. Once he was issued with his army uniform he was not permitted to call himself Sugar Ray Robinson but had to respond to his given name of Private Walker Smith Junior when the drill sergeant barked out his commands. It is hard to conceive of a man less suited for disciplined service in the armed forces than Robinson. Colleagues recalled that he wasn't a coward and the basic training was a breeze for a super-fit athlete like him. Like millions of other draftees he considered himself to be patriotic and would sooner have fought the Germans straight away rather than endure the basic training which every serviceman had to undergo. However, because he was a world-renowned boxer he immediately attracted a great deal of attention from the officers and other leading army officials as well as from the regular soldiers, many of whom followed the sport and requested his autograph and asked endless questions about his career.

After his basic training he was assigned to the Air Corps at Mitchell Field in Hempstead, Long Island. He recounted that while he was on the rifle range being tested, he suffered from an ear infection. He was admitted to Halloran Hospital where he spent the next two weeks. Immediately afterwards, he received permission to travel to Boston twice. First was to box Freddie Cabral, whom he knocked out in one round, before he returned to face Ralph 'The Ripper' Zannelli from Providence, Rhode Island. Zanelli had fought Henry Armstrong in 1940 for the world welterweight title and had been stopped in five rounds. Ray beat him on points over ten rounds in the Boston Garden.

Shortly after this, whilst he was enjoying a period of leave, he received a telephone call from Henry Armstrong. The old world feather, light and welterweight champion had embarked on a comeback and he told Ray that Mike Jacobs had suggested that a fight between them would make a big purse. Despite boasting a career which had seen huge crowds flock to watch him win a world championship at three separate weights, Armstrong was penniless and desperate. He pleaded with Robinson to accept this fight with him and assured him that with Jacobs promoting the fight, they would both earn a really big purse. Initially, Robinson would not agree. He told Henry, "You were my boyhood idol, and I couldn't fight you."

Armstrong was so insistent that he later turned up at Ray's mother's house and pleaded with Ray to offer his agreement to fight. Ray felt that he was in a no win situation. Armstrong was regarded as a legend to all boxing followers, especially the black people, and Robinson knew that he would get heavily criticized if he hammered Henry and would suffer ridicule if he lost to the old champion. Mike Jacobs became involved and convinced him that by agreeing to fight his idol, he would help Armstrong clear some of his mounting debts and help him to lead a more comfortable life. Jacobs offered the inducement of $10,000 and Ray eventually relented and agreed to box the man he admired greatly.

The date was set for the 27th August; the venue was, once again, Madison Square Garden. 'Hammering' Henry Armstrong was a pale shadow of the once great fighter he had once been and the crowd of 15,371 raised gate receipts of $60,789. They came with baited breath to see if Armstrong was capable of recapturing, just one more time, the greatness that had seemed to come so easily. Sadly, it turned into one of the dullest, dreariest fights in the rich history of the Garden. Ray knew before the first bell had sounded that he was capable of removing his idol any time he chose. He was determined not to hurt him, and when the crowd sensed what was going happening, they started booing and shouting insults. Both fighters began by cuffing each other, pushing and feinting punches, but Robinson insisted on pulling his punches. Armstrong, for his part, fell back on his fighting instinct and tried to make a match of it. Halfway through the dreary ten rounds, Armstrong pleaded with Robinson to hit him. "Ray," he pleaded, "I've fought here dozens of times and I've never been booed before. Come on and fight!" Robinson emerged as a clear winner.

Back in the dressing rooms, the press converged into Armstrong's room, obviously wanting to hear him announce his official retirement. They asked Henry how he would have fared against Robinson in his heyday. "It wouldn't have made any difference," he replied. "I couldn't have beaten Robinson on the best night in my life. He's a great fighter." In return, Robinson spoke earnestly and said, "I wonder if people know what it feels like to fight a man you admire and look up to. I didn't want to knock him out. I couldn't. I didn't want to fight him, I really didn't. I had no heart for it. I beat him clearly but it wasn't a good fight." Armstrong didn't retire after this fight because he couldn't afford to due to his escalating debts. He fought again throughout 1944 and scored six straight knockouts over top class fighters like Aldo Spoldi, Ralph Zanelli, Aaron Perry, Al 'Bummy' Davis and Mike Belloise before he finally hung up his gloves.

Before the Armstrong fight, Ray discovered that Edna Mae was going to resume her dancing career and was planning to appear in the Chicago nightclub which was owned by his friend Joe Louis. Ray was furious and let her know in no uncertain terms that he did not want her to appear at the club. Ray had heard the persistent rumours circulating that when she was younger; Edna Mae had enjoyed a brief affair with the great heavyweight icon. Robinson was insanely jealous and instructed Edna Mae that she was not permitted to be in Joe's company unless he was present.

On 29th May, he arrived in Chicago unannounced and whisked Edna off to the home of one of her friends, where they tied the knot and were married. He was 21 and his bride, 27. The news came as a complete surprise to everybody associated with the pair. The ceremony was attended by only five people, including the preacher and two friends who acted as witnesses. It is still unclear whether he ever received official permission from the army authorities to get married, but the fact remained that he was now a married man for the second time. His mother was shocked because she maintained that Edna Mae was far too old for her son. When Edna was asked by the press to confirm that she had never been married before, she refused to answer the question and offer a confirmation.

Once back in army uniform, Robinson joined Joe Louis as they were both assigned by the War Department in Washington to tour around service bases throughout America under the command of Captain Louis Krem. They were instructed to deliver training routines and sparring exhibitions for the troops. George Nicholson, one of Louis's regular sparring partners, was also assigned to the group, along with former Robinson foe 'California' Jackie Wilson and trainer Bob Payne. Initially, they had a great time, entertaining the men with their training and sparring routines before signing autographs and giving talks about their boxing experiences. However, both men made a stand while in the Deep South where black troops were not allowed to attend the exhibitions. There were a number of instances of confrontation between the Louis-Robinson group and army officials regarding the segregation between white and black soldiers. The most serious incident occurred at Camp Sibert, Alabama. Both Robinson and Louis made telephone calls from phone boxes that were designated for whites only when a couple of over-zealous military policemen attempted to stop them. Tempers quickly flared and both fighters were taken to the guardhouse before being released and issued with an apology.

Years later, Robinson recalled another hurtful incident when he and Louis were again staying at Camp Sibert, Alabama and were in a lady's house in nearby Gadsden. They both reported to the camp base and, after receiving their instructions, they went to the bus station which was situated within the camp grounds. The buses were crowded and both men were shocked to discover that there was only one bus for black soldiers and two for the white soldiers; there were massive queues waiting for a bus in the black section.

Louis went into a telephone booth to call a taxi. Meanwhile, Robinson waited outside and pretended to be playing golf with the putter he had with him. As Louis came out of the kiosk a huge, red-faced military policeman approached. "Hey Sergeant," he bawled, "You belong on the other side of the road. This side is for white soldiers only." Louis was annoyed and asked, "Why do I have to go on the other side?" The policeman barked back, "Don't you know what colour you are?" By this time the world heavyweight champion was becoming increasingly angry and pointed out he wore the same uniform as him, "It's the same as yours and we're fighting the same war. I don't stand for being discriminated against." Quickly, a full scale ruckus erupted and the policeman started pushing Louis and attempted to grab Robinson's putter. Ray grabbed the policeman by the throat. Watching this drama unfold, the black soldiers started yelling and cheering until a team of Military Police arrived and frogmarched the two boxing legends to the guard house.

The story took flight and rumours quickly circulated that Louis and Robinson were beaten up by the police officers. The Commanding General of the camp heard about the incident and didn't want to risk any further escalation of trouble and so ordered the two boxers to be immediately released and walked around to the black section of the camp in order to show their faces and prove that there had been no beatings. Soon afterwards, the inspector general's office dispatched one of its senior officers from Washington to investigate and ordered an end to the mixed bus system.

After Alabama, the group travelled to Washington and then the Port of Embarkation at Fort Hamilton, Brooklyn, where they prepared to leave on a ship bound for England. At this point, there are a number of conflicting rumours circulating about the authenticity of the events which took place which ended Robinson's army career.

Robinson's own account of what actually happened is open to question. He claimed that on the night of the 29th March 1944, he was playing poker with

Joe Louis and some other people upstairs in their barracks at Fort Hamilton. The group were looking forward to sailing to Europe the following day. As the card game proceeded, Ray claimed that he went to the toilet, which was situated downstairs. At the top of the stairs there were duffel bags scattered all over the floor and Ray didn't know if he tripped or just fell but he tumbled down the flight of stairs. The next memory he had was waking in a hospital bed in Halloran Hospital based on Staten Island whilst Joe Louis and the rest of the team had set sail to England. There were other rumours that he had gone AWOL in order to purposely miss the sailing and another rumour speculating that he was carried onto the ship in a straight-jacket. Throughout his life, Ray passionately refuted both stories, insisting that he had never been on the ship. He said he became ill because of all the junk food he had eaten in his younger days and it affected his stomach. An army doctor said he should be discharged as he was not fit for army duty. This, said journalist, was very strange, to say the least!

When he came back to consciousness, he had asked a nurse why he was in hospital and was told that he was a patient and had suffered an attack of amnesia and hadn't been able to recall anything from the past week. Alarmed to discover that he had been in hospital for a week, he tried to piece together what exactly had happened to him. His army medical record stated that, after falling down the stairs he had suffered a complete blackout for three days.

He was then taken to a New York hospital by a stranger who had found him ill on the streets. He was then transferred to Fort Jay Hospital on Governor's Island, Lower Manhattan, where he was treated by Captain R.L. Craig, who recommended that his amnesia be tested under sodium amytal, better known as a truth serum. He was given the drug intravenously by Captain S. Stromberg, who said that "it couldn't penetrate the block to cause him to reveal how he left Fort Hamilton." Lieutenant V.H. Gill's notes state that Robinson "appeared upset when he found out that he could not accompany Joe Louis to Europe." Lieutenant Gill supported this claim and added that, "I do not believe that this patient is a malingerer."

This mysterious turn of events, however, intrigued the press, who suspected other reasons. Dan Parker, writing in the Daily Mirror, suggested that "Robinson is in a bit of a pickle. Leaving the ship which was to carry him overseas with a group of other boxers to entertain the fighting men on foreign fronts, Ray was picked up by military police after the ship had sailed and now awaits court-martial." On the 15th April, the headline of the Chicago Defender stated, 'Ray Robinson in Arrest; No Word On AWOL Charge' and went on to report that "it was apparent that the U.S. Army censorship was wrapped tightly around the Sergeant Sugar Ray Robinson AWOL incident."

It went on to report that "Robinson had been a member of Staff Sergeant Joe Louis' boxing aggregation that had been entertaining servicemen throughout the country and was reported to have 'jumped' ship just prior to the troupe's departure overseas."

Although little information concerning the incident leaked out, a sportswriter with one of the New York daily papers did recount Robinson's action in a column which was highly critical of him and accused Robinson of "conduct unbecoming a soldier" in his failure to travel to England. These reports upset Robinson, who went to great pains to stress that there was nothing in his army record that mentioned that he had left the ship. He continued to claim that he was never on the ship and he would point to the fact that he was never court-martialled for the incident but, instead, received an honourable discharge from the army as a sergeant on the 3rd June 1944.

Many authors and journalist have attempted to fathom out the real mystery of Robinson's sudden departure from armed service and much speculation rests on the belief that the figure of Truman K Gibson was a considerable influence in managing to get Robinson his honourable discharge. Truman K. Gibson was a charming man who possessed the ability to flatter anyone he came into contact with. Until his death at 93, in 2005, he was a good-looking man with a light brown complexion, straight black hair and a pair of sparkling bright eyes. Gibson hailed from Chicago and forged his name and reputation working as a lawyer who became Joe Louis's legal representative and advisor towards the end of his career. Gibson would go on to play a significant role in the later life of Sugar Ray Robinson.

During the Second World War, Gibson served as an aide to William H. Hastie, the Dean of Howard Law School, who held the government post of civilian aide on Negro affairs. Gibson was the civilian aide's adviser on Negro affairs within the War Department, which was still overtly racist and had many branches, such as the Marine Corps and the Air Corps which would not permit blacks to join their ranks. The majority of other sections within the US Army insisted on maintaining segregated units. President Franklin D Roosevelt, acting on the advice of his Secretary of War, Henry Stimson, maintained this segregation on the belief that winning the war was the first priority and that justice for blacks would have to wait until Germany and Japan had surrendered. Gibson wielded a significant influence behind the scenes at this time and much speculation rests on his admiration for Robinson and his subsequent discharge in shady circumstances, however both Truman and Robinson both denied this allegation.

After obtaining his discharge he pondered about what he would do next. The obvious answer was to return to fighting and earning money again. He and his wife Edna Mae were now living in a three-roomed apartment at 276

Saint Nicholas Avenue in New York, where the rent was $63 a month. However, he had not fought for almost fourteen months and he was concerned about how the public would perceive him after his discharge from the army and active service.

George Gainford suggested that some skilful public relations work was necessary and so he went to meet with the Disabled Veterans' Fund, which was covered in the press. Gainford, who accompanied Robinson, told reporters that "Ray has seen so much suffering while in the army that he wants to do something for all disabled veterans." He offered to donate 20% of his future purses to the fund.

Almost four months after his mysterious exit from the army, on 13th October, he re-entered the ring again and boxed a third return with Izzy Jannazzo, with a crowd of 7,347 Bostonians watching him score a second round technical knockout in the Boston Garden. He was razor-sharp. In the second he dropped Izzy for a count of five and was groggy when getting to his feet when referee Tommy Rawson Jr acted humanely and stopped the bout. He then followed this up fourteen days later with another technical knockout over Sergeant Lou Woods in the Chicago Stadium in front of a 10,622 audience and then, on the 17th November, he went the full ten round distance when outpointing Vic Dellicurti in their return match in Detroit. The Convention Hall in Philadelphia, in front of a crowd of 7,681 which cheered him to the echo, was his next stop for his fight against Richard 'Sheik' Rangel, where he notched up a second round technical knockout. His last fight of the year took place on 22nd December in Boston, where he stopped Georgie Martin in the seventh round. The Martin fight was a particularly impressive display of finishing from Robinson, who had opened up with a punishing mixture of two-handed punches which opened a wide gash over Martin's left eye and forced referee Johnny Martin to stop the fight. A gathering of 8,464 people were thrilled to watch Sugar Ray in action.

Sugar Ray reminded the press that the Veterans' fund received its full share from all of these contests. It was also the start of Robinson's habit of occasionally fighting for charity. He once proudly boasted that "I fought for more charitable causes than any other boxer." He was pleased to offer his entire purse to the Infantile Paralysis Foundation and the Damon Runyon Cancer Fund when he defended his world welterweight crown against Charlie Fusari in 1950. He also donated large sums from his purses whilst touring in Europe in 1950-51. George Gainford acted as his adviser regarding which charities to offer his support. "Give a lot or don't fight for them at all," Gainford told him. After the Martin fight, Robinson also lavished praise onto his trainer for all the help and support he had given him after he came out of the army.

During this period towards the end of 1944, the Robinsons' marriage experienced its first problems. They were both desperate to start a family but Edna suffered a miscarriage. Both were heartbroken and this grief was made worse when she discovered a number of extramarital affairs which her husband had been conducting. Despite this betrayal, she was still determined to be fully supportive of him when he was preparing for his fights. She later suggested that "no matter what he did, including being a philanderer, a gigolo and a scoundrel, I forgave him."

******

His first action of 1945 saw Joe Louis sat at ringside to cheer him on against Billy Furrone in Washington's Unline Arena. After rocking Furrone repeatedly in the first, Sugar decided to end it in the second. He scored four knockdowns of 1, 9, 7 and 4 before the referee protected Furrone from himself and called an end to the slaughter.

Six days later he met Youngstown, Ohio's hot prospect, Tommy Bell, in the Cleveland Arena. Bell had a tall, lean physique like Robinson and came with a big reputation and a hefty dig in either hand. He had been repeatedly demanding his chance to meet Robinson for quite some time and had been frustrated that boxing politics had prevented it happening. 10,966 excited fans turned up in anticipation of seeing Bell, who had won 28 straight fights with 18 on stoppage, deliver on his own promises and give his foe a real challenge. Robinson, however, prevented any onslaught and boxed his head off to win a one-sided ten round unanimous decision. In the final round, he had hurt Tommy with vicious combinations which had floored him for an eight count after connecting with a stunning right hand to the jaw. In his eagerness to conclude the contest, Ray became arm-weary and failed to finish him off.

His next outing was on Valentine's Day 1945, when he faced George 'Sugar' Costner at the Stadium in Chicago. Costner was a popular and likeable man, although he decided to attempt to belittle Robinson in the newspapers before their fight. He claimed that he "was the 'real' Sugar" and that he would prove it in the ring. Gainford was amused by this attempt to drum up publicity for himself because he understood that, like the majority of black fighters during this period, Costner hardly rated more than a few lines in his local newspapers. Robinson, however, was privately seething at these disrespectful remarks and declared that he would teach this mouthy upstart a lesson he would not forget in a hurry.

Before the fight the Chicago newspapers added to Robinson's ire by running stories relating to his "dishonourable discharge from the army", which continued to upset and embarrass him. Robinson seemed to be experiencing some measure of guilt about carrying on his career while other fighters were away from home serving their country in the armed forces. George Gainford, seeing how upset Sugar was, contacted Mike Jacobs in New York and asked the promoter to get Robinson's honourable discharge papers from his apartment and have copies sent to every newspaper in Chicago. Afterwards, the discharge issue was dropped, although some journalists sneeringly asked why Robinson didn't sue their newspapers for false and malicious accusations if the claims were so ludicrous.

The Chicago Stadium was a volcano of undiluted passion and noise as the two boxers paced the ring floor while the introductions were being made. Robinson later suggested that the volume of noise from the 20,193 spectators "sounded more like 100,000 people". The attendance was the largest indoor professional boxing crowd at this venue since the Jack Dempsey-King Levinsky exhibition and from the chimes of the first bell it was virtually a 'no-contest'. Sugar Ray exploded across the ring and was snarling as he attacked Costner with wave after wave of awesome punches to both the head and body; it was obvious that there was no way this scheduled ten rounder was going that far. Before facing Robinson, George had won 23 straight fights, all inside the distance, but he was made to look like a rank novice as he was rendered sideways on the canvas, unable to rise, within two minutes and 55 seconds of the first round. He had not even had opportunity to land a decent punch. The press reported that after a close-quarter tussle, Sugar had suddenly cut loose with a whiplash left hook to the jaw which could be distinctly heard by those sitting close to the ringside. This hurt and staggered the Cincinnati man and within a second, another left hook had whistled onto his chin which knocked the sleepy-eyed Costner to the floor.

After his army discharge Robinson had boxed in various towns and cities across the States but was eager to return to New York. Ten days after his sensational knockout over Costner he came face-to-face with the Bronx Bull LaMotta for the fourth instalment of their feud. Mike Jacobs had made the match, confident of securing a sell-out for it. Ray had argued long and hard with Jacobs about his fee. He argued that he alone had attracted over 20,000 fans to watch his last bout against George Costner and he knew his power at the box office and wanted paying accordingly. This was a crucial difference between Robinson and others fighters of that era and he enjoyed these negotiations, where he demanded the lion's share of purses. He wasn't bothered that he developed a reputation as arrogant, conceited and selfish by those who entered into these protracted discussions. He told Jacobs that if he didn't pay him what he was worth then he would fight for other promoters who would pay him more. Jacobs knew he was serious about this threat and did come up with the necessary funds for Sugar Ray and he was delighted that 18,060 paid to enter Madison Square Garden to watch these two legends cross gloves once again.

In the first round LaMotta, boxing out of a crouch which he adopted for the full ten rounds, caught Robinson with a swishing left hook to the chin and staggered the Harlem stylist. Once he quickly recovered Ray sought to stamp his class by the relentless use of his accurate left jab and speedy footwork. The excitement which the crowd were displaying for this clash of styles reached a crescendo at the end of the third round and convinced Jake to go for Sugar's slim waist and hammer away in an attempt to weaken him, but Robinson's elusiveness ensured that he missed a great deal of the time. Late in the eighth, the Bull lurched forward and crashed two rights to his tormenter's jaw, but because Robinson was leaning backwards the momentum of the punches was lost but, playing to the gallery, he beckoned Sugar to 'come on and fight'. Sugar Ray was keen to oblige and many witnesses were surprised that LaMotta remained upright from the battering that resulted. Robinson romped his way to another victory over his stout-hearted opponent. Judge Eddie Joseph gave it to Robinson by six rounds to four; another gave six rounds to Sugar, three to LaMotta with one even, whilst Jack Gordon appeared to concur with most observers and awarded seven rounds to Sugar, one to Jake with two rounds even. Robinson reflected on LaMotta after the fight and said, "This guy, you just hit him with everything and he'd just act like you're crazy."

After the Costner obliteration Robinson was dismayed when he received an official letter ordering him to report to the Grand Central Palace on Tuesday the 27th February 1945 for a medical for re-introduction into the armed services.

A few days after beating LaMotta, on the 27th February 1945, Robinson went to Fort Jay Hospital where he spent several days. Many newspapers were still querying the circumstances surrounding Robinson's 15-month army service and there were a number of letters written to the Senate by parents of those fighting in the war in Europe demanding to know why Robinson had been medically discharged from the army, yet was now back actively fighting in the ring. The New York Times reported that Robinson was called to hospital to be re-examined. These reports were then sent to Washington. The report suggested that Robinson was acceptable for service and Colonel Arthur V. McDermott, the New York City director of Selective Service, announced that Robinson was indeed physically fit for military service and he suggested that he could possibly be called up in May.

Truman Gibson died in 2005; he was 93. Ray McCormack is a retired sergeant from the New York City Police Department and was a former amateur boxer. Now a boxing historian with an extraordinary collection of boxing books and photographs, he currently resides in Las Vegas. Ray became quite friendly with Truman Gibson in his later years. He praised Mr Gibson's dignity and good manners. He used to have long conversations with the former lawyer and official of the International Boxing Club about boxing and obviously Robinson was mentioned a great deal. Ray said Truman had all his mental facilities and was 'as sharp as a tack'. Clear-minded and not bitter. Just before he died Mr Gibson wrote a book: 'Knocking down Barriers - My Fight For Black America.' He writes about Sugar Ray: "Robinson looms in my memory as one of the most difficult men I ever had to deal with. Beset by his own devils, spawned out of hell that defined his upbringing in an America where blacks were worthless, Ray could quickly turn from hail-fellow-well-met to a scheming, conniving, mistrustful foe. The demons from his background made him a tortured soul but also made him something of an actor."

Truman then writes about 1943, when he describes a black soldier who was found wandering around the New York port claiming he didn't know who he was. As it happened, a writer for one of the Hearst newspapers recognised the man as Sugar Ray Robinson. An army officer, Colonel Robert Munson, had a physician examine Robinson. By a quirk of fate, the physician happened to be non other than the nephew of none other than promoter Mike Jacobs. The outcome of the examination determined Robinson had a ruptured eardrum and he was discharged from the army. Then, apparently all hell broke loose in the corridors of power of the American War Department. It was intimated that money was paid. "To smooth things over," wrote Mr Gibson. "Robinson agreed to a series of five fights for the Hearst Milk Fund. Ray had a way of being guilty of doing wrong things that eventually would turn out right in the end." There was also an article that appeared in the Washington Post on the 28th August, stating that Robinson had agreed to box five times and would contribute 20 percent of his purse money to the Disabled Veterans' Fund.

Unfazed by this, Robinson took a couple of months away from the rigours of constant training and spent time with Edna Mae. During this period, she had caught him in the act of bedding a couple of women in a local hotel. Ray blamed Joe Louis, who was with him, and although Edna accepted it, privately she knew different. He worked hard to make it up and took her to the cinema and nightclubs.

On the 14th May in Philadelphia, Robinson returned to action and fought the Puerto Rican tough-guy, Jose Basora. Basora was brought to America by Lou Brix, who managed former world bantamweight champion Sixto Escobar. Basora was a teak-tough fighter who spent a career hovering around the fringes of world class. He was six feet tall, wide-shouldered and had a well-founded reputation as a puncher. His list of opponents indicate his class and included Ezzard Charles, the heavyweight champion, Kid Tunero, Holman Williams, Fritzie Zivic and LaMotta, whom he met three times with one draw, one loss and one win.

Before the fight the Puerto Rican was classed as a 7-1 underdog, but he managed to cause a major surprise by holding Robinson to a ten round draw in front of a 14,653 crowd, the first tied fight of Robinson's career. It was a physically hard duel, but Sugar Ray thought he had just done enough to edge it. Both men demanded a quick return.

However, two more fights followed in quick succession. Washington's Jimmy McDaniel had fought Eddie Booker, Henry Armstrong and Jack Chase but Robinson accomplished in less than five minutes what no other fighter had managed in 65 previous fights. He hardly wasted a move and made every punch count. He dropped McDaniel in his own corner but was foiled by the bell. In the second, he blasted his stricken opponent with a string of left hooks before referee Benny Leonard, the former world lightweight champion, stepped in to halt the assault. The 11,210 spectators in Madison Square Garden were not disappointed. Just over eight weeks later, 4,500 Buffalo fight fans watched him score a fifth round stoppage over Jimmy Mandell.

These two fights were considered as sharpeners before he faced Jake LaMotta for the fifth time. The venue was Chicago's Comiskey Park and 14,755 made the trip for the latest in this dynasty. The Bull declared that he knew victory was assured and he supported his assertions by storming forward throughout the entire 12 rounds and forcing Robinson to box off his back foot. Robinson adapted comfortably and made brilliant use of his accurate left jab, which repeatedly jerked LaMotta's head back on his sinewy shoulders. The affair ebbed and flowed and split opinions in the crowd before Ray was awarded a very close points decision. Referee Johnny Baer and one judge voted for him. "I was lucky to come away with my life," Robinson uttered on his way back to his dressing-room.

Robinson's final fight of the year was a return with Vic Dellicurti in the Boston Garden. The 6,428 fans were not particularly impressed with his third victory over the cagey veteran because it was evident that Robinson could have ended the fight at any stage of the ten rounds but instead seemed content to use his shorter opponent merely as a punch bag.

Boxing journalists repeatedly sought for Sugar Ray to get what they considered to be his rightful chance to fight for the world welterweight title. Freddie 'Red' Cochrane had never defended it since he beat Henry Armstrong in July 1941 due to being on active service in the American Navy. He had returned to action in June and August of this year when he fought Rocky Graziano twice and was knocked out both times in the tenth round. Ray, however, told the press that he was prepared to be patient.

******

Robinson brought in 1946 by stopping Dave Clark in two rounds at Pittsburgh's Duquesne Gardens. He had floored Clark three times for counts of nine before the referee Ernie Sesto stopped it. He followed this by having a further three bouts before he was due to meet the former world lightweight champion Sammy 'The Clutch' Angott again in Pittsburgh.

He boxed at the Elizabeth Armoury, New Jersey and beat Tony Riccio in four rounds. He donated his 30% fee to the Infantile Paralysis Fund. Ten days later he was back in Detroit appearing at the Olympia Stadium in front of 14,922 fans, which was the venue's record attendance for the previous three years. He fought O'Neill Bell, who only two weeks earlier had fought and beaten Fritzie Zivic. He had also previously defeated California Jackie Wilson and George Costner and so could not be considered as a pushover. In the opening round, however, Robinson connected with a powerful left hook which decked Bell. By the second, Robinson had moved up into a higher gear and finished the fight within a minute and a half. Twelve days later, he journeyed to St. Louis to meet Cliff Beckett, the Canadian middleweight champion. Some press observers later commented that the Canadian should never have been allowed in the same country, let alone the same ring, as Robinson and a complete mismatch was concluded within 40 seconds of the fourth when Beckett was left prostrate on the canvas.

A fortnight later heralded the concluding part of the Sammy Angott trilogy. Sammy told the Associated Press that if he "didn't beat Sugar Ray this time, I will retire," and so Robinson began the fight determined to end Angott's career as he stamped his authority on the contest and completely out-classed and thrashed his opponent. He moved fluently around the ring and used his stinging left jab to open him up before bringing his two-handed combinations into play. The former lightweight champion was floored twice for brief counts. The 7,000 crowd in the Duquesne Gardens in Pittsburgh, another record for this venue, enjoyed the spectacle and applauded Robinson throughout the ten rounds, of which he won nine and drew one. Angott's promise to bow out of the game was forgotten, however, as he went on to record a further 23 fights before finally retiring in 1950 with a total record of 133 fights (98 wins, 27 losses and eight draws).

After this masterclass, the press christened Robinson as 'the uncrowned welterweight champion of the world' because the champion Freddie Cochrane had now been discharged from the Coast Guard and instead of fighting Robinson, chose to defend it against Marty Servo for a $50,000 purse. Robinson had defeated Servo twice in 1941 and 1942 but the cunning, well-connected Al Weill, who would later guide Rocky Marciano to the heavyweight championship, ensured that his man received the first shot, which proved prescient as on 1st February, Servo knocked out Cochrane in four rounds to become the new world champion.

Eddie Eagan, the Chairman of the New York Athletic Commission, responded to the press criticisms by instructing the new champion to defend the title against Robinson in his next fight. Eagan believed that Robinson deserved his title opportunity, but Weill evaded his petitions for a date and instead matched Servo against the ferocious right-hand hitter Rocky Graziano in a non-title fight for a $40,000 purse. Servo was knocked out in two rounds and sustained a nose injury. This defeat strengthened Eagan's position and he publicly spoke out on Robinson's behalf and insisted that Weill sign a contract for Servo to fight Robinson.

Robinson travelled to his usual training camp, which he called his 'cabin in the sky' camp, in Greenwood Lake, New York. The fight was scheduled to take place at the Yankee Stadium, but because the Yankees were required to play a postponed match, the fight was then put back. It was destined never to take place as Servo chose to relinquish the title, citing the injury to his nose as the reason for his retirement from boxing. Hastily drawn plans to fight Beau Jack ended after a long series of negotiations and so Robinson did what he knew best and kept busy.

He embarked on a nine fight schedule which would ensure that he was ready and sharp in case a world title suddenly materialised. It started with his fourth bout against Izzy Jannazzo in Baltimore, which he won by a clear ten round points decision. He then graced the Golden Gate Arena, New York and had no trouble with Freddie Flores, knocking him out just before the end of the fifth. He then seamlessly demolished Fred Beadle in two rounds at the Worcester Auditorium before meeting, once again, Norman Rubio, who he had stopped in eight rounds in 1942. The crowd of 6,000 enjoyed the ten round contest which Robinson won clearly. Afterwards, he announced that the profits from the tournament were being donated to the Italian Relief Fund.

12,353 Madison Square Garden devotees saw him meet Newark's Joe Curcio and witnessed a chaotic match. A fraction of a second after the bell sounded to end the first round, Robinson smashed a tremendous left hook on to Curcio's jaw and stretched him flat on the canvas. Curcio's seconds didn't try to move their man to his corner but elected to try and revive him on the ring floor. The fight doctor, Dr William Walker, examined the stricken fighter and as this scene took place, the bell to signal the new round sounded. Curcio, still stretched out, was unable to answer the call and so Billy Cavanagh, the referee, started counting. The official time of the ending was, therefore, recorded as being with ten seconds of the second round. When the crowd realized that the fight was over and that Robinson was not being disqualified for punching after the bell, a number of Curcio's followers climbed onto the ring apron to attack the referee and Robinson. A small riot ensued and the police had to intervene to restore calm. After the fight, both Robinson and the referee claimed that they had not heard the bell sound. Curcio disagreed and argued that he had heard it and immediately dropped his arms, leaving himself wide open for the finishing punch. Cavanagh responded by reminding him of his final instruction to "defend yourself at all times".

In August he travelled to the Hawkins Stadium in Albany, New York to knock out local boy Vinnie Vines in six rounds. Sidney Miller, from Youngstown, Ohio, was his next victim at the Twin City Bowl, New Jersey, and was hammered to a third round defeat. Following this, Ossie 'Bulldog' Harris fought ten rounds at Forbes Field. Robinson won every round except the sixth on his way to an entertaining victory. Previously Harris had fought LaMotta, Tommy Yarosz, Fritzie Zivic, Jose Basora, Tony Zale and Charley Burley; he was no mug! Robinson then treated 8,614 spectators jammed into the Olympia, Detroit to a six round demolition of local favourite Cecil Hudson. Hudson was downed twice before being counted out.

Just before his next engagement his frustration got the better of him and he took the opportunity to publicly lash out at Mike Jacobs via the newspapers. Robinson declared that it was Jacobs who had constantly blocked him from fighting for the world lightweight championship and for the world welterweight title. He growled that "Mike Jacobs will manipulate anybody for a buck" before suggesting that Jacobs was annoyed that he fought for other promoters without his permission. "If you don't do what he wants, he'll try to prevent you from getting fights anywhere. You don't earn the world championship on merit any more, you buy it," he said.

8.

The Hardest Puncher
I Ever Fought

ROBINSON'S NEXT fight took place in Cleveland against the middleweight Artie Levine, who was a former US Marine. The Cleveland boxing fraternity fans had championed Brooklyn's Levine after he had started his career in May 1941 with an impressive two-round victory over Carl Jones. Robinson received a purse of $12,500, which, he suggested after the fight should have been trebled. It turned out to be a great deal, hotter than what Robinson had hoped or expected.

Once the fight was signed, promoters Larry Atkins and Bob Brickman got busy with the publicity and 16,000 spectators responded and packed into the Cleveland Arena, setting a new state record. Levine, a 21-year-old Jewish-American who stood at 5'8" and possessed powerful shoulders and a bull-like neck, was a fully-fledged middleweight and had won 30 of his previous fights by knockout. He was classed as a 5 to 1 underdog, partly because he had dropped a surprising ten round decision to little known Jimmy Sheppard in his previous fight (this was later avenged in a chilling six round annihilation a few weeks after the Robinson bout). Significantly, it ignored the fact that previous to this, he had flattened his last seven opponents. Levine, weighing ten pounds heavier than his foe, signalled big trouble for Robinson.

The first four rounds witnessed some intelligent boxing from both men with Robinson edging the scoring with his classier style. Levine issued an early signal that he possessed TNT in both fists in the second round when he rocked Sugar Ray and he later commented that this "made him aware that this man could take my head off my shoulders if I got complacent." In the fifth round, an upset appeared imminent when Artie landed with a short and snapping left hook before following it with a thundering right cross to the jaw. The 16,000 spectators clambered to their feet to witness Robinson crash to the canvas face first. Instead of taking up the count, the referee walked Levine to a neutral corner before returning to the prostrate Robinson and beginning the count, which Ray struggled to beat, shakily finding his feet at the count of nine. Robinson recalled these long moments: "I remember being on the floor and looking out of the ring and seeing

George Gainford. His face was frozen; he looked like he was about to die." Groggy, cut and bruised, the fans screamed themselves hoarse demanding that Robinson's challenge be terminated. Gainford screamed above the noise that his charge should "box and move", but Robinson's legs were later described by newspaper reports as being "like a new born giraffe trying to stand for the first time." Slowly, he managed to gather his scrambled senses and keep away from Levine's wild attempts to complete the job. As the tenth and final round was about to commence, Soldier Jones, one of Robinson's seconds, leaned between the ropes. "Gamble son," he whispered to the beleaguered Sugar Ray. "Now's the time to take a gamble." Although dazed and hurt, Ray nodded and dug deep into the reserves of courage, pride and class to deliver a left hook to the body that dropped Levine to the bottom rope where he was counted out with only sixty seconds remaining of the fight.

Afterwards, Levine was furious. "In the fifth round I caught him with a powerful left hook, my favourite punch. He hit the canvas and I went to a neutral corner and the referee follows me to make sure I stay there, he then moves across to where Robinson was lying on the canvas and starts counting from one! Robinson was actually on the floor for 19 seconds." Robinson's recollections were more generous. He claimed that Levine "was the hardest puncher I ever fought" and he agreed when Levine asked him for a return fight but the fight never came to fruition.

After his retirement, Robinson always maintained that the Levine fight was his toughest. He recalled the moment when he stared defeat in the eye. "Levine started to throw a right cross and I prepared to block it. When I looked in my glove it wasn't there. He hit me with a hook and the next thing I remember was the referee shouting out the count of four." Eddie Futch, the trainer who would later guide numerous world champions to success, recalled that "I had a fighter on the bill when he fought Levine. My guy was on last so I watched Robinson starch Artie, who was a damn good fighter and a hell of a puncher. In the tenth round Robinson caught Artie with a terrific punch on the chin. Levine backed into the ropes, Sugar Ray swarmed all over him hitting him with two-handed punches. Levine tucked up and had both arms up, blocking beautifully. Within a split second Robinson had noticed Levine had left his body unprotected and switched a fast right to his body, down he went and the referee counted him out. What I vividly remember was when Artie came back into the dressing room; I was getting my guy ready. Levine was mightily upset and I tried to tell him plenty of fighters get knocked out and not to let it bother him because he was still a top class fighter. Levine ignored me and shouted: 'That was a fast count. The referee just said ten, and it was all over.' I told him that ten was the last number the ref counted, not the first. The poor man had been concussed, out cold. "

In mid-1975, boxing journalist Mike Silver wrote a story about Artie Levine which appeared in The Ring magazine. Artie was living in Hollis Hill, New York with his wife Miriam and children, Gary and Deena. His memories of the fight were still sharp. "I can describe it best in one word - awesome," he smiled. "I respected Robinson, I knew he was a great fighter but I was out to win the fight. I was in great shape. In the ring with Robinson, it was like fighting a machine. He was ahead of you all the way, very sharp. And you didn't get any openings with Ray. He was moving away from me, and just as I was getting ready to punch, he would touch me on the shoulder knocking me off balance and nullifying the punch." He recalled that in the tenth round Robinson had caught him in his Adam's apple and he lost his voice for a week afterwards. "In the tenth, Ray got lucky and knocked me out. But the fight was close all the way. I gave him a beating and cut him up pretty bad." His only regret was that he "didn't fight Robinson the year before because I was at my best then." Levine boxed for a further three years before retiring in 1949 aged 24.

Robinson moved on and there were quite a number of fighters in the welterweight ranks who were touted as possible challengers for him to meet to contest the vacant world welterweight championship. Eventually, Ohio's Tommy Bell was accepted. In truth, Bell was the only welterweight who was prepared to meet Robinson for the vacant world title; the other welterweights declined the offer. This would be their second meeting after Robinson had beaten him over ten rounds nearly two years earlier, but he was respected as a solid, tall stylist with a fair dig in each fist.

The reason Bell was the only challenger prepared to meet Robinson for the world championship was answered by Tony Pellone, AKA Jimmy Pell, who was born and raised in New York. Tony was a top ten welterweight at this time and had two victories over Billy Graham and won and lost to world lightweight king Bob Montgomery. "Quite a few of the top ten fighters were offered the fight with Sugar Ray, but we turned it down," said Tony. He said later in life they turned it down because Robinson refused to 'carry' them, meaning let them go the distance. "He was a damaging puncher and could ruin you," added Tony. "No welterweight wanted to fight him." (He mentioned that Robinson agreed to carry Charlie Fusari, whom Robinson would defend his world title against in 1950.)

Robinson went to his customary training camp in Greenwood Lake to prepare for his title shot. Gainford knew that he only needed sharpening up because he had already boxed fifteen times that year and so his physical conditioning was fine. His preparations were, however, interrupted by Ray's own candour.

One day he sat and spoke with some journalists who came to report on his preparations. The discussion moved on to the proposed Marty Servo title fight that never happened and Robinson recalled that a well-dressed man had entered the gym and mumbled an offer to him of $25,000 not to even try and make the weight for Servo. Robinson later said that he had forgot to report this encounter, but it soon exploded when a story was published suggesting that Robinson had been offered a bribe. He was then hauled before the New York State Boxing Commission and asked to explain why he had not reported this matter. He was fined $500 and suspended for 30 days.

9.

World Champion at Last!

SUGAR RAY Robinson met Tommy Bell on 20th December 1946 at Madison Square Garden in front of 15,673 spectators. It was a bitterly cold winter night and the snow tumbled down making the huge skyscrapers look like giant Christmas trees. It was only six weeks since the ferocious Levine fight and the memory of that draining night, along with an annoyingly persistent cold, left Robinson feeling perturbed.

He struggled to find a rhythm in the early rounds and complained to Gainford that he felt slow and sluggish. In the second round, Bell connected with a left hook which felled the overwhelming favourite. Robinson jumped up at seven and seemed embarrassed and tore around the ring after Bell, who never appeared to believe that he could repeat his luck and put him down again. The fight proved an absorbing contest before Robinson finally caught the Ohio fighter with a viciously effective combination left and right cross in the 11th round. He dropped to the canvas but regained his feet before the count reached eight but then had to withstand uppercuts, bolo punches and left and right hands, thrown like machine gun bullets, by a now invigorated Sugar Ray. Bell managed to weather the storm and last the distance. It had not been one of Robinson's greatest fights, in fact it was desperate at times, but at the finish the throng stood and cheered, clapped, stamped their feet and yelled their appreciation. Edna Mae, his mother and sister Marie were sat ringside and had cheered themselves hoarse as the MC made the announcement. Referee Eddie Joseph gave Robinson ten rounds and Bell five. Judge Artie Schwarts concurred and Jack O' Sullivan scored it eight rounds for Sugar Ray, six for Bell with one round even. Sugar Ray Robinson was the world welterweight champion at long last. An emotional champion said, "I have waited so long for a world title fight that I never thought I would get my chance in my 76th fight."

He received $20,000 as his share of the purse money. He obviously wanted much more but Jacobs told him that if he had fought a white contender instead of Bell, who of course was black, the money would have been much bigger. Despite this he was gloriously happy.

Instead of celebrating his victory and new status as a world champion in his customary manner, he focused on becoming a property magnate. Robinson drove to Seventh Avenue in Harlem and purchased three flats. He had agreed to pay almost $100,000 and handed over a $15,000 deposit. This purchase had followed his acquisition of a tavern. He used Winfred Springer as his broker after he had met him living in the same apartment block as his mother. He helped Robinson to set up a company called Robincrest Inc. He then hired a leading architect, Vertner Tandy, to draw up the plans for his new tavern, called 'Sugar Ray's', which opened on Christmas Eve. Later he would add Sugar Ray's Cleaning and Dye Shop, which employed seven workers before The Edna Mae Lingerie Shop was opened, quickly followed by the Golden Gloves Barber Shop, which was next door to his office and which he claimed belonged to George Gainford.

Also during this period of frenzied commercial activity, Ray fell drunk for the first time in his life. He was relaxing at home with Edna Mae when he found a bottle of champagne. He tried it and finding that it tasted like ginger ale, he filled the glass to the brim and gulped it down. Unused to alcohol, he then started behaving strangely and Edna became alarmed and called his mother. She arrived and smelling the drink, proceeded to shake him like a rag doll before whacking him straight in the face. "I thought Jake LaMotta had hit me," he later joked. "My mother was the only person who scored a knockout against me throughout my entire career."

During this period, Mike Jacobs suffered a cerebral stroke which left him a semi-invalid. Robinson had a number of dealings with Jacobs and his 20th Century Sporting Club but was reassured that the business would continue and be led by Sol Strauss and Harry Markson. Markson was a cultured man who loved listening to the New York Philharmonic at Carnegie Hall and expressed his determination to resist any involvement with Frank 'Blinky' Palermo and Frankie Carbo and the other underworld figures who lurked around the boxing business.

A number of other organisations looked to capitalise on Jacobs' misfortune, including James Dougan Norris, the 41-year old millionaire who owned the Chicago Stadium, the Detroit Olympia and the St. Louis Arena. It was a commonly known fact that Norris operated closely with the mob and had notorious underworld figures like Frankie Palermo and Frankie Carbo acting for him. Another promotional outfit which emerged was The Tournament of Champions, which was jointly owned by CBS, Music Corporation and Allied Syndicates. They actually made an offer to Robinson and he agreed to fight Steve Belloise for them.

The company which did emerge as the leading force, however, did so quietly. Joe Louis wanted to retire but was keen to cash in on the title he had held for over ten years and so, acting alongside Truman Gibson, his attorney, they signed Ezzard Charles, 'Jersey' Joe Walcott, Lee Savold and

Gus Lesnevich to contracts to contest the heavyweight title when it was vacated. This move allowed The International Boxing Club to wrestle control from Jacobs. They then asked Harry Markson to run the boxing business in Madison Square Garden, a position he held for nearly forty years.

******

Robinson opened the New Year with three routine contests. In March, he travelled to the Dorsey Park Arena, Miami. After coasting through the first two rounds, he opened up with a vengeance and stopped Bernie Miller in three rounds, including putting the hapless Miller down five times in the third round. The small crowd of 3,477 were thrilled with his display. Less than a week later he knocked out Fred Wilson in three in a return bout at Akron Armoury, Ohio. In the third he decked Wilson for nine. Back on his feet, Robinson then finished him off. It was an accurate right uppercut which knocked Wilson into oblivion. His pace was relentless as five days later he appeared in the Memorial Hall, Kansas City and stopped Eddie Finazzo in the fourth round. In the third round he had Finazzo on the canvas twice for counts of nine before finishing off in the following round with a tremendous left hook. During this period, Jack Solomons, the top British promoter, was attempting to sign Sugar Ray to box the British welterweight champion Ernie Roderick, but Roderick was beaten in Paris by Robert Villemain and Solomons decided not to complete the deal.

On the 16th May, he returned to the Garden to face the robust and experienced Georgie Abrams, a balding flat-nosed block of concrete. Abrams had an impressive pedigree, fighting the great French fighter Marcel Cerdan over ten rounds before losing on points, as well as losing on points to Tony Zale in a 1941 unified world middleweight title fight. Abrams had secured his status as the outstanding challenger after claiming three victories over Billy Soose, the former world middleweight champion. He had also drawn with the man many believed Robinson was avoiding, Charley Burley! Georgie weighed in 15 pounds heavier that Robinson and declared that he was "determined to teach Sugar Ray a few lessons."

In the first round, Abrams opened a cut over Robinson's right eye which caused him problems. The welterweight champion's advantage in height, reach and speed helped him tremendously. The cut eye caused him problems. He was guilty of throwing over twenty punches below the belt and lost the seventh and eighth rounds because referee Eddie Joseph penalised him for this repeat offence. It went to the scorecards and Marty Monroe voted six rounds for Abrams and four for Robinson; Judge Frank Forbes and referee Eddie

Joseph, however, both voted for Sugar Ray by a score of six rounds to four. This however had been a physically tough encounter for Robinson, Abrams had extended him all through the fight.

Robinson had been so confident of securing victory that he had signed to defend his title against Jimmy Doyle in Cleveland an amazing four days after beating Abrams. Because of his eye injury, he phoned the promoter, Larry Atkins, to request a postponement. Atkins was annoyed, believing that Sugar Ray was up to his old tricks of pulling out of a fight for more money, but this was not the case. He agreed to a new date of 10th June, but Robinson asked for longer because he couldn't feel sure his injury would have fully recovered. The promoter was seething. Within days, the newspapers were once again full of stories suggesting that he was "ducking the challenge of Doyle". He eventually agreed to defend his crown on the 24th June.

Jimmy Delaney (Doyle was his ring name) was a beetle-browed welterweight from Los Angeles. The newspapers incorrectly reported that he was from Irish stock but both his mother and father were actually French-Canadian. His manager Paul Doyle (no relation) was being helped by Art Winch, the experienced co-manager of Tony Zale, the former world middleweight champion. Doyle had secured a return bout contract for his man. The championship fight was being broadcast live on National Radio.

Doyle's career up to this challenge provided a great deal of media interest and concern. When he had first turned professional he was regarded as an unadventurous fighter. During 1945 he left Los Angeles and moved to New York. He trained in the famous Stillman's Gym in New York. After watching him spar a trainer told him that if he wanted to make a name for himself and big money he would have to change his style and become more adventurous and aggressive and score knockouts. As a youngster he had read a book about the former heavyweight champion Jack Johnson. He later met Johnson in Los Angeles and asked if he would teach him a few techniques. As a result, he started to win regularly. The fans, however, were far from enamoured by his brand of boxing. This was why he went to New York.

Afterwards he ignored Johnson's teachings and became aggressive. He was winning and fought quite a few times in the Cleveland area. He was reported to have won 46 of his 53 pro fights. He was then matched with the dynamic-punching Artie Levine and acquitted himself incredibly well as he was said to be winning quite comfortably before Levine dropped him backwards in the ninth round, and, as he fell, he struck his head against a metal turn- buckle on the ring ropes. He was then rushed to hospital, suffering from sustained concussion and a fractured skull. This injury prompted Willie Ritchie, the Chief Inspector of the California State Athletic Commission, to prevent Doyle from boxing in their jurisdiction on medical grounds, which forced Doyle to seek fights in Pennsylvania and New York. He looked impressive winning his five fights before his challenge for Robinson's title.

Despite the misgivings the fight went ahead. Jimmy Doyle was to receive 20 percent of the net receipts. The Cleveland newspapers were delighted that their city was staging a world championship match, a rare occurrence. However, Franklin Lewis of the Cleveland Press was extremely critical of the fight. He wrote that the ease of Robinson's victory would be determined "by how quickly and easily he found the soft spot on the head of Doyle." He sounded an ominous warning that "it is quite possible that Doyle could be seriously and permanently harmed. It is possible, quite possible, I fear, that Doyle could be seriously and permanently harmed by another thorough lacing." How poetic!

It was reported that the medical officer of the Cleveland Boxing Commission, Dr Arthur Hegedorn, was also against the fight taking place. To counter this negative criticism Larry Atkins asked how was it that Doyle had passed all the medical tests if he wasn't fit to box. "I'm no doctor," he said, "but I take their word if they say he is fit to fight. I can't see how I'm taking a chance." He then attempted to denigrate Robinson. "Believe me; Robinson was on the floor when he beat Tommy Bell for the title. Doyle could always handle Bell. This fight may be tougher for Robinson than anybody thinks."

Whilst in Cleveland, Sugar Ray based himself in his friend Roger Price's house. The training and preparations had gone well but Robinson slept fitfully the evening before the fight and was visibly disturbed. He told George Gainford that he had dreamed that Doyle would die following their fight. Gainford reassured him and urged him to forget about it. Robinson was so disconcerted by it that he asked Larry Atkins to postpone the fight but was rebuffed. He asked again at the weigh-in and Atkins brought a Roman Catholic priest to speak to Robinson. The priest told him to concentrate on fulfilling his legal obligations to the promoter. On the way to the Cleveland Arena he still had bad feelings about the outcome.

Referee Jackie Davis gave them their instructions and once the bell sounded, Robinson was forced to use every trick in his considerable repertoire to keep the irrepressible Doyle at bay. Doyle was giving a good account of himself and even cut the champion's right eye brow. In the eighth, Robinson launched a counter left hook which landed on its intended target - Doyle's jaw - and as he went down, he banged his head on the canvas. He attempted to regain his feet but couldn't make it. The bell to end the round sounded and so referee Davies shouted that the fight wasn't over, but Paul Doyle, the manager, knew his fighter was through and went over to Robinson's corner and lifted his hand in victory.

Doyle was then rushed to the St. Vincent Charity Hospital where Dr Spencer Braden, an eminent brain surgeon, operated on the blood clot. A distraught Robinson visited the hospital with his friend, Dr. Middleton Lambright, but they were not permitted to see the stricken Doyle. Robinson insisted on waiting until Doyle regained consciousness but was persuaded to rest by Father James Nagle, who had administered the last rites to Doyle before he died. Father Nagle proved a great solace to the champion in the following days as he attempted to come to terms with the tragedy he had sensed.

Robinson was distressed when he heard the news and even the embrace of Edna could not console him. At the inquest into the tragedy, he was questioned about the fight by the Coroner, Samuel J. Gerber, who asked why he had chosen to fight Jimmy Doyle. Robinson replied, "Mister, I didn't pick him. I got $25,000 to defend my title against him. That was a lot of money." Gerber later asked Robinson if he had intended to injure Doyle. Robinson looked straight at the Coroner and told him that it was his business "to get Doyle into trouble". He was cleared of any blame but left Cleveland a very sad world champion. Gerber, however, later claimed that a great deal of pressure had been put on him to withhold the investigation but refused to divulge the identities of those who allegedly had tried to influence his investigation.

Shortly after the tragedy, George Gainford received a telephone call from Manila. It was from Barney Peller, the manager of a Philippine boxer called Flashy Sebastian. He offered Robinson $35,000 to fight Sebastian in Manila; Robinson's biggest ever purse. Gainford passed on the message and Robinson spoke to Peller, who told Robinson that he could get to Manila from San Francisco by boat in two days. After the discussions, he talked it over with Gainford and instructed him to send a telegram to formally accept the offer. His upbeat mood quickly disintegrated, however, when he discovered that the journey from San Francisco didn't take two days but two weeks. Gainford suggested that they fly instead, but Ray turned the suggestion down flat; he didn't like flying and there was no way he was staying two weeks on a boat.

A number of boxing reporters saw this as a chance to poke fun. They gleefully recalled the time when he mysteriously ended up in hospital instead of accompanying Joe Louis overseas to England when he also claimed that he "had an allergy where boats were concerned". Eddie Eagan, the New York Boxing commissioner, helped Robinson out of this situation. He was organising a charity tournament in aid of the American Legion in New York and he suggested that Robinson offer his services and get the press off his back. Robinson readily accepted his offer with one proviso - he must fight Flashy Sebastian. Instead of earning a career-best purse, he agreed to fight for just $5,000.

World Champion at Last!

He insisted on a warm-up fight before meeting the Philippino because he wanted to gauge how he would feel back in the ring after the tragedy of Jimmy Doyle, and so, on 21 August, almost two months to the day after the Doyle fight, he climbed back through the ropes of a ring in the Rubber Bowl in Akron, Ohio. It was billed as the first of the 'benefit' bouts for Jimmy Doyle's family and despite his nerves he flattened 'Sailor' Sammy Secreet in one round with a missile of a right cross that hit Secreet flush on the chin and knocked him out cold. He declared himself satisfied with this return, but the local promoter was disgruntled that a small crowd had shown to watch a whole tournament which lasted a mere 16 minutes.

28 days later he entered Madison Square Garden to face Flashy Sebastian. This meeting lasted only seconds longer than his previous fight before Sebastian was dispatched with ease. It later emerged that Sebastian had been stopped six times before this fight and was hopelessly unqualified to meet a fighter of Robinson's stature. Afterwards, Robinson gave Barney Peller $1,000 for expenses relating to the Philippines trip which was cancelled. He was also proud to give $2,500 to Jimmy Doyle's mother.

In October, he travelled across the country to Los Angeles to box his old army friend, Jackie Wilson. This was another benefit in aid of Doyle's mother. The contest was like a sparring session between the two close friends until referee Abe Roth visited Robinson's corner at the end of the sixth and told him, "You're supposed to be a world champion, well fight like one." The crowd had started booing and Sugar's pride was stung by the referee's remarks. He opened up with a whistling left hook which stretched Wilson flat out on the canvas. Wilson amazed onlookers by climbing back to his feet, but his legs were like rubber. Robinson showed no mercy by knocking him through the ropes and forcing the referee to stop it. The tournament made $6,500 and Ray added this to the earlier $2,500 and then he established a trust fund in the Union Trust Company and insisted that his press agent, Pete Vaccare, become a trustee of the company which then paid Mrs Doyle $50 a month.

His next fight was scheduled for New Jersey in December against Billy Nixon (his actual name was James Lewis). A few weeks prior to fighting Robinson, Nixon had fought Kid Gavilan to a split decision before losing and was, therefore, expected to extend his foe, but he quickly found himself out of his depth. Robinson employed his jab to find his range in the opening three rounds before starting the fourth with a solid left hook to the temple which floored Nixon for a count of eight. A wicked right cross sent him back down again for a further count before Nixon rallied and caught the champion with a couple of left hooks. Unfortunately for him, this only annoyed Sugar and his response was lethal. A hurtful right to the pit of the stomach saw the Philadelphian Nixon take another eight count before this same punch was repeated in the sixth and forced the referee, Paul Cavalier, to intervene.

Ray sat at ringside to watch the heavyweight title fight, with his dear friend Joe Louis defending his crown against the boxing craftsman 'Jersey' Joe Walcott. After winning the title in June 1937 by knocking out James J. Braddock, Joe had been elevated to one of the most popular and loved champions in the history of the sport, but now, eleven years after this reign had begun, Sugar Ray was concerned that Louis had looked so bad. He had met with him and Joe talked, in confidence, about retiring. Robinson listened intently and suggested to Joe that when the time to hang up his gloves arrived, he wouldn't need anybody to tell him. "When it comes to my turn to retire," said Robinson, "I won't need anybody to tell me." He also said boxing will never have to hold any benefit nights for him.

Soon after, he defended his welterweight title for the second time when he faced the awkward Chuck Taylor from Coalport, Pennsylvania. The contest was staged in the city where he thought he was born, Detroit, and the fans were buzzing in anticipation of seeing their home town man perform before them once again. Tickets had sold out within days of going on sale and more than 16,975 people shelled out $83,522 to set a new record for the Olympia.

Buoyed by this, and determined to treat them to a spectacle, he boxed with power, confidence and precision to dominate the proceedings. Taylor was game and made a last defiant gesture at the end of the fourth round where both fighters had slugged toe-to-toe in the centre of the ring apron. Taylor smiled at Robinson and cockily sauntered to his corner. Robinson was incensed and from the start of the fifth round until he drunkenly groped for the ropes in the sixth, Taylor never smiled again. Sugar put him down twice with seven kidney punches which hit him like a loud clap of thunder. Taylor's manager, Jack Laken, shouted to Johnny Weber to stop the fight but the referee ignored his pleas, which prompted the manager to throw the towel in the ring to end the fight. After the fight, Taylor was rushed to hospital and Robinson's worst nightmare appeared to be repeating itself. He rushed to The Women's Hospital and discovered that Taylor was suffering with an enlarged kidney. He was overcome with relief when Taylor was released the following day.

Since the Doyle tragedy, Ray and Edna Mae grew further apart, which she attributed to the death of the boxer. On occasions, he would physically assault her and he moved back in with his mother. During this period at home, he began conducting a number of discreet affairs with other women. This aroused Edna's jealousy and she beseeched him to return to their marital home, which he eventually did.

World Champion at Last!

******

It was March 1948 before Robinson fought again. During this period, he found it hard to keep his weight down and knew his days as a welterweight were numbered. He travelled to Toledo, where he won a routine ten round decision over Ossie Harris, the second time 'Bulldog' Harris had taken him the full ten rounds. Ten days later, he outpointed Henry Brimm (real name Henry O'Brien) over ten rounds. The nearly 12,000 fans were ecstatic, clapping and hollering as the willing local youngster from Buffalo stayed the distance with the world champion. Sugar won seven rounds, Henry two with the other round even and referee Ed Stanton congratulated both boxers for an entertaining contest.

George Gainford received an offer for Robinson to defend his welterweight title against 21-year old Bernard Docusen, known as the 'Big Dook', in Chicago's Comisky Park on the 28th June. Docusen, from New Orleans, was heralded as a sensation and a future certainty to win a world championship. He had only dropped two decisions over fifty nine fights and had the experienced trainer, Whitey Esneault, honing his considerable talents.

Robinson accepted the fight and quickly got down to training. His camp went well, but his struggle to make the weight was more difficult than ever before. Because of bad weather, the fight was twice postponed before finally being staged in front a meagre 8,883 fans. They were treated to a great match up as Docusen matched Robinson inch for inch and gave him a torrid time over the first ten fast-paced rounds. When they emerged for the next round, ringsiders noticed an uncharacteristic snarl across the champion's lips, which seemed ominous. Robinson employed his left jab to back up Docusen against the ropes and then rained two-handed body punches in on him. A whiplash left hook exploded to deposit him onto the canvas for a nine count. The following round saw Bernard attempt to fight back and he inflicted a cut under the champion's right eye. But he lacked the necessary power and looked to be weakening with every passing second, but his resolve prevented Robinson finding the finishing punch. Ray was announced as the clear points winner and still world champion but he was bitterly disappointed. He had negotiated a percentage of the gate receipts and he was dismayed to only receive $7,500.

10.

The Sugar Man versus
The Bolo Kid

FOR MANY boxing connoisseurs, the 23rd September 1948 was a date that was etched in the diary in indelible ink. The Yankee Stadium in New York hosted an evening when the charismatic, world welterweight champion fought the equally flashy, cocky, confident 'Bolo' punching sensation Kid Gavilan, the Cuban Hawk. Gavilan, whose real name was Gerardo Gonzalez, had been fighting in America since 1946 and had gained a considerable reputation amongst fans and journalists alike. Robinson's 90th professional fight would not be for his world title, just a mere ten round contest. But the bill did include Ike Williams meeting Jesse Flores for Williams' world lightweight title.

Gavilan was predictably as tough as nails and made Robinson work hard. The Cuban swarmed forward, but most of his punches landed on the arms and gloves of Robinson and had no discernible impact. Ray didn't extend himself but seemed content to go the distance, despite the hisses and booing from the vociferous Cuban support. Judge Frank Forbes voted 7-2, Judge Arthur Aidala gave it 6-4 and referee Eddie Joseph had it 7-3, all for the champion. Afterwards, Robinson expressed his disappointment and said that he was getting weary of boxing as a welterweight and disenchanted that the quality of his challengers hadn't allowed him to make the kind of money a world champion of his calibre could expect.

There was an interesting aside concerning the Gavilan fight which indicates that Robinson's troubles making the weight were well documented. Angel Lopez, Gavilan's manager, asked him to deposit a $5,000 bond with the commission as a guarantee that he would not weigh more than 150 pounds. At the weigh-in, Robinson came to the scales at a half-pound over the agreed weight but Lopez thought better of claiming his forfeit. He later said the reason he didn't claim the $5,000 from Sugar Ray was because Robinson might not agree to a world championship match with Gavilan at a later date. But he told friends he didn't wish to anger Ray, in the event they did fight he feared Robinson would go all out and do a 'number' on his fighter - Gavilan.

He ended the year with yet another ten round points victory when he beat Bobby Lee in Philadelphia. Lee was a short, stocky fighter who had a knack of making great fighters look ordinary. Robinson was listless and Lee showed him complete disdain as he chugged relentlessly forward throughout the ten rounds. Referee Charlie Daggert gave Robinson the fight 7-3, the judge Harry Lasky saw it 6-4 for the champion while Leo Costello carded 6-2-2 for Robinson. This result prompted a number of critics to suggest that he had peaked and now lost his knockout punch because 1948 was the first (and only) year of his career in which he didn't score an inside-the-distance victory.

He was scheduled for one more fight in the year when he was due to fight Steve Belloise in Boston. While training for the fight, he used a fighter named Tiger Wade as one of his sparring partners. Wade was a respected light-heavyweight who was employed to give Robinson the feel of fighting a fighter as strong as Belloise. After the first day of sparring, Robinson told Wade he could not pay him the agreed fee. Wade was aggrieved but continued to help Robinson for a couple more days. Eventually, however, his agitation got the better of him and the two boxers had to be separated. After the training session, the two men walked outside where Wade, according to Dan Daniel of The Ring magazine, "gave Ray a going over on the street." The Belloise fight had to be postponed.

******

Robinson got 1949 off to a flying start on the 10th February when he knocked out 'Young' Gene Buffalo within 52 seconds of the opening bell in Wilkes-Barre, Pennsylvania. Gene had fought the highly respected Holman Williams and had a victory over Fritzie Zivic and was no pushover. Buffalo, an experienced veteran who had turned professional in 1929, stunned Robinson during the fight's introductions when it was announced that he was entering the ring weighing considerably less than the welterweight limit. Gainford had to explain that Buffalo had weighed in wearing his shoes and tights to appear heavier. (The reason Robinson was concerned was because his opponent had weighed in under the championship poundage, if he won, he could claim his world title.) Sugar was unsure about his tactics in this unexpected situation and asked Gainford what he should do. Gainford kept it simple: "Just knock him out."

Five days later he boxed a return with Henry Brimm, a foe he'd comfortably outpointed just eleven months earlier. Brimm was hugely admired by all after he had been left for dead on the Normandy sands on D-Day and had been reported as killed in action. This respect increased when he held Robinson to a creditable draw. Robinson expressed his admiration for

Brimm and described him as "a good, tough fully-fledged middleweight." This last comment, however, gave an indication about his increasing weight concerns, especially as he had regularly given weight away to bigger fighters, such as LaMotta, in the past.

After this he journeyed to Chicago and, once again, outpointed Bobby Lee over ten rounds. He then boxed in Omaha, Nebraska and thrilled 3,648 fans with the smooth boxing skills he exhibited when decking Don Lee twice on the way to a clear victory on the judge's scorecards. The promoter Max Clayton told the local papers that he had "never seen a fighter as graceful as Sugar Ray Robinson." Nine days later, he stopped Earl Turner in the eighth round in the Auditorium in Oakland. Sugar dropped Turner with a flurry of whiplash two-handed punches in the fifth and it was eight rounds before referee Billy Burke called a halt to this one-sided bout.

Robinson then received notification that he would, once again, be meeting the flamboyant Kid Gavilan, but this time his title would be at stake. He then quickly organised some warm-up fights to reach a peak of conditioning for his Cuban challenger. On 16th May he faced Al Tribuani in a four round exhibition, and then two weeks later, in the Page Arena, New Bedford, he had another return and demolished Freddie Flores in three fast-paced rounds. To give an indication of Freddie's capabilities, he had lost a close decision to Steve Belloise and won and drawn against the murderous punching of Artie Levine. Robinson then moved to Providence and finished off Cecil Hudson in five breathtaking rounds. A terrific right hand smashed into Hudson's solar plexus and he had to be carried from the ring.

Then came the defence of his world welterweight title, which took place on 11th of July in Philadelphia's Municipal Stadium before 27,805 paying fans. Robinson was delighted to receive his biggest ever purse of $51,196, which helped his mood as he set up his training camp in the Cabin-in-the-Sky in Pennsylvania. Gavilan's preparation was far plusher as he based his camp in the upmarket Lash Hotel in Parksville, New York. Gavilan fascinated the well-heeled guests with his presence as he insisted on enjoying his evening meals in the main dinning room and dancing the rumba until well after midnight; hardly ideal preparation to meet Sugar Ray Robinson over a 15 round contest. His ebullient trainer Mundito Medina was equally popular as his charge. Mundito was a keen songwriter who entertained guests by playing the guitar and singing his melodies. The hotel guests were in full agreement that Gavilan need not worry unduly if he lost his challenge for Robinson's title because the hotel management would willingly employ both the Kid and his trainer as entertainers. Gavilan, however, appeared unconcerned about meeting Sugar Ray and told the reporters that he "wasn't impressed, in the least, by Robinson's reputation." He boldly announced that he was going to beat the world champion and proudly take the title back to Cuba. Gavilan's charming manner won the critics over, and a groundswell of opinions started to form which suggested that Robinson, at 29, was slipping from the lofty heights he had attained. They pointed out that his long amateur record along with his 98 professional fights and hectic lifestyle had taken their toll.

Sugar Ray, along with an entourage of 20, left his Cabin-in-the Sky training camp in Pennsylvania where he had completed the bulk of his preparation and moved to Pompton Lakes in New Jersey for his final preparations. Whilst training enthusiastically, he mixed it with games of golf and relaxed by playing the drums in a four-man band. He was also in deep conversation with George Gainford on business matters.

Although Robinson purposely set out to portray an air of confidence, they masked his growing concerns about making the weight. The Gavilan camp played on these worries and openly said that Robinson would weaken himself by trying to come in at the welterweight limit. Gavilan also tried to gain another advantage by employing Charley Goldman, one of the most famous and respected trainers in boxing, to work with him. Goldman advised Gavilan that the key to victory was by keeping on top of Robinson and using the bob-and-weave tactic to evade Robinson's potent two-handed combination punching. The experienced boxing reporters said having Goldman in his camp was a massive factor in his favour.

The reason why the fight was held in Philadelphia was that the infamous Boxing Managers' Guild were on strike, but it didn't deter over 2,000 Cuban fans attending and making a cacophony of noise. Doctor Oscar Gans, the Cuban Ambassador to the United States, was also in attendance and sat alongside the Cuban fighting legend 'Kid' Chocolate, the former world feather and junior lightweight champion, in what many respected pressmen suggested was going to signal the passing of the baton.

Once again for a Robinson title fight the atmosphere was fantastic and the noise from the Cuban contingent made it an event. After the usual introductions and issuing of the referee's instructions, the ring was cleared and the two gladiators did their final limbering up exercises. Before the sound of the opening bell had diminished, Kid Gavilan pounded out of his corner and immediately unleashed a two-handed avalanche of punches. As in the first fight, Sugar Ray adopted a side-on position and took the blows on his arms or slipped them with ease before issuing his own responses. By the fourth round, the ringside observers were suggesting that the hectic pace of the fight couldn't be sustained. Gavilan's followers screamed with delight when they noticed that the champion had blood running down the right side of his face coming from a deep cut over his right eye and believed that this helped to make it a pretty evenly scored event. This, however, was a razor-sharp world champion Gavilan was facing on this occasion.

In the eighth round, Robinson had the Cuban Hawk in trouble but Gavilan's instincts, which had prevented him being knocked out or stopped, nullified Robinson's attacks by bobbing and weaving and avoiding his lunging punches. Charley Goldman's tactics of bobbing and weaving and throwing a range of body-punches disturbed Robinson's rhythm slightly, but Ray was warned by Gainford that he was spending too much time retreating to the ropes which didn't allow him to find the range to get his own punches off and deliver the cleaner, crisper punches of the two men. Ray soon rectified this fault and boxed and countered superbly. He was class personified. The huge crowd were delirious with excitement, Gavilan was flashy but Robinson was chastising him with solid, crisp punches.

Coming into the last quarter, Gavilan noticeably moved up into a higher gear but was surprised when Robinson matched him and appeared to grow stronger. In the fourteenth round, Gavilan became desperate in his attacks and managed to catch the champion with a few punches that seemed to bother Robinson, but the Cuban fans seemed to know that their man required a stoppage or knockout to gain a victory. In the final round Robinson sauntered through the three minutes, which encouraged Gavilan to go for the kill. Robinson's tactics, however, lulled him into a false sense of perspective and when he let fly with a short left hook and followed through with a power-packed right uppercut doubled with a lightning left hook, Gavilan walked straight into it and nearly dropped.

Throughout the 15 rounds, Robinson had exhibited brilliantly skilful boxing, while the Cuban was an exhibitionist. That was the main difference in this championship encounter.

At the final bell, the referee Charley Daggert scored it to Robinson by nine rounds to six and Judge Harry Lasky scored it the same, whilst Frank Knarsborough saw Robinson as a clear twelve rounds to three winner. Gavilan was seething and told the press that Robinson had never hurt him throughout the fifteen rounds. He expressed his disbelief with the scoring and demanded a third fight. Robinson was more sanguine and, looking tired and weary, said, "I must be getting old. A few years ago I'd have finished a fight after hurting an opponent like I hurt Gavilan tonight. But I'm pleased I won clearly."

Despite Robinson's disappointment, the reports acknowledged that they had been too swift in penning his demise. Nat Fleischer captured the general mood in The Ring: "Weight problems and Kid Gavilan's rushing tactics failed to check Robinson. He gave a great exhibition in retaining his world welterweight title." He also suggested Robinson possessed one of the finest brands of boxing seen in a championship match in many years.

A few weeks after the Gavilan victory, he returned to action in the Yankee Stadium against Steve Belloise, rated number two in the world middleweight ratings, in an eliminator for the world middleweight title. Many journalists expressed surprise at taking on such a reputable opponent so soon after the tough test Gavilan had provided. Robinson had been due to meet Belloise in December of the previous year but his altercation with his sparring partner had led to it being cancelled.

Stephen Michael Belloise was born in the Bronx in 1918 as the middle child in a family of five boys and four girls. His older brother Mike became the only one of the three boxing brothers to become a world champion when he won the world featherweight title in 1936. Trained by Jack Friday, Steve was a big middleweight and carried a significant dig with his left hook. He had the first of his century of fights in 1938 and met a lot of top fighters, like future world champions Ceferino Garcia and Ken Overlin. He lost a close decision to former world middleweight champion Al Hostak, and also fought future Joe Louis challenger Tami Mauriello, Holman Williams and Georgie Abrams and knocked out former world light-heavyweight title-holder Anton Christofordis in ten rounds. Immediately prior to fighting Robinson, he had fought Jean Stock and stopped him in eight before he then battered Robert Villemain, cutting him over both eyes and ripping his cheek before gaining a unanimous ten round points decision; and then he outpointed Tommy Bell.

Whatever championship dreams the stout-hearted Steve Belloise entertained were ruthlessly hammered out of him in front of a huge crowd of 28,812. Belloise crumpled under the paralyzing punches of the welterweight king in the sixth round, forcing him to retire on his stool. Robinson redeemed himself in the eyes of those reporters who had criticised him for cancelling the earlier fight. This was Robinson's hundredth fight since turning professional back in 1940 and this was the 63rd early ending he had delivered.

Belloise was staggered early in the second round when Robinson hit him with a pulverising right cross. The fourth was the only round where he appeared to have any semblance of a chance when, after taking a booming right cross which shook him down to his toes, he fought back and forced Robinson to retreat to safety. This though was only a sliver of hope. In the sixth round, Robinson was connecting superbly with dynamic left hooks to his head which caused the spray from his face to explode into the arc lights. Just before the bell ended the round, he hit Belloise with such a potent right to the jaw it caused him to wobble on rubbery legs and groggily stagger back to his corner.

The noise and atmosphere in the stadium was deafening. The spectators were thrilled at watching this boxing artist return to form against a fighter who displayed amazing courage. The ending was dramatic when it came. Sugar Ray upped the pace in the seventh and smashed left and rights into Belloise's body with sickening thuds which were clearly audible at ringside. He swiftly switched from the body and aimed for the head of his ever-weakening opponent. A two-handed combination that finished with a left hook whipped in with lightning speed saw Belloise back away. His reserves of courage forced him to swarm back at Robinson and during these hectic moments before the round neared its conclusion, both fighters simultaneously threw left hooks. Belloise's missed by inches, but Robinson's didn't. It crashed straight on Belloise's jaw with a cracking thud that was heard on the radio broadcast. Belloise sprawled on the canvas but as referee Eddie Joseph reached the count of five, the bell rang and so his seconds jumped into the ring and dragged him back to his corner and doused him with ice cold water, but to no avail and his manager, Eddie Walker, called the referee and told him it was over. "I was unconscious," said Belloise. "I didn't know what hit me and I never heard the bell ending the seventh round."

"I got paid $33,138,99, for proving I wasn't afraid of fighting this man," said Ray.

Amazingly, just over a week after this contest Robinson insisted on fighting again, in a four round exhibition against Al Mobley before fulfilling his obligation to have another four fights before the year's end. Benny Evans was next in Omaha, Nebraska. After a quiet opening couple of rounds, Sugar Ray focused on entertaining the 1,703 spectators before Evans opened the fifth by smashing a powerful right hand to Robinson's chin, which quickly dispelled Robinson's desire to put on a show, and so he subsequently deposited his foe on the canvas four times in quick succession, which forced Evans to beg the referee to stop the fight.

Three days later (yes, three days!) he arrived in Houston, Texas, where he delighted the crowd with a brilliant display of boxing wizardry in the first two rounds before cracking home a vicious left hook onto the chin of Charlie Dotson in the third. The 'Purple Heart' veteran Don Lee gave Sugar Ray another hard tussle in Colorado and forced him to go to the judges to gain his ten round points victory.

In the final fight of 1949, he appeared at the Coliseum Arena in New Orleans to fight Vern Lester from San Francisco. A few months before meeting Robinson, Lester fought Jake LaMotta to a close spilt decision. It was a Sunday afternoon fight staged by Abe Katz, whom the matchmaker Louis Messina had convinced that it would be a tremendous fight in front of the 3,532 fans that had turned out. Lester, who also fought under the alias Jimmy 'Top Row' Allen, had recently lost a close points decision to Jake LaMotta and was tipped to extend the champion.

Prior to the fight, Ray was sat in his hotel room completing his final preparations when the phone rang. His sister Marie called from the Sydenham Hospital in New York to excitedly give him the news that he was now the father of a baby boy. With his hands trembling and his voice cracking with emotion, he was eager to rush home and tried to postpone the fight. George Gainford persuaded him to get the fight over first, and begin celebrations back in New York.

He took Lester out in five rounds but the fight was notable for an amusing incident which occurred just seconds before the bell sounded in the third round. Whilst extracting himself from a clinch, Lester sent a left hook toward Robinson, but the punch accidentally hit the poor referee, Battling Ferdie, on the whiskers and sent him down as if shot by a bullet and laid him out for thirty seconds. After the victory, Ray dedicated the fight to his new son, Ray Robinson the second.

Before he could finally pack up and head home, however, he had to fulfil his commitment to appear at two venues and box a six round exhibition against Gene Burton. The first destination was in Shreveport and the second in Dallas. He did consider withdrawing but was mindful of the continuing bad publicity about his repeated withdrawals. Additionally, Burton, a good fighter in his own right, had been a huge help to Robinson in his preparations for a number of important fights.

He finally got home on 16th November. Sugar Ray was deliriously happy with Ray Junior and declared his intention to be a better influence on him than he had for his first son, Ronnie, who was now ten years old and living with his first wife, Marjorie. He wasn't well suited to domesticity, but he tried. He spent long hours whispering to his new son that as a child growing up in the ghettos of Detroit and New York, he had seen enough of people living from hand to mouth and he intended to get the most out of his talents to prevent his children experiencing that.

A few days later, he heard the news that his old dancing mentor, 'Bojangles' Robinson, had passed away. The old dancing master had been good to the young Sugar Ray and he attended the funeral with a heavy heart.

******

Despite all of his success in the ring Sugar Ray had not received the acclaim of the American public that Joe Louis had enjoyed. Television was still in its infancy and the majority of ordinary Americans heard about their sporting stars through the medium of the newspapers, magazines and the wireless. Although he had demonstrated undoubted class and was perceived as being the boxer of his generation, Robinson was not particularly liked. He was the most criticised boxer of his generation and was perceived as being arrogant and this rankled with him.

On his 28th birthday he decided to address a number of critics by telling his side to a chosen group of journalists he felt were sympathetic to him. He tackled the criticisms of being difficult and his reputation of withdrawing from fights. He expounded that there appeared to be a general consensus of opinion amongst many in the boxing hierarchy that a boxer couldn't and shouldn't speak up for himself. He asked why the majority of fighters ended their careers with hardly a penny to their name before answering his own question. "It's quite simple," he said, "because they leave all the negotiating to their managers and promoters, who are looking after their own interests not the boxer who gets into the ring." He suggested that he was only labelled as a troublemaker after he had started to ask questions relating to money. He emphasised his point further by using former world heavyweight champion, Gene Tunney as a prime example. "Everybody knew that he was his own man and would only do what he thought was right for himself, but today he is worth millions of dollars; he's a very rich man." He contrasted this with the plight of two former world champions who were both huge drawing cards and popular fighters: Henry Armstrong, his boyhood idol, and Beau Jack. "What happened to them and their money?" He boasted that he was the only boxer who could account for every cent of his money since the first time he laced up the gloves in 1940 for his first professional fight. He claimed to keep meticulous records of every financial detail from all of his professional fights. "I know where every quarter I have spent from my purse money from every fight has gone. What other boxer could state that? Every black boxer that ever lived, outside of heavyweight Harry Wills, ended up with no money and broke! I'm not going to make the same mistakes as they did and act the way they acted," he vowed.

The issue of television was another thorn in his side. He acknowledged that this represented a considerable income stream for the promoters which was not trickling down to the fighters. "It's the fighter the viewers are watching, not the promoter. If the promoter was getting nothing for it, I wouldn't want anything either, but if they get paid, I've got to be paid as well."

He believed that his independence - from the boxing authorities and from the financial control of the promoters - was a significant factor in his bad press. "Perhaps people knock me because I am not obligated to any organisation and don't owe anybody a dime." He recounted that Mike Jacobs was forever trying to loan him money. "He [Jacobs] would pull out his cheque book and ask me how much did I need. I always refuse the offer and Jacobs can't understand me because most of the top fighters he promotes are always borrowing money from him and he knows that they owe him both money plus favours for lending them the money."

**The 12-year old Walker Smith Jnr., already showing signs
of the future style which, as Sugar Ray Robinson,
he would thrill the boxing world.**

Sugar Ray's sisters, Evelyn and Marie. Both played a major role in their brother's rise in what was a close-knit family.

Sugar Ray's mother, Leila. It's easy to see where he got his good looks from.

**The delightful Edna Mae, Sugar Ray's wife and confidante
for most of his boxing career.**

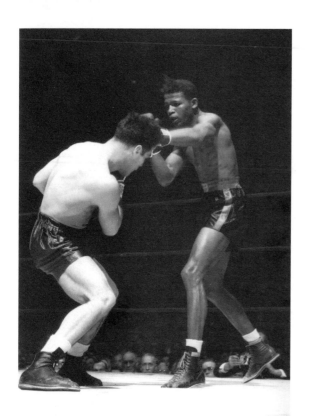

Left: Robinson connects with a solid punch on Sammy Angott in Philadelphia in 1941.

Below: Also in Philadelphia a few fights later - Marty Servo gets ready to deliver a right as Robinson leans backwards ready to block the punch.

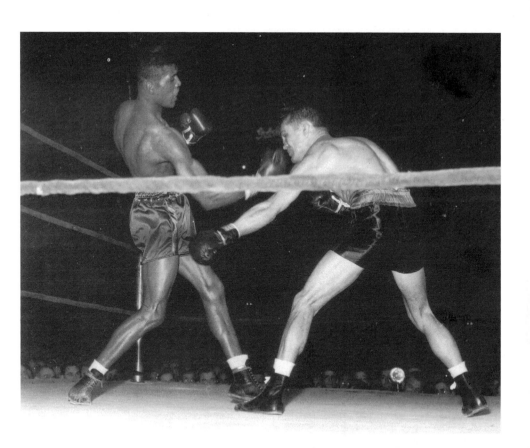

Above: In his final fight of 1941, Robinson connects with a power-packed right uppercut on tough Fritzie Zivic.

Right : Robinson gets set to throw a left hook at Fritzie Zivic in their January 1942 re-match in Madison Square Garden when Sugar Ray stopped the vastly experienced Zivic in the 10th round.

Above: Sugar Ray knocking out Cowboy Ruben Shanks in the second round of their bout in Madison Square Garden in 1942

Left: Robinson in his army fatigues with top promoter Mike Jacobs

Sugar Ray looks the consummate GI in this portrait.
However, the manner of his mysterious exit from the army
was to dog his footsteps for many years to come.

Sugar Ray slumps to his first defeat in a ferocious 10-rounder with the Bronx Bull, Jake La Motta, on the February 5th 1943. Just three weeks later Robinson was to get his revenge at the same venue in what was to be the second of a series of five contests the two fought up to 1951.

For his final fight of 1943 Sugar Ray fought his boyhood hero, the great Henry Armstrong. Despite boasting a career which had seen huge crowds flock to watch him win a world championship at three separate weights, Armstrong was penniless and desperate and pleaded with a distraught Robinson to accept this fight with him.

A champion at last!
Shortly before Christmas 1946 Sugar Ray took on and beat Tommy
Bell in 15 exhausting rounds to win the world welterweight title.

The attorney Truman Gibson oversees the finer points on a contract with Sugar Ray. Gibson came to the fore when Mike Jacobs suffered a cerebral Haemorrhage.

A fateful night. Above: Robinson sends Jimmy Doyle to the canvas
during the world welterweight title defence on June 24th 1947.
Below: Anxious officials and cornermen gather round Doyle's prone
and lifeless body. He died a day later in a Cleveland hospital.

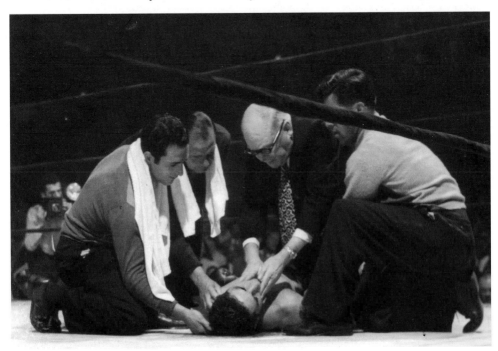

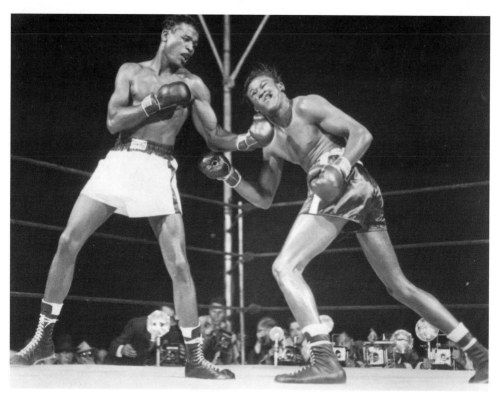

Above: Sugar Ray shows the power of his punching as he overpowers Kid Gavilan to retain his world welterweight title in July 1949 in Philadelphia, followed by, below, a TKO in seven rounds over Steve Belloise in New York City.

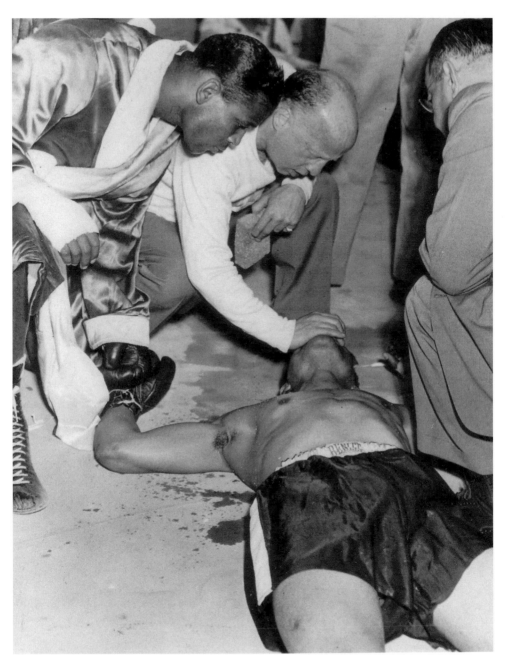

A worried looking Sugar Ray is concerned as doctors and officials attend the stricken Jose Basora, whom Robinson flattened in one sensational round in 1950 in Scranton.

A Sugar Ray right whistles past Charlie Fusari in their world welterweight title fight in 1951 in Jersey City.

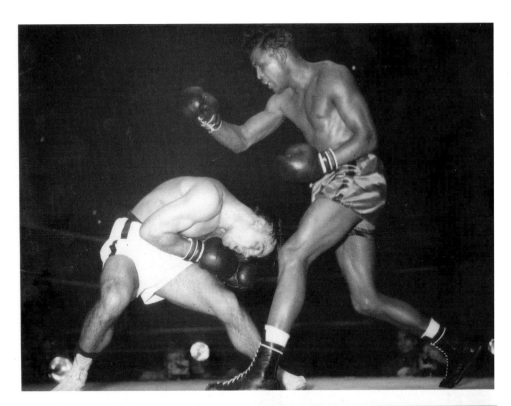

Sugar Ray made his first trip to Europe at the end of 1950, where he was feted wherever he went. Amongst a number of bouts was the one above with Frenchman Robert Villemain, who dives low after a Robinson combination during their encounter in Paris.

Sugar Ray adds the world middleweight title, right, with a convincing 13-round stoppage of Jake La Motta. This was their fifth and final confrontation.

**By the time Sugar Ray took on Randolph Turpin in London in the
summer of 1951, he had lost only once in nearly 150 contests and was
undisputed champion at two different weights.**

He addressed the topic of the bad reputation which he had acquired in the press and argued that "I don't own a newspaper and so I can't argue with them. Because of this the public only gets one side of the story about what I am supposed to be like." He gave the example about the recent exhibitions he had featured in. He had agreed the terms to meet his stablemate Gene Burton with the local promoter. He was, however, unaware that Burton was suspended from fighting in Texas and so the promoter had quickly engaged a fighter named 'Cocoa' Kid to take Burton's place. When he heard about this change, he demanded more money because the terms of the contract - to box Gene Burton - had changed. Rather than engage him in negotiations, the promoter immediately informed the press that Robinson had pulled out of his tournament. "People read the papers and believe what it says. What can I do?" He claimed to have been the victim of "more phoney stories than any other boxer in history." The one story that particularly aggrieved him concerned the story about him receiving a dishonourable discharge from the army. "One newspaper reported that I jumped ship, punched an officer, got court-marshalled and put in the guardhouse. What a load of trollop! I actually joined the army as a private and received an honourable discharge as a sergeant. Enough said!" (After reading this, many people wondered why he had not sued the source of these accusations? He would have received thousands of dollars if these libellous and slanderous allegations about his character were wrong.)

He then warmed to the topic of the numerous advisers and experts that seemed to surround many fighters. "If I went into my barber shop and told the barber how to cut hair, everybody would think I had gone mad, but everybody in the world tries to tell a fighter what to do. I don't try to run anybody else's business but everybody tries to tell me how to run mine." He then made the surprising claim that the respect he so craved was to be found amongst his own; he was often sought out by his pugilistic peers to act as a manager. "People would be surprised at the boxers, both white and black, who wanted me to manage them. I turn them all down because I have my own career to take care of. If I was as bad as I am made out to be, would this kind of thing happen?"

Finally, he attempted to show that his esteemed position had not blinded him to the needs of past greats. "I've boxed more charity events than any other champion in the ring," he said "but few ever mention this charity work that I do. They say I'm cheap but I take more people around the country with me when I fight than any fighter around and it all comes out of my own pocket." He said that he had reached a point where he didn't care what anybody thought of him. "One thing I can tell you, they'll not need to run any benefits for Sugar Ray Robinson!"

At this time, Robinson's confidence in his future financial independence was well-founded. He was ranked as one of the wealthiest residents in Harlem and owned almost an entire block on New York's West side of 7th Avenue, between 123rd and 124th streets. Additionally, he also owned three businesses consisting of a bar and grill, a barber shop and a cleaning establishment. He had also recently bought the house in the Bronx where his mother lived as well as proudly owning his two cars.

He opened up 1950 in fine style by boxing at the New Haven Arena in front of 4,000 fans where he met Philadelphia's George LaRover. LaRover, like many of Robinson's opponents, appeared to be petrified of his fearsome reputation before they had even stepped into the ring. LaRover, despite having 93 fights preceding this meeting, showed little inclination to cause an upset. Robinson was able to ease his way into the fight and began boxing calmly and using his left jab like a wand to conjure a spell over his hapless foe. He snapped jabs and left hooks into his opponents face whenever the mood took him. Several times he hurt the Philadelphian and had him in trouble but chose instead to drop his hands to his side and wait until LaRover had composed himself. This was the manner of the fight until the fourth round arrived and he decided to end the show with a devastating display of two-handed punching. He hit his man just over the eye with awesome power, which deposited LaRover to the canvas for a count of six. He gamely regained his feet but was no more than a sitting target and George Fitch, the referee, was forced to wisely halt the fight and save him from further punishment.

He continued to set the hectic pace of previous years by meeting Al Mobley at the Coral Gables Coliseum in Miami, Florida in front of 4,500 spectators. The Newark fighter was fresh from losing a ten round decision to world lightweight champion Ike Williams just prior to boxing Robinson and, over the course of his 81 bouts, had earned a reputation as an able and experienced campaigner, but Robinson took him out in six clinical rounds when the referee, former world featherweight champion Pete Sarron, was obliged to stop the fight.

Within a fortnight, Robinson arrived in Savannah to face his former sparring partner, Aaron 'Tiger' Wade, at the Municipal Auditorium. Robinson had been requesting this fight for quite a while and had instructed George Gainford to secure it at all costs. Wade was the fighter who had complained loudly about his sparring partner fee and subsequently engaged his employer in a street brawl which resulted in Robinson being forced to pull out of the Steve Belloise fight. In an ironic twist, Robinson was almost forced to postpone this fight due to other injuries he sustained a few days earlier when he was travelling as a passenger in his car, which was being driven by his friend Warren Jones through Melbourne, Florida, when it crashed and left him with minor cuts on his arm and feeling shook up. His determination to meet Wade though was enough to ensure the fight would go ahead.

Wade brought a respectable pedigree to the meeting and had been in with the top fighters of the era. He held a points victory over Archie Moore and had also fought class fighters like Holman Williams, Bert Lytell, Charley Burley and Jack Chase. This didn't appear to be any concern to the vengeful Robinson, who entered the ring looking solemn and focused. After he spent the first round moving briskly around the ring, he exploded into life in the second and battered 'Tiger' from pillar to post, flooring him four times with dynamic and venomous two-handed punches. Robinson was mean and merciless and allowed Wade to last seconds into the third round before knocking him senseless. Afterwards, he claimed that the victory was "a vindication in more ways than one."

Five days later he arrived in St Louis to fight Frenchman Jean Walzack and ensured that he fulfilled a promise to the promoter Hans Bernstein to box on one of his tournaments. The blonde haired Walzack was the French welterweight champion and during the first three rounds, Robinson took it easy and engaged in a little showboating until Gainford told him to "cut the fooling around and get down to business", which prompted him to start throwing punches in clusters. Suddenly, and against the flow, the durable and aggressive Frenchman decked Robinson and caused the crowd to rise in anticipation of a shock. Despite Robinson's protests that the knockdown was the result of a low blow, which were ignored by referee Dick Young, Walzack continued to bulldoze forward and inflicted a troublesome cut over Robinson's left eye. By the end of the ten rounds, Robinson did enough to ensure that he emerged from the bruising and challenging encounter as a points winner.

Sugar Ray Costner had spent many months telling the Philadelphia press corps that he would exact his revenge on his more famous namesake after he had entered their first encounter under-prepared and unwell. Robinson agreed to grant his opportunity on 22nd March in the city's Convention Hall. Privately Robinson was irritated by the irksome comments and felt that it showed a distinct lack of respect. Costner's declarations paid dividends at the box office though and tempted 11,747 fans to pack into the hall and watch the fireworks. The opening bell rang and Robinson moved like a panther. He threw a short left hook which immediately wobbled Costner. Robinson sensed an opening and immediately struck, throwing a devastating right uppercut to end the proceedings within two minutes and forty nine seconds. After the fight, Robinson told the Nat Fleischer, the esteemed editor of The Ring magazine, that he "still didn't know what style George Costner used."

Despite the mocking words of Robinson and the disgusted jeers of his local supporters, it would be many years later that George Costner revealed the real reasons for his disappointing show. A year earlier, Costner had fought a Cuban fighter named Chico Varona and was cruising to a comfortable win when he was caught with a hard left hook on his right eye. He suffered a pain like a ball of fire and, afterwards, doctors informed him that he had only burst blood vessels. It was, in fact, a detached retina. By the time he was due to meet Robinson again his vision in his right eye was almost non-existent and he couldn't see punches aimed at him from his right side. He didn't want to call the fight off because he feared his opportunity and the $12,000 pay day would not come again. His plan, therefore, was simple. "I figured I'd try to get to him quickly, but I knew if I didn't, I'd have to go down myself." After this contest, Costner won his next three fights but his eye condition continued to bother him and forced him to accept his retirement. His condition continued to deteriorate and despite six operations over the next seven years he became totally blind in both eyes.

Robinson's repeated requests to be granted the respect he felt was his due was some way met in a Ring magazine article written by Ted Carroll. Carroll questioned whether Robinson was the greatest boxer of the last half century. He cited a recent poll which had named the former heavyweight champion Jack Dempsey as the best and ranked Joe Louis as the runner-up, but a large number of boxing experts believed Robinson to be the best all-round fighter. Jimmy Bronson, a promoter since the turn of the century and a recognised boxing authority, was especially lavish in his praise. "I can't see how anyone can fail to name Ray Robinson the best fighter of the past 50 years for the simple reason that he can do anything any other boxer could ever do and maybe just a little bit better. Pound for pound, I can't recall a harder hitter. On the other hand, I have never seen anybody who is harder to nail with a good punch. He's a great hitter and a great boxer. What more can one ask?" Joe Gans said that he couldn't rate anyone above Sugar Ray. "His four victories over LaMotta convinced me. It was a great achievement. A welterweight licking a good, tough middleweight!" Frank Erne, the oldest living former world champion, waxed equally lyrical. "Robinson is a natural and does everything as well as any fighter I have ever seen." The finest tribute, however, came from Harry Markson, the matchmaker for the International Boxing Club. "To be better than Ray Robinson you have to improve on perfection."

After the Costner meeting, Robinson squeezed in another two quick fights. Firstly, he fought Cliff Beckett from Ontario, Canada, in the Memorial Hall in Columbus, Ohio. It was a complete mismatch and referee Mutt Schartz used his good judgment to stop the one-sided spectacle after three rounds. A week later he returned to his hometown Detroit to face the promising Ray Barnes at the Olympia Stadium. Robinson's popularity was still high as nearly 9,000 spectators packed into the stadium. Over ten rounds of action-packed excitement, the fans roared and cheered themselves hoarse as the two fighters gave a marvellous exhibition of the noble art. Robinson won clearly and in the sixth he put Barnes down with two lightning fast left hooks to the chin; this cemented the emphatic victory. As the final bell sounded, Barnes was the happiest fighter in Detroit to have made it to the end of the scheduled contest.

During this period, Robinson had been publicly begging Jake LaMotta, the new world middleweight champion, to grant him a crack at his title. The promoters were queuing up in anticipation of signing the two most exciting middleweights to a contract and promoting what they considered to be a surefire sell-out. LaMotta, however, was not answering the calls and was refusing to respond to the challenges. John 'The Ox' DaGrosa, a former American football star and chairman of the Pennsylvania State Athletic Commission, intervened. He had watched Robert Villemain, the French middleweight, outbox Jake LaMotta to snatch a ten round points decision in Madison Square Garden. He contacted the National Boxing Association and asked them to support Robinson's claims for a title shot and urged them to make the forthcoming Villemain fight for their title. They refused and so DaGrosa announced that Philadelphia would recognise the Robinson versus Villemain fight but only Pennsylvania gave the fight their blessing as far as the world title was concerned. Villemain, standing only at 5 feet 5 inches, was a squat and well-muscled brawler. He had fought 40 times before meeting Robinson, losing only three times. The standard of his opposition was exceptional. Only three months before his fight, he defeated Kid Gavilan, but Ray beat the courageous Frenchman on points over the 15 round championship distance.

Robinson was determined to continue his public charm offensive and win over the critics. He offered to give the Damon Runyon Cancer Fund his entire purse from a proposed world championship contest against Charley Fusari in Jersey City on August 9th but many critics refused to believe it. The New York Daily Mirror journalist, Walter Winchell, was one of the most respected journalists and broadcasters in America, and chairman of the cancer charity. He received a warning phone call from one New York Times journalist who urged him not to trust Sugar Ray, suggesting that he would pull out with some excuse. A worried Winchell felt obliged to call the champion and outline his concerns. "Don't believe those people. Believe me," Robinson replied and after all the negotiations were completed, Robinson agreed to take just one dollar. After his career had finished, Robinson frequently said that this was the biggest thrill he had ever got from boxing.

Fusari wasn't keen to box Robinson. It was rumoured that Robinson had even agreed to split the purse with Fusari, which was in the region of $25,000, but Charley was still unwilling to accept a career-best purse and was prepared to forego the chance of fighting for the welterweight crown. His manager, Vic Marsillo, was far braver, however, and secured the fight after conducting a publicity campaign on the radio and in the newspapers by asking, 'Where is Robinson hiding?' The real clinching factor, however, was more poignant. One of Robinson's friends and a one time opponent from his Golden Gloves days, Louis 'Spider' Valentine, had recently died of cancer. The capacity to donate his fee to the Damon Runyon Cancer Fund was enough to persuade Charley to fight. According to Madison Square Garden matchmaker, Teddy Brenner, Robinson did insist on receiving $5,000 to cover his training expenses. This generous spirit rubbed off on others and before the fight, Abe J. Greene, the chairman of the New Jersey State Athletic Commission, helped Robinson a great deal. Ray was finding it increasingly difficult to make the welterweight limit and spent a lot of time in steam and Turkish baths. Commissioner Greene was sympathetic to his difficulties and insisted that he could weigh at a different time than Fusari, when only he would be present to verify matters. (Robinson actually made three attempts before making the welterweight limit.)

The match was held at the Roosevelt Stadium, Jersey City. Fusari, the 23-year old former milkman, was classed as local boy but had actually been born in Sicily and emigrated to America when he was six. He had knocked out a highly touted prospect named Vince Foster in one sensational round to record his tenth consecutive victory and extend his record to 36 knockouts in 64 fights, losing only four decisions. He had established a growing reputation when he fought the unbeaten Tippy Larkin, the world junior champion, and stopped him in nine rounds. He came into the fight ranked within the world's top five welterweights. 30,000 spectators came along to see a fight which promised lots but delivered little. The fight went the full 15 round distance with Sugar Ray winning thirteen of the rounds with ease. In his autobiography, which he released after his retirement, Robinson claimed that he had agreed to carry Fusari, stating that it was Marsillo's idea after he had told Ray that his opponent was not good enough and that he raised no objection because he didn't want another Jimmy Doyle.

"You can't argue with this man," George Gainford told Sugar Ray, after a meeting with the multi-millionaire tycoon Jim Norris, the head of the International Boxing Club. "He controls Madison Square Garden, Chicago Stadium, the Boston Garden, the Detroit Olympia and all the big indoor arenas," added Gainford. Norris had agreed to meet Robinson to discus what he had to do to get Jake LaMotta into the ring for his world middleweight title, and seeing that Jake was now controlled by Norris and his organisation, he thought that it would facilitate events.

Norris, possessing a sophisticated presence, greeted Robinson with a big grin and a warm handshake. He knew Robinson was desperate for a title fight with LaMotta. Robinson opened the meeting bluntly by telling Norris that he deserved a shot at the middleweight title. The promoter nodded in agreement and suggested that the IBC would be able to guarantee it only if he worked solely with them. Robinson retorted that he shouldn't have to do this to earn his rightful shot, but Norris cautioned him to be smart. The sticking point for Ray, however, was the television money, of which half had to be received by Norris. Robinson left the negotiations frustrated but Norris did not give up his quest and secretly phoned George Gainford in an effort to get him to change Robinson's mind, who advised him that his charge was very definitely his own man and would not budge on his principles.

Sixteen days after despatching Fusari, he returned to the ring to defend his Pennsylvania version of the world middleweight title against Jose Basora. The Puerto Rican had forced Robinson into a draw in May 1945 and the newspapers built up the meeting on this result. The 4,145 crowd in the Scranton Stadium was reduced significantly by the fact that the fight was going out live on radio and television. Another, more bizarre, reason was that the local papers published scare stories suggesting that Robinson may cancel the fight again after he had let them down previously when citing a back injury and withdrew from a previous date. The Pennsylvania Boxing Commission had fined him $1,000 and awarded promoter Ernie Genell $4,500 expenses for this cancelled tournament, which still left him feeling aggrieved, and he decided to release his anger in the ring. The fight was all over within 52 seconds of the opening bell.

As soon as it sounded, Ray sprinted across the ring and took the Puerto Rican, who had yet to leave his corner, by surprise. Basora hadn't even had time to put his hands up in defence when a left hook hit him with devastating effect and tremendous force, on his ear. He then delivered a terrific right cross with a thud to the side of Basora's head and watched him drop in a heap. The dazed Basora got to his feet without a count but another lightning-fast left hook came whizzing in and returned him to the canvas, hurt and bemused. Again he clambered to his feet. Referee Johnny Kelly was watching the Puerto Rican carefully, whilst the sparse crowd was howling with excitement as Robinson's punches hit him like bullets from a machine-gun. Ray dipped to his left and delivered two brilliant left hooks with a follow through right cross and all three venomous punches landed flush on the chin. Basora was badly hurt and Dr Freds, of the State Athletic Commission, rushed into the ring before the count had been concluded. Initially, the crowd began to boo and yell that it was a fix but soon realised that he was badly hurt after ten minutes of treatment. Eventually, the doctor declared that Basora had suffered an ear puncture.

The manner of his victory stunned ringsiders. Basora was certainly no ordinary opponent and this was brilliantly spectacular! Nat Fleischer suggested that the chilling approach of Robinson should concern LaMotta: "This fight proved that Sugar Ray is the top man in both the welter and middleweight divisions. His great performances against middleweights have earned for him the designation of 'uncrowned king' of that class." However, it was still not enough to dispel the doubts which some observers held about Robinson's character. Ring magazine correspondent, Ken 'Duke' Stigner was in raptures of this thrilling victory. This fight for Pennsylvania's version of the world middleweight title saw Robinson at his best: "Robinson's speedy knockout was quite amazing!," he wrote. He also reported that many ringsiders had believed that he "had hastened the 'kill' because he only received a small purse for the fight, and was angry at having to pay the $1,000 fine."

A few weeks later, Robinson returned to fighting in New York and boxed, for the first time in his career, at the Coney Island Velodrome. His opponent, Hartford's Billy Brown, surprised the crowd and Robinson himself, by giving a good account of himself over the full ten round distance. Robinson still had more than enough in reserve to ensure that he won every round. He then customarily destroyed Boston's rugged warrior, Joe Rindone, in six rounds in Ridone's home town, the Boston Garden. 12,086 fans turned up to watch Rindone, a warhorse whose features catalogued a career of fighting. He tried desperately but failed to bridge the huge gulf in class. In the fifth Ray connected with his vaunted left hook, which landed with force on Rindone's outsized jaw; he fell forward and referee Johnny Martin tolled ten over him.

Ten days later, he arrived at the Philadelphia Convention Hall and prepared to meet Carl 'Bobo' Olson from Hawaii. Robinson systematically shattered the dreams of the ambitious Honolulu youngster. Sugar Ray was like a craftsman and had everything his own way against the 22-year-old Olson, who had an unusual style of fighting. He kept his gloves high and his elbows protruding, therefore presenting himself as a difficult target. Olson's plan appeared to be to tire Robinson out before finishing him off in the later rounds. Once he stepped into the squared circle, however, the islander realised that he was mixing in the wrong league. Gainford's early instructions to Sugar Ray were to target his opponent's body, which he did to great effect, whilst occasionally switching powerful rights to Olson's exposed chin. Olson presented very little in the way of an offensive threat as he was too busy defending himself and the frustrated 5,034 fans clapped their hands for more action. Robinson responded by upping the tempo and in the 12th round, he hammered his challenger. This was the fateful and final round as far as Olson was concerned. Sugar Ray was angry and had a determined glint in his eyes. A sweeping right cross decked Bobo as if he had been felled by an axe. He couldn't get to his feet, even after the referee, Charlie Daggert, counted him out. Later, Robinson was magnanimous and told reporters that it was one of his toughest fights in his long career. He used the opportunity to again taunt his ultimate target and direct a challenge via the reporters. The next day's press led with his question to LaMotta: "Well, Jake, how about it?"

He followed up his victory in Philadelphia by making the journey to Chicago to defeat one of the most promising young fighters of the new generation coming through. Bobby Dykes from San Antonio, Texas, stood an imposing six feet tall and carried an impressive punch. Dykes, however, was cruelly exposed and Robinson toyed with the younger man and gave him a boxing lesson. Whenever it appeared that he was close to ending the education, he repeatedly backed away and allowed Dykes to regain his composure. It was no more than a brisk workout for Robinson before he departed for Europe.

11.

Europe Welcomes Sugar Ray
and his friends

JUST BEFORE the end of the year Ray felt increasingly frustrated by being avoided by the now elusive Jake LaMotta and he pointed the finger of blame firmly at Jim Norris and the dark figures of gangsters Frankie Carbo and Frankie 'Blinky' Palermo who surrounded the 'Bronx Bull'. Since winning his title, LaMotta had successfully defended it twice against European opposition when easily outpointing the Italian Tiberio Mitri and then stopping the French fighter, Laurent Dauthuille, with only thirteen seconds left in the fifteenth and final round of their contest. After this closely fought battle, he declared that he had no intention of fighting again in 1950.

Lew Burston, an American who had spent time in Paris and America and worked with various promoters throughout the world, suggested that Robinson follow the champion's trail to Europe. Burston was instrumental in bringing Marcel Cerdan to America to defend his world tile against LaMotta. He told Sugar Ray that Charlie Michaelis, the leading Parisian promoter, would help them arrange a series of fights which would stand him in good stead for a future challenge to LaMotta as well as allowing Robinson to earn a substantial fee. Once all the details were settled Robinson prepared to leave America. Burston gave Robinson a piece of advice about his approach to the fights in Europe, and suggested that he must never take it easy on any opponent, as he had done in the Charlie Fusari fight, but instead endeavour to knock them out as fast as he could. He reasoned that his style, punch and sheer magnetism would turn him into a hero amongst the European fans.

On the 11th November, Robinson, along with Edna Mae and his sister Evelyn, George Gainford and his wife Hazel, Harry Wiley, 'Pee Wee' Beale, Shelton Oliver - a golf professional, Roger Simon - his personal barber - and a male friend named June Clark - a purported secretary - boarded the SS Liberté to begin their trip. All of the other passengers and crew came out on the deck to witness the colourful sight of the Harlem party coming aboard. However, everything was not as it seemed, with the smiling Ray and wife Edna Mae. A few hours before boarding the liner an argument had ensued between Ray and Edna Mae. It was believed that argument concerned Robinson flaunting with another woman and Edna Mae found out. He hit his wife and she had a discolouring under her eye. This act of violence apparently was a regular occurrence. A member of the Robinson family said he would slap his wife or anyone who upset him for the slightest reason. The Robinsons sued the Amsterdam News for $50,000, a tremendous amount in those days. The newspaper headlined their front page with a story that Ray had kayoed his wife. The trial lasted two days after Dr C.B. Powell, the owner of the paper, contested the libel claim. He told the court that the word 'kayo' meant emphasis. The jury upheld the charge, but awarded the Robinsons only $25,000.

Nearly 20,000 fight-saturated Frenchmen and women, many of whom were fashionably dressed folks from the city's high society, were gathered round the ringside and could merely gasp in wonder - they were too dazed to cheer - as they watched the world welterweight champion completely engulf Jean Stock, one of three fighting Parisian brothers, who was his first opponent, and cap a spectacular entrance to the continent. Robinson, who had been front page news in France ever since he arrived in the French capital ten days earlier, entered the ring at the Palais-des-Sports on a wintery Monday evening with all of the glitter and showbusiness glamour which the crowd expected of the American showman. He wore a luscious new dressing-gown and strutted into the ring surrounded by his four seconds and electrified an already excited audience.

Stock did not lack any of the courage for which his fighting family were famed for. Just three weeks earlier he had beaten the respected American Bobby Dawson over ten riveting rounds, and he had also stopped Britain's Randy Turpin in five rounds only two years earlier. He was eager for the action to start and at the first bell, he launched a swinging right hand onto Robinson's chin, which forced him to immediately fall into a clinch and clear his head. After being caught by this sucker punch, Robinson appeared to decide that he would terminate proceedings as quickly as possible and collect the £5,000 for this 'personal appearance'.

Ray replied with a fast accurate left to the head and Stock's knees began to sag. The huge throng of spectators switched allegiance and began cheering for him and US reporters later wrote that a section of the crowd had shouted, "You are an artiste". Robinson heard this and was moved at receiving the kind of acclaim which had eluded him in his own country, and this seemed to change his sinister mood. And so, for the remainder of the round, Robinson then treated his foe as if he was merely a friendly sparring partner in the gym. He tapped him lightly with punches from each fist, easily moving out of distance when Stock tried to hit him back. Robinson evaded the blows and allowed Stock to return to his corner. George Gainford used the break to refocus his emotional fighter and when he emerged for the second session, he immediately advanced toward his rival, whipped over a lightning fast short left hook, and watched Stock sink to the canvas. He gingerly regained his feet as the count reached nine, and so Robinson neatly planted a ram-rod right to his stomach and returned him to the prone position. Displaying the stubborn nature which had earned him respect within the fight game, he managed to get to his feet again but looked in some distress. Robinson repeated his body punch to finally put Stock out of his misery. As he landed, a white towel came fluttering into the ring from Stock's corner and the audience sat silently spellbound by the virtuoso performance they had just witnessed before breaking out into rapturous applause. He was chaired back to his dressing room by the crowd, eager to get close to him.

Sitting at ringside were a quartet of Britain's most powerful boxing figures. The leading promoter, Jack Solomons, Sam Burns, his manager, British Boxing Board of Control secretary Teddy Waltham and the British welterweight champion, Eddie Thomas. All were in complete agreement that Sugar Ray was simply incredible. Later that same night, Solomons travelled to Claridges Hotel, situated on the Champs Elysees, to meet the world champion and his manager, George Gainford. Robinson agreed to attend the Harringey Arena on December 12th as a special guest of the persuasive promoter. Robinson refused to give an exhibition because he was scheduled to fight Luc van Dam, the Dutch middleweight champion, in Brussels just three days before.

Jack Solomons was steeped in boxing history, having had a brief one fight career before his wife Fay successfully convinced him to retire and concentrate on his considerable fish business. In the 1930s he had returned to boxing in the capacity as a manager of a popular fighter called Eric Boon. He had then branched out as a promoter and then became a matchmaker for the Devonshire Club in London and became famed for hosting exciting events. He became a household name after the Second World War when he promoted Britain's best heavyweight prospect, Bruce Woodcock, and the lion-hearted light-heavyweight, Freddie Mills. After the war, the British public were looking for heroes and both fighters became huge drawing cards and his tournaments attracted royalty, politicians and film stars, and he was determined to add Robinson to his star billing.

Ray Sugar Robinson….World's Fistic Phenomenon!
20,000 Frenchmen See Him 'Toy' With the Tough Jean Stock
Five Minutes Display of Dynamic Punching
First Time Stock Had Taken Counts

Sugar Ray had been sensational and Europe, especially the French, treated him like royalty. Above are some of the headlines from a few newspapers after his first fight in Europe.

Before his next engagement, Ray and Edna Mae were determined to enjoy themselves and could be found dancing in the city's top nightclubs. People would gather to watch the couple jiving and jitterbugging and other dancers would stop and applaud them. In some of the clubs, the compere would request that the champion go on to the stage and sing or play the drums, opportunities which he eagerly embraced. Older Parisians recalled Battling Siki and Panama Al Brown visiting their city, but they said Sugar Ray and the gorgeous Edna Mae were a class apart. Lew Burston would translate the press coverage and confirm that he really was a hero in France. Robinson would contrast the accolades with his own public image back home and lament on why he couldn't be afforded the respect he felt he deserved.

The buzz which his presence created encouraged 15,000 people to pack into the arena in Brussels on the 9th December. His opponent was the Dutch middleweight champion, a swarthy, curly-haired brawler named Luc van Dam. In the third round, the Dutch fighter crashed to the canvas in agony from what appeared to be a low punch. His cornermen dragged him back to his corner after the bell had rang and they saved him from taking the full count despite the fact that he lay with his head sticking through the ropes and his gloves clutching his lower abdomen. After receiving treatment, van Dam walked on rubbery legs to meet Sugar Ray's power-packed punches. Robinson dipped his shoulder and unleashed a deadly left hook which stretched the Dutchman for the full count. When the referee, Gustave de Baecher, raised Robinson's arm to signal victory, the capacity crowd began booing their derision. They believed that van Dam had held his own in the first three rounds and he had been cheated. In his dressing room afterwards, van Dam asserted that it was a low blow which had incapacitated him and he claimed that he would be complaining to the authorities. Dr F. J. Thoolen examined the Dutch fighter and said it was a low blow, indeed a very low blow, it could not have been lower. Susan van Dam, the Dutchman's wife and business manager, said she had lodged a complaint with the Belgian Boxing Federation. Ray was unperturbed and maintained that he had "hit him in the stomach above the belt." He was delighted to receive $9,000 for his thirteen minutes work. He then moved to Geneva to box a return with Jean Walzach, whom he had outpointed a few months before in St Louis, and a 10,000 crowd were thrilled when the lightning-fast champion dropped the Frenchman in the ninth and tenth rounds to run out a clear winner.

He returned to Paris with a new addition to his entourage, whom he introduced to Peter Wilson, a respected old-school British journalist, who had arrived to conduct an interview with him. It was a 3ft tall 'Arabian Knight', whom Robinson described as 'my bodyguard' and who was to become a permanent feature on the tour. "Ray Robinson is a fistic phenomenon," said Wilson. Adding that Sugar Ray was not only a great fighter, but also a scientist. "In his fists lay brains and brawn. He's like a well-oiled machine…He is as great in his weight division as was Joe Louis at his best in his division." He told the journalist he believed he could beat most heavyweights. He also confirmed that he was finding it harder and harder to make 10st 7lbs, the welterweight limit, and was considering relinquishing the title and launching an all-out offensive with the middleweight crown as his objective. The journalist then confidently predicated that Sugar Ray would be the middleweight champion of the world. "Who is there to stop him?" he asked.

His next fight was six days after the Geneva contest and the crowds in the French capital again turned out in droves to watch him box another return against the French champion, Robert Villemain, who had extended Robinson over the full distance only a few months earlier.

The two gladiators didn't waste time engaging in any subtleties, but instead pitched straight into battle from the opening bell. The French fighter was determined to avenge his defeat and beat the man he had christened as 'The Black Angel' and 'Death Ray'. It was Sugar Ray, however, who was first to the punch and he smashed home two right 'bolo' uppercuts followed by a couple of dynamite-laced left hooks to the head, which had Villemain tottering and clinching to avoid a visit to the floor. Robinson had left his mark and subdued his opponent's early fire and then chose to settle down and box his way to victory from a distance. The crowd had never seen punches like the American was delivering and were in raptures and the salubrious, packed Palais des Sports was rocking with the noisy acclaim He continued to throw lightning-fast combinations, but Villemain seemed to read his role and contented himself in burying his head into his black gloves and using his rugby forward's build, protected by his elbows, to keep moving forward into his tormentor. The French spectators, who seemed to have been collectively holding their breath and waiting for Robinson to end the fight, drew inspiration from these crude tactics and began to roar noisily every time their compatriot barged forward. They cheered on every occasion their man threw a punch, most of which were absorbed on Robinson's arms and gloves.

In the fifth it started to appear that Villemain's bulldozing technique, allied to Robinson's hectic schedule and regular nightclubbing, could all combine to bring about an unlikely victory as Robinson appeared to visibly wilt, and in the seventh round, it looked to have been confirmed when Villemain connected with the best punch of the fight; a dizzying left hook, which left Ray hanging on as the fans erupted into a sustained frenzy of yelling and clapping. As the ninth round started, Robinson later recalled that he had become "fed up with everyone roaring and shouting for my opponent" and he unleashed a right cross which landed with a brute force onto the Frenchman's square jaw. Time seemed to stand still as Villemain faltered, tried to hold onto the evasive American and then dropped to the floor. His pride forced him to stand up and the referee gave him an eight count, but the breakthrough seemed to breathe fresh life into Robinson, who was like a new man and he drove him back into the ropes, where he delivered a merciless barrage which dropped Villemain at his feet. The local hero's brave attempt to continue was stopped by the referee, Robert Vaisberg, who grabbed him under the armpits and did a crazed, drunken dance across the canvas to prevent him suffering any further damage.

The Parisians gave him a tremendous ovation, accorded only to those they considered artists, and cries of 'Magnifique', 'Brilliant', 'L'artiste', 'Ultimo' thundered around the stadium.

"What a champion," enthused Peter Wilson. "What a superb, magnificent champion. He dignifies boxing."

His final appearance in Europe was scheduled to take place on Christmas Day in the open-air of Frankfurt, Germany. This was the first occasion in the history of German boxing when a world champion was actually seen in action in the country and Robinson was determined to conclude his tour in style. His opponent was former German middleweight champion Hans Stetz. A large crowd of 7,000, many of whom were American GI's stationed in the city, were keen to witness a spectacular show and at the end of the first round, George Gainford cautioned Robinson to slow down and prolong the contest for the benefit of the crowd. Ray complied and went through a showcase of his best moves before he finally decided to end the one-sided affair in the fifth round, and drove the willing German to the ropes and threw a six-punch combination which put Stretz on the floor. As the count reached eight, he made an effort to rise but his legs refused to obey and he fell backwards and allowed the referee to conclude the count. During the contest the game German had been down eight times.

After the Stretz victory Ray was sat in his hotel relaxing and having a conversation with his team. "I've been fighting professionally now for ten years," said Robinson. "And you've fought over a hundred times against all-comers," remarked George Gainford. This was perfectly true, of course. However, many knowledgeable boxing connoisseurs were convinced his best days were behind him, and they had a point. Although Robinson was one of those once-in-a-lifetime fighters, no matter how fit and well prepared any athlete remain, there is no doubt that a slow deterioration takes place mentally and physically, more so in the case of a boxer. This of course is only normal procedure, it happens to the majority of us, but in boxing it can prove fatal. There are, of course, exceptions to the rule and Archie Moore, Willie Pep and Jersey Joe Walcott, to name but three, had longevity. Sugar Ray would also fall into this category, an exceptional human being, for a few more years. What would eventually become crystal clear through the ensuing years, though, was his remarkable speed and co-ordination and reflexes would sadly diminish. However, we are running ahead of the story. There were still more unbelievable and unforgettable nights of pure magic and nostalgia.

The news of Robinson's European success was eagerly reported back home in America, and his absence seemed to add to his prestige and precipitated a media campaign for Sugar Ray to be given his chance against Jake LaMotta. The US press were impressed with the manner in which Robinson had left unforgettable memories of how a truly stupendous American world star should perform and they reported that the Europeans had taken him to their hearts. Charlie Michaelis, the promoter who helped arrange the tour, told the press that once Robinson had secured his world title by beating Jake LaMotta, he would return to perform once again in front of his new fans. Michaelis described how the French press disliked LaMotta because he had beaten their idol, Marcel Cerdan, who was tragically killed in a plane crash on his way back to America for the return. "I have insisted the next time he comes he must bring his pink Cadillac," said Michaelis.

The trip also added to the myth and enigma which Robinson represented to many of his peers. In later years, the trainer Eddie Futch recounted how he trained a bright young welterweight prospect named Lester Felton in 1950. Felton was matched against Ike Williams in a ten-round non-title fight. Futch assured him that after he had beaten Williams, they would throw open a challenge to Sugar Ray and gain plenty of newspaper headlines and coverage. Lester was delighted and told his wife about their plans. The following day in the gym, Felton looked glum and Futch enquired what the problem was. Felton explained that his wife had banned him from ever challenging Robinson in the ring. Needless to say, he lost the Williams fight and Futch maintained that it was the mere thought that he may have to fight Robinson which was the significant factor in his defeat to the world lightweight champion.

Apart from the respect which he so desperately craved, the European tour was also a financial success for him and had netted over $50,000. However, by the time he arrived back in America, much of this money had been frittered away in expenses and the cost of accommodating increasing members of his entourage, as well as Edna Mae and his sister Evelyn's extravagant shopping trips in the most exclusive and expensive shops in Paris.

12.

The Final Battle Against
The Bronx Bull

THE YEAR OF 1951 started well. On 9th January, he attended the Waldorf Hotel in New York to receive his award from the Boxing Writers' Association, honouring him as their 'Fighter of the Year'. He was awarded the Edward J Neil Memorial Trophy, a plaque which was named in honour of the great American boxing writer and war correspondent who died in the Spanish Civil War. He was now able to see his name ranked alongside previous winners like Joe Louis, Jack Dempsey, Barney Ross and Benny Leonard. The honour was a double celebration for Robinson when it was also announced that the International Boxing Club had finally bowed to public pressure and declared that Jake LaMotta would defend his championship against Robinson. During the usual heated negotiations prior to contracts being signed and sealed, Robinson had refused to sign a contract which gave the IBC exclusive control of his services. Norris and his cohorts equally refused Sugar Ray's demands for 45% of the gate after he claimed that it was he who was the drawing card.

When the formalities were finally concluded, Sugar Ray moved to his training quarters at Pompton Lakes, New Jersey. He arrived in a great frame of mind and his preparations were going well. One quiet Sunday afternoon, however, he received an unexpected visit from Frankie Carbo, also known to Robinson as Mister Grey on account of his grey hair and his reputation for operating in the shadows.

Ray walked outside to meet the mobster, also known as an associate of Jake LaMotta's. Carbo, dressed immaculately in a black cashmere overcoat and a grey fedora, told Sugar Ray that he was speaking on behalf of the Bronx Bull. He outlined a proposal for a further three fights: "You'll win the first; the Bull wins the second and the third fight is 'on the level'". He explained that all parties would stand to make a great deal of money. Robinson remained courteous and clarified whether this meant that he had to take a dive in the second fight. Carbo's voice remained still and his eyes burned deep. "It's either that or you don't put out," he responded. Robinson politely informed him that he had the wrong man and he asked Carbo to give LaMotta a

113

message: "Keep your hands up and your ass off the floor." With that Robinson turned and walked back to his quarters.

St Valentine's Day 1951 is a date which is forever etched on the memories of those that were fortunate enough to possess tickets for the Chicago Stadium on the evening when it was announced that Sugar Ray Robinson would finally meet Jake LaMotta to contest the world middleweight championship after months of negotiations and debate.

When it was finally confirmed, LaMotta told the press that he "was tired of hearing them spouting on about how great Robinson was" and cautioned that "you forget that he is only a welterweight but now this welterweight is in for a night of absolute pain!" He reminded them that "I've beaten him before and I'll demolish him on the night of the fight." LaMotta seemed sensitive to the growing popularity of his old foe and keen to demand the respect he felt the champion merited. "You say I'm not a smart fighter but I always seem to keep hitting these clever guys. Just because a fighter doesn't stand up straight and dance around, you think I'm dumb. How could a little guy like me ever be able to stand up and jab? Instead I roll with the punches and I don't get hit anywhere near as much as it may look to people outside the ropes." LaMotta argued that he had won at least two more of their five fights. All the time he spoke, Robinson just smiled.

The Robinson - LaMotta fight was the most talked about fight for many years. When Ray heard about Jake's remarks in the newspapers he smiled. It was reported that he and Gainford had received a $75,000 guarantee from San Francisco's Bill Kyne to box light-heavyweight champion Joey Maxim if successful against LaMotta. It was believed that the same deal would be offered to Jake if he disposed of the Harlem dancing master. This news added extra spice to the fight between these two gladiators.

The night before the contest Jimmy Cannon, the New York Journal's inimitable sports columnists, visited Sugar Ray's hotel room. The two men respected each other and Cannon had been a long time admirer of Robinson's brand of boxing, although later, they would have a bitter difference of opinions. Cannon wanted to discus the LaMotta fight. Robinson looked the newspaper man in the eye and told him: "I'm going to try and take him (LaMotta) out early, in one round." Robinson was serious, this was no publicity stunt. He meant it. Then Ray elaborated: "If I don't manage to do it, then I'm going to make him do road work. I'll run him crazy until I'm ready to finish him." Cannon was delighted. He'd got his scoop!

14,802 lucky fans handed over record gate receipts of $180,619 to feast upon this battle royal between two world champions, who appeared to be such contrasting exponents; the embodiment of the slugger and the scientist. The interest in this match was truly global and the fight was being covered by both television and radio broadcasters around the world and included, for the first time, remote destinations such as Australia and New Zealand.

LaMotta bounded into the ring wearing dark shorts, whilst Robinson sauntered in and wore his customary white satin shorts. As both boxers limbered up in their corners, the master of ceremonies, Eddie Quick, made the official announcements in homage of those great fighters who sat at the ringside, including the great light, junior-welter and welterweight champion Barney Ross, the former world bantamweight king Johnny Coulon, Tony Zale, the former world middleweight ruler, former world welterweight title-holder Jackie Fields, and Johnny Bratton, another former welterweight champion. When the referee, Frank Sikora, beckoned the two gladiators to the centre of the ring to issue his final instructions, Robinson performed his ritual of lightly jogging on his feet and appeared to be a study of absolute concentration, oblivious to the screaming hordes and the ringside celebrities. He fixed his gaze only on one thing - Jake LaMotta. In the opposite corner, the champion prowled in circles, keeping the hood of his dressing gown pulled down over his forehead. George Gainford quietly reminded Robinson of their fight plan and repeated the words, "Remember the matador and the bull" into his ear. They knew that LaMotta was a famously slow starter in his fights and they intended to establish a blistering pace in the early rounds and use Ray's potent left jab and balletic footwork to grind the Bronx Bull down methodically.

At the sound of the opening bell both fighters circled each other like alley cats, waiting for their moment to pounce; LaMotta acted first and threw a huge left hook which grazed Robinson's chin. Robinson responded and within the first minute, LaMotta's nose had begun to redden and his right eye started to bruise from the effects of the challenger's accurate left jab. For the next eight rounds, both men then appeared to fall into a rhythm which suited their own individual purposes. The middleweight champion chugged forward in a relentless and remorseless manner, with his head dropped low. This was done to entice Robinson close into his range from where he would lash his punches into his foe's chiselled abdominal region and weaken and slow him down. He enjoyed success in the third and fourth rounds when he countered with heavy-handed left hooks that shook him up, forcing him to retreat quickly. Robinson's rhythm was, aesthetically, far more pleasing for the purists. Using nimble footwork combined with a text-book style of side-on left sided boxing, he looked the superior fighter. His piston-like left jab constantly picked off the rampaging LaMotta and also gained notable successes; in the third round Robinson caught LaMotta with a variety of twenty six punches in under two minutes which all landed flush on the champion's head and body.

Robinson was repeatedly reminded by Gainford to stick to their plan to tire out the champion, but LaMotta continued to remain strong and kept steaming forward looking to land his own brand of bombs on Robinson's head or body whilst refusing to take a backward step. LaMotta's plan was simple in its conception but difficult to execute, yet he stuck to it throughout and attempted to get as close to the fleet-footed welterweight as possible and wear him down by banging punches into the midriff. It was the archetypal clash of boxing cultures and ringsiders sensed that a classic was being written before their very eyes as the rounds flashed past.

As the bell for the seventh round sounded, LaMotta's face catalogued the marks of the battle taking place; some of his lumps and bumps coloured spectacularly to look like slabs of raw meat. He heroically stuck to his battle plan and refused to bow to Robinson's increasing superiority and continued to battle away and connect with a left hook that would stun the classy challenger. He maintained one metronomic pace and never looked in danger of becoming fatigued like Robinson was hoping, but ringsiders were forced to cringe when Robinson started to land with explosive punches that were like bullets from a machine gun, yet LaMotta took them without blinking. It was becoming clear, however, by the ninth round that LaMotta's furious pursuit was starting to lack some of its fire. Just before the end of the round, it looked like Robinson had found the fight-ending punch and hit LaMotta with a left hand direct to the kidney. Hardened pressmen close to the ring heard the leather glove being driven into the target and visibly flinched in sympathy for the excruciating pain which resulted from it, yet the world middleweight champion drew on his deep reservoirs of courage and ploughed forward.

In the eleventh brutal round, Robinson, by now enjoying his march to the title he had campaigned so vigorously for, flung punches at his foe which were described in the following day's papers as "raining down on him like a thunder storm." Amazingly, not only did LaMotta absorb the punishment but he found enough resolve to drive Robinson back onto the ropes, where he trapped him in a corner and flayed away with two-handed power punches as if his very life depended on the outcome. Robinson was shocked by this unexpected response and bent from the waist, tucked his chin into his chest and took many of the punches on his arms and gloves whilst managing to slip others. Still, such was the raw energy of the champion's assault that a great deal still got through and shook him up. The crowd recognised this phenomenal courage and rose, as one, to their feet and acknowledged it. He rained punches in from every conceivable angle and Ray, with his back against the ropes, started to look tired and weary. LaMotta, however, couldn't sustain his attack indefinitely and became arm weary at trying to end the bout in convincing style and it signalled the beginning of the end. As if the shellacking he had received only seconds earlier had not happened, Robinson felt the fury subside and he pushed his way off the ropes and turned the tables to despatch LaMotta back to the sanctity of his corner on wobbly legs.

LaMotta was a spent force and the following two rounds were like watching a slow execution. Robinson dished out merciless punishment and the champion was forced to take it without flinching. Robinson moved with the stealth of a panther, knowing that his prey was ready to be taken. His jabs were precise and the combination of four and five left hooks in succession forced many spectators to shout for the referee to halt the slaughter. LaMotta's cheekbone was cut and his nose and mouth oozed blood and Frank Sikora, the referee, began to take a keen interest in LaMotta's welfare before Dr Houston, a physician for the Illinois State Athletic Commission, jumped into action after two minutes and four seconds of the thirteenth round and signalled that Sikora should hold Robinson's hand aloft as the new world middleweight champion.

This fight really lived up to expectations, a truly memorable contest in every respect. It was a championship encounter of artistry, courage, excitement in abundance, and irreplaceable performances from two special men who would be Hall of Fame inductees. It was a fight that would live in the memory of everyone who saw it. It was superb in every phase of the 13 rounds it lasted. This championship was won with blood, sweat and tears, with the rivalry between both Jake and Ray showing the utmost respect they had for each other.

James P. Dawson wrote in the New York Times: "Never in his life has the Bronx strong-boy been subjected to such a hammering," He said that this sixth meeting saw Robinson, the master craftsman, do "everything short of battering LaMotta unconscious to register his fifth triumph of their series."

Afterwards, the referee explained that Dr Houston had hinted before the start of the thirteenth round that LaMotta had given all that he could and that it was nearly time to rescue him. He had then seen the signal from the doctor that LaMotta's reign was over and had then moved quickly to halt the fight. Both men, however, were physically bankrupted by their clash. LaMotta looked disillusioned and completely spent. His seconds worked frantically to attend to him and allow him to regain his faculties. The pride of the vanquished Bronx Bull still shone through and he disdainfully waved away the willing hands that reached up to help his descend from the ring. He was determined to depart from the ring steps under his own power but still stopped several times to signal to his fans his disappointment at being stopped.

Once back in the sanctity of his dressing room, oxygen was administered to the fallen champ and the press were made to wait for an hour and half before they could hear about the views of the fight through the badly discoloured eyes of the Bronx Bull. He explained that making the weight had cost him dearly and drained him of his much needed strength. It was only years later, when he was enjoying a renaissance on the after dinner circuit, that he made the claims that if Frank Sikora had not stopped the fight when he did, Robinson would have dropped through exhaustion. It was, however, not the opinion he offered in the immediate aftermath when he was only able to leave the stadium assisted by a trainer under each arm.

Back in his dressing room, Robinson cringed as he inserted his severely swollen left hand into a bucket of ice to try and reduce the bruising. George Gainford worked away at the bruising which coloured his left eye. These were the only injuries sustained from the battle and he reflected on the achievement of becoming only the fourth boxer ever to win both the welterweight and middleweight world championships with a number of reporters inside the little room. Most of the pressmen agreed that they had witnessed a contest which would come to be regarded as a magnificent example of boxing for as long as boxing and its great bouts were discussed. Regarding his immediate plans, Robinson suggested that he would be prepared to accept the offer of meeting Joey Maxim for his title but would first of all like to embark on his second European tour.

His phenomenal capacity for recovery enabled Robinson to return to action in April. He outboxed Holly Mims of Washington D.C in front of a 5,500 crowd in the Miami Stadium. Mims, from Washington D.C., was a craftsman but lacked the charisma or personality to make an impression at world level. Sugar enjoyed a comfortable points victory over ten rounds, but the fans recognised that Mims was tough and durable and cheered him for his courage and willingness to have a go, although the gulf in class was evident when he knocked Mims down in the second round, the first time he had been dropped in his fifty three bout career. The promoter, Major W.H. Peeples Jr., along with the IBC, suggested that "Sugar Ray Robinson is a unique talent and should be enjoyed as such." Just four days later, before he left for his European sojourn, he knocked out Don Ellis within a minute and half in the Municipal Auditorium, Oklahoma City.

Just six months earlier Robinson had promised Charlie Michaelis that he would return to Europe as soon as he had won the middleweight title. This time, however, his entrance to the continent would be far more spectacular. He had spent months arranging how to ship his 17-foot Flamingo Pink Cadillac with his name painted on the side. With him as well were 32 trunks and 15 suitcases which contained three radio sets and over 140 jazz records. Edna Mae, Gainford and his secretary also returned with him and set up his base in the French capital's Claridge's Hotel on the Champs-Elysess. The French were fascinated when viewing his car and wherever he drove he was followed by a horde of cars like a procession. The French were indeed fascinated with Ray and his retinue, Edna Mae, his sister Evelyn, his barber Roger Simon, Pee Wee Beale, George Gainford and his wife Hazel, Danny 'Bang Bang' Womber and Don Ellis, who sparred and helped prepare him for his fights while also fighting on the udercard. Male secretary June Clark, golf partner Joe Roach, Harold 'Killer' Johnson, chauffeur Jean Roger and the midget Jimmy Karoubi, whom Robinson described as his bodyguard, right-hand man and interpreter. Robinson revelled in this adulation and walked about wearing a black beret.

He quickly threw himself back into the fray and on May 21st he fought the French middleweight champion Kid Marcel in the Palais des Sports. Although it was billed as a non-title fight, over 6,000 spectators turned up to watch the new world champion toy with their own champion for the first four rounds whilst Marcel tried, in vain, to make a fight of it. The end came only fifty seven seconds into the fifth round. Robinson hurt the Frenchman with the power of his hard, accurate punches and left him bleeding and groggy and unable to defend himself. His seconds decided they didn't want their man to suffer any further and they insisted that the fight was stopped. After the fight, Robinson's standing amongst the French public rose still further as it was revealed that he would receive only a symbolic franc for his endeavours. The rest of his purse was donated to the French Cancer Fund.

Five days later he headed over the border to Zurich to face Jean Wanes in front a large number of enthusiastic American GI's stationed in Germany. It was another one-sided affair and the rugged French fighter visited the canvas five times but still managed to last the full ten round distance. Immediately after the fight was over, he headed back to Paris, eager to sample the city's vibrant night life.

It was during this return to the city that Jack Solomons arrived determined to speak business with Robinson and entice him to finally fight in Britain. Robinson, however, left a message with George Gainford that he didn't wish to be bothered and that discussing boxing deals was strictly off his agenda and so he left his trusted trainer to meet with Solomons, who offered the opportunity for Ray to defend his world title against the European middleweight champion, Randolph 'Randy' Turpin in London that July. Gainford promised to relay the offer to the champion, who eventually declared that he would accept the challenge for $100,000. Solomons nearly choked on his cigar and immediately stormed away from the meeting. When Gainford gleefully recounted the outcome of the meeting to Robinson, he shrugged his shoulders and told his trainer not to concern himself because there were other European promoters only too wiling to pay his price and he would not have to defend his world title. He was proven right. Instead of going to London, they quickly moved to arrange a fight in Turin later in the tour, which was promoted by the wealthy owner of the Fiat car plant, Signor Agnelli. Gainford successfully negotiated a $20,000 purse which would be deposited in Robinson's bank account the day before the fight. Robinson, used to the cynical negotiations with US promoters, was suspicious until the American consulate authorised the cheque. He could only thank Gainford for his efforts. Signor Agnelli, after more discussions, also agreed to pay the train and hotel bills for the entire Robinson entourage, or circus as the press called his team.

The Belgium city of Antwerp was the next stop for the Sugar Ray Robinson bandwagon. He was scheduled to meet a fair-haired Dutch middleweight called Jan de Bruin and over 8,000 spectators packed the city's Sportspalais arena. De Bruin was still feeling humbled because just five weeks earlier he had been peeled off the canvas after Randolph Turpin had flattened him in six dynamic rounds in Coventry, but this result never entered Robinson's thoughts as he was all business.

At seven' o'clock on the morning of the fight, the unshaven champion walked out of his hotel and went to Mass at a Roman Catholic Church near his hotel. This was a little-known ritual with Sugar Ray. Before every one of his fights, he would insist on going into a church, no matter what denomination, to pray. After this, he would enjoy a light breakfast before he would sit and read. For the de Bruin fight, this was interrupted by the requirement to attend the weigh-in at 11.30am before he could return to his customary approach and head back to his hotel to sleep. He would make his way to the fight venue in the late afternoon, where Harry Wiley, whom he affectionately called 'Papa', would take a clean linen sheet out of his carefully packed bag and drape it over the rubbing table. He would then put Robinson's clean woollen socks and his crisp white boxing shorts (for the de Bruin fight, Ray broke this tradition and opted to wear purple) and his boxing boots with brand new laces onto the table. Robinson always insisted on being ready about half an hour before he was officially due into the ring. After his hands had been carefully wrapped, his protector fitted and his gloves laced on, he would start the process of loosening up his taut, sinewy muscles, whilst Wiley and Gainford made it their business to relax him by laughing and joking around. When the time finally came to take the long walk to the ring and the noise started to grow louder and louder, he would begin jogging rhythmically and trying to disguise the effects which the atmosphere and tension would etch on his solemn face. The laughing and joking would cease and Robinson would focus on becoming the master craftsman.

In truth, the de Bruin fight was like a race meeting between a thoroughbred and a carthorse. The Dutch fighter suddenly looked frail in stature and had nothing in his arsenal to bother the sleek Robinson, who was able to box well within himself. He employed his much-vaunted left hook to terrific effect and the crowd responded to these flashes of brilliance with hearty appreciation. At the first break, the wily Gainford advised his man to hit de Bruin in the stomach and Ray followed his instructions to the letter and flayed into the Dutchman with lightning fast jabs, hooks, uppercuts and bolo punches which crashed through his meagre defences until the referee was moved to call a halt to the proceedings half-way through the eighth round after be Bruin held up his hand in a token surrender. De Bruin had simply had enough and later told reporters that he "was beginning to feel like a toy in the hands of Robinson." They asked him about the difference between the world champion and Britain's Randy Turpin. "Robinson is the better boxer but that Turpin is the harder hitter," he readily informed them.

The respected British journalist, Peter Wilson, followed up his earlier piece on the champion from his last visit and was granted an audience from the willing Robinson after this fight. His feature contained a fascinating insight into the mind of the American superstar. Many ringsiders had been puzzled by Robinson's reluctance on a number of occasions to deliver the coup de grace when de Bruin had obviously been dazed and helpless. Instead, he had repeatedly stepped back with a half smile playing on his lips. Wilson challenged him and Robinson suggested, "I seem to be losing the killer instinct." He mused that he "once killed a kid in the ring and maybe that's always at the back of my mind." Later, when faced with the US press, he had changed this explanation and told them that he had "let De Bruin off lightly because I wanted the practice for when I meet Randolph Turpin." Wilson's interview touched on boxing, sportsmanship, politics and philosophy. Wilson was moved to write that "Robinson is one of the most fluent boxers I have ever heard speak." Finally, he witnessed a touching scene which gave an insight into Robinson's humane side. An old black man, claiming to be a former fighter, had been selling chewing gum in the arena and managed to get into the dressing room. Before he could be removed, Robinson ordered them to allow the obviously poor former fighter inside and proceeded to shake the man's hand and make him feel important and on level terms. Wilson described it as "a wonderful, humane gesture by a wonderful and humane fighter."

After the newspaper interviews Sugar Ray showered and dressed. He wore a conservative blue suit, white shirt and tie and black shoes. He read his messages that officials had handed him. He studied them like a conscientious businessman leaving the office. "Whew," he uttered. "I'm glad that's over, that guy could punch." He then left his changing room and posed for photographers with a group of doctors to whom he had presented a $10,000 cheque in the name of the Damon Runyon Cancer Found. Then he returned to his hotel where he wrote letters to the fund treasurer Walter Winchell, whom he considered a close friend, and crooner Billy Eckstine. By midnight he was in bed because he had a game of golf to play the next morning at St Cloud.

Six days later, he moved across the country to Liege to meet Jean Walzack in a repeat from his first European tour six months earlier. On that occasion, he had been forced to complete the full ten rounds and 10,000 fans flocked to see if Walzack could improve on this showing. Instead, Robinson treated them to nineteen murderous minutes of action and mayhem as the former French welterweight champion was forced to hit the canvas six times in the last three rounds of this massacre before pounding him to a standstill in the first minute of the sixth round.

Ever since he had first arrived back in Europe and stepped off the boat at Le Havre, invitations had been pouring in at such a rate that he was forced to employ another secretary to help sort them into categories - yes, no and maybe. The ones which fell into the affirmative pile was a white-tie benefit event, where Robinson impressed by taking to the dance floor and his jitterbug stole the show from Edith Piaf and Louis Jouvet. He also accepted an invite to unveil a plaque in honour of the great French middleweight, Marcel Cerdan. He judged the mood of the event perfectly and behaved with dignity at the ceremony, which endeared him to the French public even more, especially as Jake LaMotta was the fighter who Cerdan was on his way to America to fight when the airplane he was on crashed. He also received an award from a French boxing magazine as 'The Best Boxer of the Year' and he gave a modest acceptance speech, praising the French public for their knowledge and appreciation and even compared his treatment to his own country's attitude.

Despite this hectic round of socialising, Robinson's discipline for training was still healthily maintained. Every morning at six o'clock he religiously completed his six miles of roadwork, which was overseen by Harry Wiley, before he would rest and then head to the gym of the Central Sporting Club at three o'clock every afternoon where his routine consisted of three minutes of shadow boxing to loosen up before going through six rounds of sparring, two with each of three sparring partners, before three minutes on the heavy punch bag and then three minutes on the speed ball. He would then end by using his skipping rope. He didn't skip in a conventional manner but danced using the rope at his side while doing a kind of jitterbug routine, which he boasted made him razor-sharp and helped him maintain his status as the world's greatest boxer.

The Final Battle Against The Bronx Bull

The treatment he received in Paris was exceptional and made Ray reflective on the status he had successfully acquired. Whenever his fuchsia-coloured Cadillac convertible purred away from the Claridges Hotel and he drove along the Champs Elysees, local gendarmes would stop the traffic whilst cyclists would swarm behind him, like seagulls after an ocean liner, all singing his name. Robinson entered the spirit of it and would reply in his newly acquired French. Simply, he loved Paris and Paris returned his affection in kind. He told one US journalist that the huge crowds that followed him and begged him to sign autographs had started to make him appreciate just how fortunate he had been. The sense of his own boxing mortality, which he had first revealed to Peter Wilson, seemed to be more prevalent in his thoughts. "I know that one day it's all going to end for me because boxing is a young man's game." His eyes scanned the room thoughtfully, as if he always wanted to remember this precise moment of this particular day. He reflected on his friend Joe Louis and how he had adapted to the slower pace of retirement. "Perhaps Joe needs the money but it is the excitement of the crowds and the prestige of being a world champion that he really misses the most." He ruminated on the discipline required to stay at the top of the fight game and suggested that being based in Paris made him appreciate this characteristic. "Boxing isn't an easy life because of the constant temptations. It eats away at your will power and will power doesn't last forever."

Some journalists began to suggest that Robinson was starting to seriously contemplate retirement from boxing. Given that he was now over the age of 30 and placed such great emphasis on acquiring enough money to ensure that he didn't need to work again made this a plausible view. Robinson, however, still hankered after earning really 'big' money, which he believed was his due as boxing's leading man. He, therefore, instructed George Gainford to re-enter negotiations with Jack Solomons to meet Randolph Turpin. He also started to publicly suggest even bigger fights, such as Joey Maxim's light-heavyweight title. Although he was too diplomatic to mention it, the light-heavyweight title was now the only major world title not held by a black fighter and the businessman inside Robinson calculated that this fight would mean big money.

Fight number five on his European tour was imminent though, and he arrived in Berlin to face twenty four year old Gerhard Hecht, a tall, dark-haired fighter, who looked more like an academic than a pugilist. Looks were deceiving, though, as Hecht came into the fight boasting an unbeaten record in his previous twenty four contests prior to this match on a balmy Sunday 24th June afternoon. Over 30,000 spectators seated themselves inside the open air Walbuehne Stadium eager to catch a glimpse of the American boxer which the German press had been featuring since he began his European tour on the 21st May. Robinson's wife and sister also attracted attention, when they assumed their seats at ringside along with the promoter Lew Burston.

When he was introduced before the contest, the German crowd abandoned their partisan support for their local challenger and greeted Robinson to a tremendous standing ovation. Shortly afterwards, as the opening bell signalled the two men to move from their corners, Robinson unleashed a series of devastating left hooks to the German boxer's unguarded right side. Hecht appeared stunned and badly hurt as he fell to the canvas clutching his side and making exaggerated agonised facial expressions. The huge crowd was stunned at the speedy and dramatic ending when the referee, Otto Nispel, counted him out.

Hecht's manager, who had been screaming obscenities whilst Nispel was conducting his count, jumped onto the ring apron and protested that Robinson had floored his man with foul blows. This prompted the fans to begin booing and yelling their displeasure. Robinson, who had returned back to his corner believing that he had won, merely looked perplexed at the commotion. The confusion was increased when the bell - to signal the end of the round - rang. On the orders of the judges, the loudspeakers then announced that there would be "a short interruption" in the fight.

Doctors leapt into the ring to examine Hecht, whilst his seconds also aided him by rubbing his back; the crowd continued to boo vigorously and Nilsen lost complete control. He instructed Robinson to keep fighting and then ignored the voluble protests from Gainford, who pointed out that Hecht had been counted out. Incensed and determined to end the fight, Robinson flew off his stool and cracked home three vicious punches to despatch the hurt and visibly distressed German down again.

The crowd's anger seemed to increase at this and bottles, cups, programmes and other debris began to rain down onto the ring and some racist chanting was later reported. The loudspeakers kept appealing for calm but the crowd took no notice and the missiles being hurled got heavier. Robinson, by now wrapped up in his blue and gold silk dressing gown, jumped from the ring and ducked under the ring apron as more and more beer bottles were flung into the ring. Edna Mae was hit before she could join him under the ring. Eventually, thirty policemen drew their batons and cleared a way through the hostile mass and pulled the Robinson party back to the sanctity of his dressing room. Hecht, meanwhile, was taken to hospital and diagnosed as suffering with broken ribs. The news of the riot made headlines across the world.

Robinson refused to go back to his hotel but insisted on jumping aboard a military train bound for Frankfurt. William Hamsher, a young journalist, also managed to jump on the same train and spoke to the world champion about the frightening scenes. He denied that he had won with a foul punch but claimed that the referee had insisted that he keep fighting because "he feared being killed by the angry crowd." In his report, referee Nilson stated that the final punch was a kidney punch, which was not classed as illegal in America. Lew Burston told Hamsher that "a right hook to the liver did the damage and how can a fighter hit his opponent in the back if he doesn't turn his back?"

The night after the fight, the West Berlin Boxing Committee debated the referee's verdict for over four hours before adjourning. They later resumed and clarified that "a punch near to the kidneys is legal in the States but not in Germany." The final outcome was that the commission suspended Nilson for "officiating the contest in an improper manner" and they then declared the fight as 'no decision'. Robinson declared that he would never return to Germany again. He also suggested that "the people throwing bottles were Communists." He also told the press that he "had been approached by Communists who told him that Communism was good for black people" and were upset by his refusal to join them.

Nine days later, he fulfilled his obligation to Signor Agnelli at the Palazzo dello Sport arena in Turin. Cyrille 'Tarzan' Delannoit, a former European middleweight champion hailing from Belgium, was a respectful opponent to face only ten days before he had agreed to defend his world crown against Randy Turpin. It seems unbelievable now that he actually fought ten days before defending his world championship! This would not be permitted today. Although Delannoit had a decent record, including beating Marcel Cerdan to win the European crown, from the opening bell it was obvious to the 25,000 spectators that he didn't belong in the same ring as the world champion. He quickly slashed a deep cut over the Belgian's left eye with the very first punch of the fight and the Belgian then attempted to play on the events of Berlin by complaining that Robinson had struck him with low punches. The referee ordered the boxers to continue and Robinson proceeded to slam him all over the ring and just seven seconds before the end of round three, the Belgian threw up his arms in surrender. Immediately after the fight, Ray altered his plans and decided to leave for Paris where he was going to travel to catch the night ferry to England.

At this time, Nat Fleischer wrote a long editorial in The Ring magazine which conceded that Robinson was the idol of 'Gay Paree' and was an ambassador of good will, and that he now appeared to surpass the great Jack Dempsey and Joe Louis in terms of the affection he received on foreign shores. He contrasted this goodwill, however, with an assessment of why Robinson could not claim to be the sport's richest or most popular fighter in his own country. A man who could argue to enjoy both these titles was the "club-fighting brawler" Rocky Graziano, who was drawing $100,000 gates. Fleischer suggested that American fight fans "preferred watching a slugger to a boxer" and were "almost bored by Sugar Ray's cold, businesslike perfection in the ring."

Robinson responded to these claims by arguing, "I'm a boxer, not a fighter." He pointed out that he had beaten some of the most rugged fighters in the light, welter and middleweight divisions because most of them were predominantly either "one-handed or they have a good right cross or a good left jab but rarely combine the two." Robinson's repertoire, he reminded everybody, were "thrown with equal speed and power in either hand and include every standard punch from a 'bolo' to a hook and even a few I make up on the spur of the moment." He claimed that he varied his style depending on his opponent's approach and gave the example of when he had fought Robert Villemain in December 1950 and he was faced with a technique adopted by the Frenchman called "the defensive shell". Robinson reacted by threading his devastating uppercuts between the Frenchman's gloves. Against the flashy Kid Gavilan, Robinson employed his dazzling footwork to keep out of range and avoid the Cuban's punches before beating his man convincingly with a brilliant exhibition of counter-punching. "Whatever the opposition is capable of, I will always come up with the right answer and cut loose with two-handed combination punches from both hands,"he said. Tommy Bell, the man whom Robinson had beaten to become the world welterweight champion, supported these claims and said that "Robinson came at me with two punches, a left and a right, and I am still not sure which hit me first. The punches didn't really hurt me but when I started to move, my legs just wouldn't go with me and I fell over on my head."

Sugar Ray revealed that a huge part of his success came from careful planning and shrewd coaching from his corner. During his fights, George Gainford and 'Pee Wee' Beale studied the fighters, hawkishly looking for any problems before they occurred, and were quick to spot something his opponent might be doing wrong. "My trainers can see better than me. I'm busy watching my man and looking for any openings or guarding myself against any danger but they can spot things like where he leaves his right hand after throwing a punch. They tell me to draw his right hand, which leaves me with an opening to counter." Robinson recounted his latest victory over Jake LaMotta as a triumph of close teamwork, careful strategy and calculated risk. "The 'Bronx Bull' was a solid, crowding fighter with menacing strength and a stubborn pride in never having been knocked down but our team strategy was one from the bull ring, with me dancing out of danger from LaMotta's angry charges while using my left jab to weaken him. In the eleventh round, our strategy changed and I stood my ground, purposely absorbed his best punches and when I was satisfied that Jake was no longer dangerous, I moved in for the finish."

13.

Welcome to England

THOUSANDS OF French men and women turned up at the port in France to see him off to England, where he prepared to defend his world title against Britain's hard-punching 23-year-old British and European middleweight champion, Randolph Turpin. The heartfelt farewell he enjoyed in France was soon mirrored by the reception he received when he stepped from the Paris boat train in London and was besieged by thousands of British people who were eager to catch a glimpse of him. Althea Gibson, a young black American women's tennis champion whom Robinson had sponsored, rushed forward and gave him a big hug and a kiss. The scenes around the station were frenzied with cameramen and reporters jostling to get the best vantage point to this extraordinary boxer. When the party finally got away they drove to the Cumberland Hotel where he was besieged again by hundreds of fans waiting outside. The manager of the hotel was worried. He had never seen scenes like this before. Robinson then attended a press conference at Jack Solomon's gym in the centre of London. It was a press conference the like of which had never been seen before in the British Isles (until a decade later, in fact, when Mohammed Ali first came). It was absolute bedlam!

Sugar Ray was enlightening, and the press lapped him up. He answered their questions, smiled, posed for photographs and pleased one and all. Back at the Cumberland hotel, thousands of fans were outside and more photographers were inside waiting to take more pictures. Fans were milling around and the manager was not happy at all. After discussions it was decided to relocate the team. But how was he going to leave the hotel? It was decided he would leave through a back door and he was whisked away in a waiting Rolls-Royce to his training headquarters in Windsor. At the same time, it was arranged that the pink Cadillac would provide a decoy and pull up at the front of the Cumberland hotel and lead the public to believe that Robinson was based there. His Cadillac was then driven over to his actual base.

Seated alongside him on the journey to Windsor was the Daily Mail journalist Geoffrey Simpson, who provided the British public with an amazing insight into the world of Robinson. He breathlessly reported that when he reached the 15th Century inn, named The Star and Garter, where he would be based throughout his stay, his staff of twelve unloaded over a hundred pieces of luggage whilst Robinson ordered his lunch of voul-au-vents, fresh salmon and a leg of lamb before he changed his mind and ordered ham and eggs. He then declared that he would have his hair trimmed and as Simpson watched on, George Gainford turned to him and pointed at Robinson and smiled, "He's my very own million-dollar corporation." Robinson sat in a chair and had his personal barber smooth out the natural crinkles in his hair.

The public clamour for more insights into Robinson was so overwhelming that the Fleet Street editors assigned their leading feature writers to work alongside the traditional sports reporters. They pored over every detail of his life during his daily meetings with the press. One of them asked him if he thought it was "wasteful to maintain a staff of twelve." With a huge grin, Robinson answered, "I like having my own people around me. It costs $1200 a week in expenses but I'd rather pay it out and have a good time rather than pay it in tax." George Gainford outlined the scale of Robinson's burgeoning business empire which consisted of "several city blocks of real estate in Harlem, a laundry, a lingerie shop, plus two barber shops, and a brewery and restaurant." The British people, still on rations after the Second World War, were overwhelmed.

The main focus, however, was the fight. He had just completed six fights in a ten week period and Robinson admitted that it was a tough finish to his tour, but stressed that it was not the actual fights that bothered him but the drudgery and routine of the training. "I'd just like to be left alone for awhile and play some golf and learn to play my piano." He refused to discuss the Turpin encounter in detail but insisted that he was "proud to be a world champion and I intend to fight like one." He wouldn't give a prediction but George Gainford was less circumspect and assured them that "There ain't any man in the world that can outbox Robinson."

The whole of the British Isles was caught up in the euphoria and excitement. British boxing was stimulated by the interest shown in the forthcoming world championship match. It was described as being "the most anticipated event since VE day." There was no live television, in fact, there was only one channel, the BBC, and so the wireless (radio) was considered as the principal luxury for most families. The Turpin versus Robinson clash was announced as being broadcast live on the BBC's Home Service at 9.30pm and the commentators charged with describing the action to over twenty million listeners were Raymond Glendenning and Barrington Dalby. On the night itself, there was uproar from thousands of these listeners because the programme which aired before the fight, the popular 'Family Favourites', overran and, therefore, the broadcast missed the explosive ring entrance in

Earl's Court, where sold out signs had been displayed for weeks after the tickets, ranging in price from one to ten guineas, had been snapped up in record time.

Barrington Dalby told his captivated audience that he believed Turpin's only hope of victory lay in his ability to score a quick knockout. This was the common consensus amongst most observers, who only gave Turpin a 'puncher's chance' of beating the flamboyant world champion. One worried reporter, Bernard McElwaine of the Sunday Pictorial, captured the general mood with his headline: 'Best of luck to Turpin - he'll need it!' McElwaine wrote that "Robinson is the greatest fighter of his weight in the world. At 31 he is not past it and at 23, Turpin is nowhere near it." He declared: "I wish Turpin was not meeting Robinson. The fight should be the most exciting ever staged in this country. Exciting, like a train wreck, an earthquake, a cattle stampede, or any other disaster."

There appeared to be only one way for Turpin to emerge victorious. Clifford Webb, writing in the Daily Herald, articulated how: "Turpin's one chance of winning must be to catch the titleholder with one of his paralyzing punches early on." George Whiting, one of England's most knowledgeable boxing doyens suggested that "Turpin cannot hope to outbox Robinson; his one chance is to knock the champion senseless." Turpin was inexperienced, possessed only one quality and was being plunged into a class way too deep for him. Peter Wilson suggested in his Daily Express article that "Turpin is being rushed. He should have waited another year." He lamented that "Turpin's long-range punching is probably superior to the American. But what's the use of outgunning the opposition if you can't land on the target?" L.N. Bailey of the now-defunct London evening newspaper, The Star, expressed his concern that Turpin might be overawed. "Randy's biggest danger might be the possibility that he might 'freeze-up' when the fight starts and numb his nerves and muscles so that they will not respond to messages of the brain."

The one lone voice in the wilderness belonged to Tom Phillips, an independent journalist writing in the Daily Mirror. He predicted a British upset. Phillips had reported on Turpin's career from the very beginning and had followed Robinson's two European tours, where he was disdainful of the hype surrounding the world champion and his "gang of hangers-on". He urged Turpin not to be fooled by the hype. "People say that the Robinson-Turpin contest should not be allowed to take place," he said. "Their reasoning was that Robinson was such a destroyer when going all-out and no British fighter could stand up with him. Well, Randy Turpin has got a chance; I know the odds will be laid heavily on Robinson to win. But I stick to my guns, Turpin will beat Robinson. In fact, I will put my shirt on Turpin to beat Sugar Ray."

The hype which Tom Phillips warned against had been steadily building throughout his stay in England. His training sessions repeatedly saw thousands of fans queuing to enter the small gymnasium. Dressed in a pure white T-shirt and shorts he would dramatically enter the gym to the music of 'Anchors Aweigh' whilst dozens of photographers' flashbulbs would pop away. Before he would step into the ring, his interpreter, Jimmy Karoubi, the dwarf whom he had christened as his 'bodyguard' in Paris, would request silence and then instruct the spectators to refrain from smoking during the training session. Robinson would then proceed to shadow box before getting his sparring partner, Don Ellis, to put on his head guard and pillow-sized gloves and then begin gently boxing each other, without going all out.

Edna Mae and Ray's sister Evelyn were present at all these training sessions and sat in chairs beneath the punch ball dressed in the finest Parisian fashions and wearing ear rings like miniature chandeliers. When Edna Mae was shown photographs of Turpin, her only observation was that "he looks vicious doesn't he?" Robinson's sister, Evelyn, gave an insight into Robinson's mental state and suggested that "He'll be glad when the next few days are all over. It's a great strain on him as he's never seen this boy, Turpin. He's not sleeping very well."

The build up, however, was shrouded in tragedy. On the Sunday before the fight, the customary huge crowds had gathered in Windsor to try to spot Sugar Ray and his team of characters. Seven year old Christine Butcher was among them, but later that same afternoon, her partly clothed body was discovered on a patch of wasteland; she had been strangled to death. Corn blonde Christine had earlier told her neighbour that she was going to show Robinson her black-faced doll. Neither Robinson nor any of his team claimed that they had seen her. The Police conducted an exhaustive enquiry and spoke to 4,300 local schoolchildren without any success in tracing her killer.

Also during the pre-fight preparations, Robinson and his entourage visited the Life Guard's barracks at the invitation of Major Cooper, who asked the hugely impressed champ to inspect the barracks before he watched two strapping Guardsmen sparring. He then visited the stables where he spent a long while admiring the well-groomed horses. He asked if he could ride one but was told that the promoter Jack Solomons would not feel quite so jolly if he found out and so this idea was quickly shelved. Robinson was described by the officers as "gracefulness personified".

While all the attention was on Robinson, Randolph Turpin kept a deliberately low profile and holed himself up in his training quarters of Cwrych Castle in Abergele in North Wales, a place he professed to love. He was joined in this rural retreat by his six sparring partners and his two trainers, including Dick, his older brother and former British middleweight champion who had made history in 1948 when he became the first black English boxer to win a British championship. Hundreds, rather than the thousands Robinson attracted, of holidaymakers visited the gym and watched with interest as the town's honoured guest prepared for the most important fight of his life. The ordinary lad from Leamington didn't attract the ballyhoo, dwarf compere or litany of hangers-on which his celebrated rival enjoyed. His quarters were once used by Queen Victoria and he would retreat there and read his collection of comic books and Westerns before conducting his workouts, which were between twelve and twenty hard rounds each night.

Dick and Randy could often be found in the castle cinema, watching films of Robinson's previous fights. He studied them so often that by the time he had finished his training camp, they had almost become worn out. After watching them, he would sit in an armchair and discuss them with his older brother and Jackie, his younger brother and the family comedian, and Jackie's constant joking ensured that Randy remained relaxed in the build-up. His deputy trainer, Hymns, summed up the difference between the two fighters when he told local newspapers that "any resemblance there is between Sugar Ray and Randolph begins and ends in the ring. Randolph likes to live and train without any fuss, unlike Robinson who seems to thrive in a blaze of publicity."

The weekend before the Tuesday night fight saw the press build up reach a crescendo and both boxers acquiesced to speak with the newspapers at length. Robinson paid tribute to the British public's appreciation of the noble art and said that he was treating this fight "as the most important fight of my career." He mentioned that "Britain is well known for its appreciation of the art of boxing" and stated that his intention was "to make you folks understand I'm worthy to be a world champion." He went out of his way to show Turpin the deference which he rarely granted to other opponents: "All respects to Randolph Turpin and his ability, which I know about from good friends in England, he is a deadly puncher and a courageous fighter who is perfectly conditioned and determined to beat me." He displayed his usual confidence, however, when declaring that "I know I can beat him because I've had more experience than him and have fought better fighters than Turpin has ever faced, and in boxing, you never stop learning from the fighters you fought, whether you won, lost or drew."

Turpin was far more circumspect and reserved in his assessment of his date with destiny in Earl's Court. "Robinson has only two hands and so have I," he said without a trace of emotion. Instead, he allowed his sparring partners to share their views on his chances. "For the last six years I have been fighting against tough opponents and sparring with the best fighters in the world," said the American Mel Brown. "That includes Ezzard Charles, the former world heavyweight champion, and until now, nobody has ever hurt me but I have certainly been hurt these past few days. Randy spars as if he was actually fighting Sugar Ray and his sixteen ounce gloves have felt like sixteen ounce rocks. My head has been going round; I never thought it could hurt like this." Then British heavyweight prospect Johnny Williams explained that "Turpin has power like the hind leg of a mule and I think that he might cause Robinson problems. I honestly believe that Randy could knock out most of our light-heavies and heavyweights." Other sceptics believed that Turpin wouldn't be able to withstand body shots that Robinson would flay him with but Arthur Batty, his physical conditioning expert, addressed this concern: "Randy can't be hurt to the body because his stomach muscles are two inches thick." Randy completed the interviews by assuring the British public that he had "never trained harder in all my life, nor felt better. I'm going to make this the fight of my life. So, watch out Sugar Ray!"

British boxing fans were a unique breed. They would follow a certain fighter either by watching or reading about him. In the case of American fighters like Sugar Ray Robinson they might have had only a glimpse of him via the Pathe Newsreels, but they would follow his career through the Boxing News and other boxing magazines. Sugar Ray Robinson was someone they had latched onto. He was a 'Superstar' of the ring. Only one defeat in over one hundred and odd professional contests! This was perceived as absolutely phenomenal. The general feeling was that most didn't believe there was a middleweight in America who could beat Robinson. And, they certainly thought that Sugar Ray and his entourage did not think there could be a boxer in Britain or Europe who could match him in talent, let alone beat him. After watching and reading about how Robinson had easily beaten the top European fighters they, like the majority of sportswriters, believed that Randolph Turpin was lined up as a sacrificial lamb

The final weekend's coverage also included some unsavoury and unsubstantiated allegations and innuendo. Mel Brown gave a controversial interview to the Empire News newspaper claiming that he had "advised Randy to be extra careful because there were unscrupulous creatures in America who attempted to fix certain fights." He insisted that he "had been offered money to lose a proposed fight against Sugar Ray" but furiously turned the offer down. Brown also claimed that he had warned Turpin about carefully guarding "the water bucket, the sponge and the drinking water bottle in his corner" because they could be contaminated with drugs. Robinson and his team were suitably furious and completely refuted the allegations.

Thousands of people descended onto the Soho offices of Jack Solomons in Great Windmill Street in Soho in London's West End, where the promoter had a gymnasium above his offices and where the official weigh-in was being conducted. For hours before the actual ceremony, hordes of fans converged and caused traffic jams in their desire to catch a glimpse of the two fighters. Police were eventually called to quell the crowds as the two boxers stood for the customary handshake before they stripped to the waist. Turpin weighed in at 11 stones and 4 ¾ pounds and looked hugely impressive. The champion took his turn and weighed a comparatively light 11 stones and ½ pound. The British Boxing Board of Control doctor, Phil Kaplin, then examined the two men and declared them fit and ready. The doctor, after examining Turpin, remarked: "What an excellent body. I wish I had half his strength. If I had a body like that I would be quite happy." Sugar Ray quietly eyed up Turpin. He couldn't fail to have been impressed.

When the day finally arrived, the mood amongst the capacity 18,200 people who squeezed into the multi-tiered Earl's Court was a strange mix. Many had been seduced by the myth of this American superstar and had come to watch in wonder at the masterclass he was expected to produce. Others were not particularly committed boxing fans but had come to see if Turpin could pull off a miracle. Many others, however, came to display a patriotic zeal and support their brave countryman. This mixture helped to create an amazingly charged atmosphere, and when the former Navy cook, Turpin, a man who had never been further than Paris in his entire life, made his entrance to the ring, the showbusiness instincts of Jack Solomons were fully utilised to great effect. The whole building fell into a complete darkness before a fanfare sounded out and blue spotlights picked out Turpin. Subsequently, newspapers claimed that "the extravaganza would have done credit to the great Cecil B. DeMille" as all the way to the ring, Turpin was carried on the deafening cheers and applause. When he stood in his corner, shrouded in his white towelling robe, he looked completely impassive and without a trace of nerves. And then the house lights dimmed again and the band blasted a sustained fanfare as bathed in the brilliant rays of multi-coloured spot lights, Sugar Ray Robinson, looking regal in a blue and white silk gown, stood hopping on his toes. He proceeded to dance down the aisle as the spectators craned their necks to catch a glimpse of the world champion. He jumped into the ring and immediately started to wind up his bolo punch and throw lightning fast combinations in an attempt to intimidate Turpin. It didn't appear to have any impact as the challenger remained impassive like a Sphinx.

Robinson was the betting favourite and was quoted at 7-2 to win in any round and 6-4 against the fight lasting beyond five rounds. The bookmakers offered odds of 66-1 for a draw and generous odds of 20-1 that the Britain would emerge as a points victor. George Gainford outlined his supreme confidence and laid a bet of £1500 that his charge would emerge victorious. The scale of this bet must be appreciated by the fact that the average annual salary at this time was around £312.

Patsy Hagate, the Master of Ceremonies, cleared his throat before making his usual introductions. Once he had completed the formalities, the referee, Eugene Henderson, beckoned both men to the centre of the ring and issued his final instructions before sending them back to their corners to await the first bell. The tension was as thick as the smoke-filled air in the arena when the first bell sounded and both men came from their corners quickly to meet in the centre of the apron. It was the British fighter who scored first with a long raking left jab which drew thunderous cheers. This early signal from Turpin seemed to carry with it a clear message that he was unmoved by the champion he faced and he continued to employ his jab to magnificent effect. In contrast, the first round offered no signs of the lightning combination punches promised by the American as the Leamington boxer calmly went about his clinical business.

The supporters were not surprised by Turpin's hitting power, but his solid straight left jab stopped Robinson ever finding a rhythm. His relentless aggression and piston-like jab carried him through the first six rounds with comfort. In round seven, there was a pivotal moment in the fight when they accidentally clashed heads. Turpin merely winced, shook his head and resumed his relentlessly aggressive approach, but Robinson came off the worst and had a deep gash running above his left eye after an old scar was reopened, causing the blood to ooze down his face. This injury seemed to suddenly jolt the watching public into a realisation that Turpin may, just may be within touching distance of achieving the impossible. Turpin showed no mercy. With a deadly intent, he jabbed his left hand into the damaged eye.

The considered opinion amongst the press pack was that Turpin's most dangerous moments would be in the clinches, where the American would overwhelm and bully him. On the few occasions, however, when they did tangle at close quarters, Robinson opened up and dug hurtful punches into the mid-section of Turpin. Many ringsiders assumed that this would signal the beginning of the end but the British boxer confounded them by responding with sickening right crosses to the chin that left Robinson holding on like an octopus and risking disqualification.

After nine rounds, Robinson sensed that he was being beaten and became disorganized and desperate. His face started to betray his true feelings and he winced from the barrage of lefts that Turpin repeatedly sunk into his ribs and he seemed to be distracted by keeping an eye on Turpin's right hand to offer any real response. He appeared to be shocked that in the later stages of the fight, Turpin knew almost as many tricks of feinting, defence and counter punching than he did. It was only the American's courage and defensive skills which kept him going, but when the final bell rang, it wasn't heeded as the two warriors couldn't hear it because the noise of the by-now partisan fans was deafening.

They erupted when referee Henderson held aloft the arm of the new champion, who was judged as winning every round except the third with two others deemed as drawn. A mob of well-wishers descended on the ring, all wanting to pat the back of the unmarked Turpin. A ripple, which started in the upper reaches of the hall, quickly cascaded throughout and a chanted chorus of 'For he's a jolly good fellow' was sounded. After Turpin was declared the new world champion, Barrington Dalby turned to Nat Fleischer: "Well, what about that Nat?" he shouted. The diminutive boxing historian replied: "Barry, you haven't seen the real Sugar Ray, he wasn't sharp tonight. He's been living the good life in Paris; he thought he had an easy touch."

Jolly Jack (Solomons) was elated! "If this contest had been staged at Wembley Stadium, 140,000 would have willingly paid to watch it," he lamented.

Artistically it had not been a great fight. There had been too much missing of punches and clinching. Surprisingly, from the spectators' point of view, it was Sugar Ray who was holding the most. He held Turpin's arms in a vice-like grip from as early as the third round. But this was all forgotten by the tide of emotion of this never-to-be-forgotten special occasion. It was an event. Not just for sports fans but also for the ordinary people of the British Isles. It was a long-lasting memory which would live with them until the day they died. We must also remember that austerity throughout the country needed a stimulant to help lift the gloom of the Second World War, which had only ended a few short years before. There were still coal shortages, power cuts, food and clothing rationing and national service conscription in force.

There was complete shock among the experienced denizens of the boxing writers' guild. The British scribes eagerly ate their portions of humble pie for doubting their man. The headlines above Bernard McElwaine's Sunday Pictorial captured the consensus, 'I'm glad I was wrong about Turpin!' He concluded his report with the statement, "Turpin wears the mantle of greatness and richly deserves it; he wears the world crown and I wear a dunce's cap - but I don't mind. This is one of the great and rare occasions when being wrong is a pleasure." However, many were also shocked at how poor Robinson had appeared. Norman Hurst, regarded as the doyen of boxing writers, wrote that "this was not the Sugar Ray we have seen before." His colleague, Clifford Webb, suggested that "Robinson was well below the standard most people had been led to expect from him and my guess is that he wasn't at the peak of physical fitness."

Immediately after the conclusion of the contest, the BBC was inundated with irate complaints about the controversial broadcast of the fight. Besides the fact that they missed the ring entrances due to a previous programme over-running, many listeners objected to the commentary from Dalby, who failed to reflect the superiority of Turpin and appeared to have him behind on points. Dalby was later forced to issue a public apology for "giving the impression that the fight was closer than it was."

Before he returned to the frenzied scenes in his dressing room, Turpin excused himself and found his way into Robinson's dressing room where he paid homage to his rival and told him that "you're the champion they all said you were." He apologised to him for beating him and Robinson, touched by Turpin's genuine sincerity, explained that "when you're the champion, you have to be the champion every night and tonight I lost to a better man." Robinson also displayed grace and dignity and told the press that "I have no excuses to make. Turpin won on his merits and he was the better man."

The result seemed to echo around the world. The British Prime Minister, Anthony Eden, was one amongst the four hundred people who sent telegrams of congratulations. The Duke of Fife, who would later become the president of the Amateur Boxing Association, claimed that King George VI was holding a private dinner party at Buckingham Palace on the night of the fight and insisted on listening to commentary of the fight. At the conclusion of the fifteen rounds and when the result was announced, the King reportedly sprung to his feet in excitement and exclaimed, "He's won it! He's won it!" before he toasted Britain's newest world champion.

"I have no excuse to make," uttered Robinson in his dressing room. At first Sugar Ray was very contrite about his defeat, but this would change later. "Turpin won on his merits and he was the better man." The sportsmanship displayed by both the winner and loser seems old-fashioned in the present world.

A couple of days after this historic event, Robinson engaged in a public spat with Nat Fleischer, who was one of the BBC's guest commentators for the fight. Robinson had denied comments attributed to him by Fleischer and reported in The People newspaper in which he claimed that "Turpin repeatedly uses the illegal rabbit punch and that the new world champion would never get away with such tactics in their return bout." Fleischer responded to this professional insult by suggesting that Robinson and George Gainford "regularly denied statements they had given to reporters." He defended himself by claiming, "I go on record with the declaration that not only did Ray Robinson make every statement published under my name in an interview but also approved the material after it had been read back to him the morning that he left London for Paris." The row did draw attention to Turpin's tendency to employ this particular punch and Lewis Burton, writing in the New York Journal-American later suggested that "it was difficult to understand why the British officials permitted such a flagrant foul as Turpin's rabbit punch, without issuing a caution."

Overnight Randolph Turpin became a hero and a world celebrity. His life would never be the same again and in the fullness of time he would pay a very heavy price as we shall see. After the Robinson victory he was besieged with offers to appear here, there, and everywhere. The day after the fight he travelled back to Warwick to visit his blind mother who had been overwhelmed by hordes of reporters and photographers outside her little house. She said she was proud of her son, and had listened to the fight on the wireless. Randy was then rushed to the Festival Ideal Home Exhibition in Coventry; where he was introduced to the large crowd as a recording of his fight with Robinson was broadcast over the loudspeakers. The following day he drove in a limousine, between the Lord Mayors of Warwick and Leamington, for a civic reception at Leamington Town Hall. The streets of Leamington were teaming with thousands of residents who came to congratulate the young coloured kid who had put Leamington and Warwick on the map. Over 20,000 excited people greeted his appearance at the Town Hall. It was a day Randolph would never forget. A jet fighter was in the sky performing loops of welcome. The streets were decked out with flags, banners and streamers, reminiscent of a carnival atmosphere with the throng dancing and singing. Randy was ushered up onto the balcony as the thousands started singing 'For he's a jolly good fellow'. Randy spotted his three-year-old son from his broken marriage in the crowd and lifted him up high in the air. He was then overwhelmed by batteries of cine cameras, newsreel cameras, radio microphones and newspaper photographers. There were civic speeches from various dignitaries but the hordes took no notice. They just wanted to hear Turpin. That night, he was the guest of honour at a private dinner given in his honour by the two mayors. His home town paid tribute to their hero.

Many reporters expressed their surprise that Turpin had agreed to a return with Robinson so quickly after his success. Many believed that he was entitled to box a few exhibitions and engage in the public appearances which he was deluged by and simply cash in on his burgeoning reputation as one of the world's leading sportsmen. What they didn't know was that Turpin had had to sign a return clause before the original fight. He had signed a legal contract which stated that if he won, Robinson was guaranteed a return contest in New York within 64 days of the original. The initial contract was heavily weighted in favour of the vanquished champ in other areas too. Despite being the challenger, he would still receive the champion's share of the money, which was 30%, while Turpin would receive the challenger's end of the wedge, which was 25%. George Middleton, Turpin's manager, responded to the criticisms that he had sold the champion's rights away cheaply by lamely arguing that Turpin had no complaints because he had to acquiesce to get the initial fight.

A few days later, George Middleton and promoter Jack Solomons tempted the British press that the return fight needn't be fought in America, if they could secure a 150,000 crowd - and million dollar gate - in a British football ground. Middleton spoke in detail about using Hampden Park Football Stadium, Glasgow because this could accommodate 149,000 fans with a further 5,000 seats added on the field. Solomons spoke with determination about his intention to keep the middleweight championship in Britain as long as he could and declared that he would announce the details of the return bout within the next day. However, within a few hours of this press conference, Harry Markson, the powerful managing director of the International Sporting Club, flexed his muscles and announced that "a return bout between Robinson and Turpin would take place at the Polo Grounds in New York."

14.

The Return

BEFORE RETURNING to New York, Robinson elected to spend time recuperating and licking his wounds on the French Riviera along with Edna Mae and selected members of his entourage. Dr Nardiello, the physician who had inserted ten stitches above his gashed eye after the fight, prescribed that he should get some sun on his face to help the injury heal quicker. Robinson stayed at the Carlton Hotel in Cannes and he relaxed on the beach and his hotel balcony, but he also lost a considerable amount of money in the casino every night playing baccarat with the two legendary film producers, Jack Warner and Darryl Zanuck. After his two weeks rest and recuperation, he boarded the Liberté ship and thousands of French people turned up at the quayside to cheer him; despite the loss, he was still regarded as a huge hero in the country.

When the ship berthed back in New York, an eager posse of reporters were granted permission to board the ship to interview him. Robinson repeated his earlier graceful and respectful comments about Mr Turpin, as he insisted on referring to him. He then displayed his customary boldness and asserted that he had merely "loaned the title" but would soon bring it back to America. He was then whisked away to the City Hall for a reception with Mayor Vincent Impellitteri and another 3,500 invited guests. Sugar Ray was incredibly gracious but repeated his promise to bring the world crown back to "its rightful place". He then appeared on the balcony, flanked by Walter Winchell, Jim Norris from the IBC, George Gainford, Soldier Jones and Ray's two nephews where the Mayor awarded him the keys to the City.

Reinvigorated by this gesture of respect for his achievements and the incessant demands of the public to rectify matters back in the ring, Robinson quickly settled back into his routine at his training camp in Pompton Lakes. He got down to some hard, physical training. Reports soon began to emanate that his sparring partners had to wear specially adapted body protectors, made from heavy leather and rubber, because of Robinson's vicious body-punching. Although he rarely watched films of his opponents, because of his belief that they would never box him the same way they fought other fighters, he started to watch the film of his fight with Turpin over and over again. The one aspect which troubled him most was Turpin's habit of bending his head backwards to avoid a punch before he would launch his own. It was the gravel voice of Soldier Jones who helped him solve the conundrum. "If you feint Turpin and he then draws his head backwards, that is the position you want him in; he can't take it back any more. Then you step in and nail him." Robinson tried this tactic out repeatedly in sparring.

On the 15th August, Randy Turpin began to make his preparations for his first defence and he left Southampton on the luxury liner, The Queen Mary, which would take seven days to arrive in New York. The International Boxing Club, who was promoting the fight, refused to sanction the champion travelling by air and so he travelled in the first class carriage. His party consisted of George Middleton, his manager and his daughter Josie, promoter Jack Solomons and his wife Faye, his two brothers Dick and Jackie, Eddie Phillips - his loyal sparring partner, Sam Burns and his wife Sophie, his trainers Bill Hyam and Leslie Salts along with his wife and daughter. He did his daily roadwork around the decks of the ship before using the liner's well-equipped gymnasium in the afternoon. He made himself accessible to other passengers and would happily recount his version of that heady night.

When he stepped from the Queen Mary, he was immediately rushed to a press conference at the Edison Hotel, just off Broadway, where he seemed startled and uncomfortable by the blinding flash bulbs and aggressive questions. The American pressmen claimed that they could not understand his accent and began to mock him. They proclaimed themselves as mystified that this Englishman had inflicted the second defeat on the great Robinson. The following few days were a non-stop barrage of press conferences, radio, newsreel and television interviews as well as the ceaseless demands of the autograph-hunters and those eager to take advantage of the innocent abroad.

Jackie Turpin later recounted this period in his book, 'Battling Jack', and described the moment that they arrived at the Edison Hotel and were introduced to a charming black lady from Harlem. They assumed that she was part of the official delegation who was assigned to look after them. The following morning, the Turpin team accepted her invitation to enjoy breakfast at her house, which featured a small band with various singers providing entertainment. In the corner of the room a beautiful-looking lady Jackie remembered as "looking like a high-class model" was introduced to the champion. Her name was Adele Daniels and Turpin was soon enamoured by her obvious charms and eagerly arranged to meet her again for dinner and to enjoy several shopping trips before the team eventually left for their training camp. Jackie later subscribed to the theory which Tommy Farr, the courageous Welsh heavyweight who had lost to Joe Louis, had warned them about. He had cautioned Turpin that "the Mafia would plant women on the boat and in the training camp in order to distract him." Randolph certainly had his head turned.

Randy and his team wore T shirts for comfort in the humid heat of the skyscraper city of New York. He was besieged by everybody. He was slapped on the back by folk who shouted, "Good luck Limey". Then photographers wanted pictures of him stood outside the Empire State Building, the tallest block in the world, 102 stories towering 1,250 feet in the air. The Americans couldn't believe that he was the man who had destroyed the invincibility of the great Sugar Ray Robinson. It was like a Hollywood success story of poor boy makes good. It was reported that Turpin stood to make more than £25,000 from personal appearances and the sale of novelties, like ties, shirts, and souvenirs which were endorsed.

His team moved to Grossinger's Airport, which was 1,700 feet above sea-level and based in the Catskill Mountains. It was a huge country club where the wealthy elite enjoyed their vacations and consisted of high-class restaurants, a golf course and a ballroom, where six hundred staff were employed to cater to the whims of the guests, who included top entertainment stars like Eddie Canter, John Garfield, Irving Berlin and Milton Berle. Turpin enjoyed full use of the Olympic-sized swimming pool and he also rode a huge white horse over the jumps until Jack Solomons discovered him and put an immediate stop to it. His training sessions were conducted in a huge hangar.

There were a number of newspaper reports which began to surface relating to friction in the camp, primarily between Bill Hyam, his brother Dick and his manager, George Middleton. Additionally, speculation that the champion was seen indulging in wild drinking parties became increasingly prolific and caused Turpin real grief. He maintained that the partying was being enjoyed by Dick, but it refused to abate the rumours, which soon claimed that Turpin had rudely snubbed British tourists who had offered their support. On a happier note, he was thrilled to receive a surprise visit from two former middleweight champions, Jake LaMotta and Rocky Graziano. Turpin was offered a number of tips by LaMotta and both Americans wished him luck before he left to return to New York. Merchant seamen from the Queen Mary, the Ocean Monarch and the Mauritania, which were berthed in New York, visited the training camp and had a wonderful time.

While the newspapers were full of stories about the British boxer, Sugar Ray was preparing for the toughest fight of his life. There were old timers, critics and officials saying his best days were behind him and he was looking for one last big payday before retiring. But he was planning how he was going to deal with Turpin's unorthodox style of boxing which he had struggled against in London. He watched the film of their previous contest for points. But there were contradicting stories emanating from his training quarters about his preparations. Early reports indicated that he was looking awesome, yet Lou Viscous, the manager of the former world featherweight champion Willie Pep, came away from a visit to the training camp and declared himself disappointed with the way Robinson had performed. This added fuel to the fires of a whispering campaign which appeared to be going around New York indicating that the fighter's 31-year old legs had 'gone'. There were further rumours that Robinson claimed that his weight was only 11 stones 4 pounds and that he needed to keep his weight up. "I can't understand why an overstuffed welterweight like Robinson should be worried about going stale when he is well with the required weight," Concluded Viscusi.

On the Monday before the midweek fight was due to take place, Randy Turpin finished his preparations by joining his brothers, Dick and Jackie, and a couple of sparring partners in a quintessential English game of cricket. They then relocated themselves in central New York. Reporters were rebuffed in their attempts to discover the name of the hotel where they stayed by George Middleton, who feared that his man would be disturbed by well-wishing admirers. "Randy is just the way we want him, on edge but not over excited; in fact he's ready to fight right now," declared the confident Middleton. Turpin was boosted further still by the unexpected news that Mick Gavin, his long-time co-trainer, was due to arrive by air into New York the following day. It didn't affect the odds, however, which heavily favoured Robinson. Turpin was nonplussed. "Odds mean nothing to me," he said. "Robinson was a 10-1 favourite in London. I had a job to do and I think I did it pretty well."

The hysteria which seemed to be growing around the contest started to peak at the noon weigh-in, held in the New York State Athletic Commission offices. Amid scenes which were reminiscent of a cattle market auction, Turpin scaled in a pound inside the middleweight limit at 11 stones 5 pounds, whilst the challenger was a slightly lighter 11 stones and 3 ½ pounds, which was still 3 pounds heavier than he had been for the London fight. The niggling issue of Turpin's alleged illegal punching was also addressed when George Gainford asked the chief boxing commissioner, Colonel Eddie Eagan, a former Oxford Rhodes scholar and Olympic boxing champion, to clear up the debate about whether the 'rabbit punch' was permissible. Unfortunately, the colonel only confused matters further with his non committal statement that "the rabbit punch is a punch with the side of the glove or wrist to any part of the body." British Boxing Board of Control secretary, Teddy Waltham immediately took issue and claimed that the rabbit punch was, in fact, a punch to the back of the neck at the base of the skull. A heated debate between the two camps erupted whilst Robinson stood like a pall-bearer at his own funeral, and in contrast, Turpin doubled up with an uncontrollable fit of the giggles. Eventually, the issue was finally resolved. Waltham reignited the debate again when he brought up the delicate subject matter of kidney punches.

After the weigh-in, Turpin returned to his hotel and sat down to a meal of steak and eggs washed down with gallons of tea, which was prepared by his own chef, Frank Nimmin. He spoke freely with his team about his plans to retire the following year, whether he won or lost, before they all rode in a specially hired car to journey to the Polo Grounds, a police motorcycle rider escorting them through the thick traffic. A full moon lit up the cloudless night sky above the city as thousands of eager spectators began to make their way to the arena. The temperature was still balmy and most fans wore shirt sleeves. The powerful arc-lights blazed down over the whole arena and made it appear as bright as day. Amongst the first to arrive was American General Douglas MacArthur, who was seated next to the chairman of the New York State Athletic Commission. Prince Monolulu arrived at his seat, dressed in feathers and flags and sat alongside a plethora of former and present world champions, Sandy Saddler, Joey Maxim, Ezzard Charles, Jersey Joe Walcott, Walter Winchell, Joe DiMaggio and Joe Louis.

At exactly ten o'clock, a roar which radio commentators described as sounding "like the engines of over a hundred jet planes" hit the night air as the sixty thousand fans rose to greet Sugar Ray Robinson's dance to the ring. A few minutes later, to the surprise of the New York fight fraternity, the champion, Randolph Turpin, emerged to a far nosier reception led by an English choir, the crew of the several British ocean liners berthed in New York, two specially chartered UK airplanes of fans and over six hundred Merchant Navy seaman from the Queen Elizabeth liner, who all came determined to cheer their countryman to a repeat performance.

Once the introductions were concluded, the referee, Ruby Goldstein, gave the fighters their final instructions before the noise of the opening bell began the battle. The champion and challenger circled each other warily and after the initial couple of minutes, it became obvious that Turpin's dominance, which he established from the off in their first bout, was not be in this fight. The British contingent expected Turpin to walk forward and jab Robinson back on his heels and keep him on the run but he didn't do it. His brother Dick, who was forced to sit in the press section and remain supervised throughout by a Commission inspector to ensure that he didn't issue instructions, writhed in frustrated silence. The ruling was a demonstration of pathetic bureaucracy by the New York commission, who didn't agree that relations could be suitable cornermen. Turpin appeared lethargic and started to get caught with hurtful punches to the body.

After this slow start, Turpin started to inch his way back into the fight; he landed with a right hook to Robinson's head, which caused him to back away. He threw another right followed by a left hook to the body, which brought roars from the crowd, but the judges awarded the opening couple of rounds to Robinson, although not by wide margins. In the third and fourth rounds,

Robinson stepped up the pressure further still and tried to knock the champion out with sharp right hands mixed with plenty of body punches. Turpin appeared wary of the right hands, which came toward his jaw like exocet missiles, but he avoided them by pulling his head backwards and nullifying the power of the punches, which drew appreciative applause. The fourth round was relatively quiet but Turpin tried to win it by rushing in and throwing overhand rights which connected but carried little power.

It was noticeable that every time the two fighters engaged at close-quarters, Robinson would grab Turpin's arms and referee Goldstein had to part them. This was part of Ray's tactics to disrupt the rhythm of Randy, but the holding and mauling irritated the crowd and brought slow handclapping and shouts of derision. The approach, however, impressed the judges and they awarded him the first four rounds. Turpin started to turn the tide in the fifth and sixth rounds and won them by close margins, but he still looked stale and sluggish. In the seventh, Robinson got his jab going again and connected with a few rib-bending punches with either hand. As a spectacle this eagerly awaited world championship was a huge disappointment for everyone concerned.

The Leamington boxer disappointed his British spectators by boxing in a manner which seemed tailor-made for Robinson and played into his hands. Turpin's cautiousness allowed the American to dictate the course of the fight and it was only in the eighth session when Turpin, at the behest of his corner who beseeched him to attack more, started to counter Robinson's punches. He forced Robinson back onto the ropes where both men flayed away at each other, but Turpin's power told and he finished the stronger. Robinson started to look tense as he tried to avoid the chopping right hand punches and his opponent, intent on victory, piled on the pressure. The ninth round featured Turpin continue to catch his prey with damaging punches and Robinson was warned for hitting on the break. Turpin began to swarm all over his challenger, who appeared to be in real trouble. He attempted to put the champion on his back foot but Randy sent him back on his heels with a hurtful left hook and Sugar Ray was glad to fall into a clinch until the bell saved him.

It continued to be a disappointing spectacle for both sets of fans. Where was the bulldog spirit that Turpin showed in London in July? Where was the flamboyant and cultured Sugar Ray? When the bell for the tenth round sounded, things were beginning to look good for the champion. He just walked through the flicking left jab which attempted to ward him off. When they clashed at close quarters, Turpin was now much stronger than the tired and weary Robinson, who suffered another nasty gash above his left eye, which pumped blood that ran down his cheek. The sight of his own blood, however, seemed to shock him into action Robinson went berserk. He tore into Turpin, who was forced to retreat from the fury of Robinson's ferocious two-handed attack. He caught the champion with a pulverising right cross to the jaw and buckled Randy's knees; he remained upright by holding Robinson's arms in a vice-like grip.

From then on, Harlem's finest was like a man possessed and attacked furiously. Turpin tried to ride the storm by keeping both hands high and slipping his head from side to side in an attempt to roll with the punches, but Robinson had the bit between his teeth and offered him no respite. Turpin tried to keep him at bay by throwing a left hook counter but was beaten to it by a stunningly potent right cross that landed perfectly on his chin and bowled him over onto his back, where it looked like he was out to the world and the fight would be over. This was a venomous punch that had knockout written all over it. Amazingly, at the count of three, Turpin somehow managed to get to his knees and remained there as Ruby Goldstein tolled the count. Turpin shook his head vigorously in an attempt to clear the fog before he got back onto his feet. Within seconds, a snarling Robinson pounced. Radio commentators suggested that there was none better in the world than Robinson in finishing off a beleaguered foe and now spectators saw the perfect fighting machine in action.

The first nine indifferent rounds were instantly forgotten. The crowd jumped to their feet and screamed and yelled with excitement. Turpin moved on unsteady legs back towards the ropes where Robinson pinned him in, and with his hair looking dishevelled and with a steady torrent of blood oozing down his face, he looked demonic as he unleashed a series of deadly punches from his full repertoire. Turpin, drawing on his deep reservoir of courage, brazened it out but remained trapped against the ropes and as the punches came faster and faster, his head was being rocked from side to side like a speedball. Robinson then switched his punches to the body and began to hammer away without mercy. The British corner screamed for their man to go back down on one knee and gain himself some breathing space to readjust but Turpin either couldn't hear or his pride refused to accede. Robinson's onslaught continued unabated; he pulled Turpin's head downwards to obscure his sight and then hit him with further devastating blows. It was an overwhelming annihilation and Turpin began to lurch forward and his knees looked ready to buckle. Fight official Goldstein seemed hesitant to stop it until he saw the conclusive proof that Turpin was not doing enough to defend himself and he then threw himself between the two fighters and clutched Turpin around the waist to stop him keeling over onto the canvas. There were eight seconds of round ten remaining.

The Leamington Lion dragged Goldstein over to Robinson's corner. Fans thought that he was going to remonstrate or complain but the reality is that his Corinthian spirit and his sense of sportsmanship meant that he wanted to congratulate the new reposed champion. "Ray, you're a great champion," said Turpin. "The title's yours; you keep it until you've had enough and then I'll see what I can do about it again."

Journalist Peter Wilson believed that Goldstein had been too eager to terminate the fight but felt that he had showed sensitivity because of the context of the fight. Only eleven days earlier George Flores, an American-Italian fighter, was boxing on the undercard of the world welterweight title fight between Kid Gavilan and Billy Graham. Flores fought Roger Donoghue from New York and was knocked down in the eighth round and fell on the back of his head. After being rushed to hospital and having two operations, he never recovered consciousness and died a few days later. The build up to the Turpin fight had been against a backdrop of debate about banning boxing. Wilson felt that in this environment, Goldstein had been urged to exercise caution. He felt that "it was extremely rare for a world title fight to be stopped after the champion had only been put down once. I doubt that Robinson, who had to have stitches in the deep wound above his eye, would have been permitted by the fight doctor to come out for the eleventh round." The journalist later claimed that when Robinson arrived in a New York night club that night, "he told me that he was sure he would not have been allowed to continue."

Turpin's brother, Jackie, who had fought and beat Joe Wamsley on points in a six round bout which was on the undercard, watched in anguish as his younger brother lost his treasured crown. He said that the wound which Robinson suffered was "absolutely horrendous" and he, like other ringsiders, felt that the fight would have to be stopped. He believed that his brother "was coming more and more into the fight the longer it went."

Gilbert E. Odd, the esteemed boxing historian and editor of Britain's weekly boxing paper, Boxing News, was sat ringside for the fight and felt that the fight's pivotal moment had been encapsulated in "one punch which was responsible for Randolph Turpin's loss of the world's middleweight title." He claimed that "the short right landed by Turpin in the tenth round that reopened the eyebrow wound sustained by the American in their London fight, turned the challenger from a careful and tiring boxer into a berserk, dynamite punching demon." Odd was critical of Turpin's lack of ring savvy and suggested that with a mere eight seconds left of the round, "Turpin should have gone down and taken a count and saved himself taking unnecessary punishment." He concluded that "we did not see the real Robinson in London last July but, equally, we did not see the real Turpin in New York."

The general consensus of the British newshounds was that Robinson had justified all of the claims that he was one of the greatest fighting machines that boxing has ever seen. Gilbert Odd suggested that "he boxed cleanly and cleverly and appeared perfectly trained and utterly resolved to win back his title. When the moment came, he proved himself a master craftsman. We offer no excuses for Turpin's defeat. He was beaten by a superior boxer."

Ruby Goldstein was happy to speak to the press afterwards and answer their criticisms of his officiating. He claimed that "Jack Solomons, the British promoter, has told me that I should never have stopped the fight with only eight seconds left in the round." He paid tribute to Turpin's approach and suggested that "he looked harder to hit when you were in the ring with him than when you watch him from outside. He was a persistent guy and constantly stayed on top of you." He confirmed that the fight had been close, "I had Robinson and Turpin each winning four rounds, with one even, going into the tenth" and recalled that Turpin had seemed "dazzled by Robinson's speed in the early rounds and took a few solid punches but was coming back and getting stronger." He confirmed that "Robinson's cuts, above both eyes, meant that Ray was bleeding and getting desperate because time was running out on him." Goldstein also confirmed that "if he had another bad round and the bleeding around his eyes couldn't be checked, the commission doctor at ringside would have told me to stop the fight."

Jackie Turpin watched his younger brother in action and said the cut which Robinson suffered was absolutely horrendous and he, like other ringsiders, thought that the fight would have to be stopped and that Randy was "coming more and more into the fight the longer it went." He also mentioned Robinson's tactic of pulling Randy's head downwards.

Goldstein's account of the last round offered an insight into the fight's intricacies. "In the tenth round, Robinson tore into Turpin and they fought all over the ring and then Robinson nailed Turpin with a helluva punch - a right-hand blast to the chin. Turpin was hurt and dropped his hands to his sides. In his eagerness to finish the fight, Robinson was wild but Turpin just dangled before him like the heavy bag that fighters punch in the gym. When Robinson hit him on the chin again and he sagged, defenceless, into the ropes with his hands still down and his head hanging now, I knew that although he was game he couldn't defend himself. That's a terrible situation to find yourself in against a puncher like Robinson. I have always maintained that it is better for a fighter to walk out than be carried out; it's better to stop a fight one punch too soon than one punch too late. With only eight seconds left to go in the tenth round, I stepped in and I stopped it. At the time Turpin didn't complain and his corner didn't complain, either. Truthfully, I didn't know there were only eight seconds left but if I had, it wouldn't have made any difference. I never regretted stopping it."

Afterwards, Turpin told the press and his British followers that he had "tried his best but, on this occasion, my best wasn't quite good enough." He was magnanimous and congratulated Robinson on winning back the title and said he "admired Sugar Ray as a boxer and a man." Robinson reciprocated the respect and insisted that Turpin visit his nightclub. Turpin was amazed to see people tap dancing outside the club and laughed in wonder when the newly reposed champion joined them and gave a wonderful exhibition of his dancing skills.

Turpin was accompanied by Adele Daniels on this evening. The fears of his team would later prove well founded when in October 1953, he returned to the city to meet Carl 'Bobo' Olson for the vacant world middleweight title. He was involved in a scandal when Daniels complained to the police and had him arrested and charged with assault. Before he was permitted to sail back home, he had to deposit £10,000 as security, in case he should have to go back to face civil charges. Daniels later withdrew the charges but claimed she would instead sue the British man for $100,000. Rumours continued to circulate that she was offered money to withdraw her complaint; a charge she always denied.

******

Six months after the dramatic victory over Turpin, the champion returned to the ring to defend his title against his old foe Carl Olson in the Civic Auditorium, San Francisco. A disappointing total of 11,000 fans turned up on the 13th March 1952. Robinson told the press that he was "dismayed, especially after my last victory." The turnout seemed to capture the mood of the lacklustre spirit which the fight was conducted in. It lacked thrills or drama and Sugar Ray appeared lethargic and ring rusty.

Olson gave the champion quite a few uncomfortable moments and made Robinson miss with his punches too often. The Hawaiian still seemed to have his previous experience of Robinson's capability seared into his brain and appeared to be wary of his punching power to ensure that he didn't get too close to exploit the champion's lack of spark more than he could have done. A number of ringsiders believed that Olson had still done enough to win the decision but the officials didn't agree and awarded the unanimous points decision in favour of Robinson. Referee Jack Downey voted 86½ for the champion to 79½ for Olson. Judge Frankie Brown scored it 85½ to 79½ and Toby Irwin gave it clearly to Robinson by 84½ to 80½.

Afterwards, Robinson conceded that he "had had a close call". Swathed in a Turkish towel bath robe and sat in the sanctity of his dressing room, he was generous in his praise for Olson and declared that "he belongs to be up with the top level middleweights." He also admitted the six month break since he met Turpin had started to dim his speed and reflexes. When he was asked if he would be willing to give Olson a return, he smiled and replied, "Not for another one dollar purse!" He then revealed that his purse would go towards the Damon Runyon Cancer Fund and he would accept a token dollar plus his expenses for this defence of his world title.

15.

The Rock versus Sugar

BEFORE THE Olson defence, there had been increasing newspaper talk concerning a fight which most fight fans had dreamed about for years; Robinson versus the original 'Dead End Kid' from the East Side of New York - Rocky Graziano. Graziano was the legendary tough guy who had served time in Leavenworth's Military Prison and had eventually been dishonourably discharged from the army after attacking an officer. The speculation ensured that fans had their hopes raised but in March 1952, the Illinois State Athletic Commission threw a spanner in the works when they announced that although they supported the proposed world title fight between the two men, they wanted to investigate Graziano's alleged friendship with a convicted murderer.

In a January newspaper interview, Graziano had admitted that he had ended his association with Eddie Coco, who was described as an 'undercover' manager and who was currently defending himself in an appeal from a murder conviction in Florida. This was the latest charge in a long criminal record which dated back to 1931. An objection to the heralded Robinson fight was lodged by the Chicago television and radio sports announcer, Tom Duggan, who stated that the fight should not be given official approval because the links to Coco risked polluting the sport's reputation. The International Boxing Club, who were due to promote the fight, were incensed and IBC secretary Truman Gibson and Duggan conducted a bitter argument through the pages of the press. Lou Radzienda, a commission member, also became embroiled in the messy exchanges as the details began to slowly become clear.

It appeared that Rocky had admitted that he had an agreement with Coco ever since he had turned professional in 1943 that necessitated paying him 11% of his purse money. This agreement ended, by mutual consent, in January because they acknowledged that the association was harming his career and that he might as well retire from the sport if it wasn't ended, especially after Coco was convicted of second degree murder for the slaying of a black parking lot attendant in 1951.

Eventually, the arguments were resolved and the fight arranged with undue haste, lest opinions change again, to take place a month after the Olson fight. Robinson was delighted with the outcome and both he and George Gainford had

149

attended the committee meetings to state his case for the fight. The agreed venue was the Chicago Stadium and the instant clamour for tickets was incredible; every fight fan wanted to be present when these two knockout merchants started unloading their bombs on each other.

Rocky Graziano fitted the sport's reputation for producing some of life's most unique characters. His real name was Thomas Rocco Barbella and he was born on the 1st January 1922, as one of the first rebels without a cause. He was classed as a juvenile delinquent and seemed to be always engaged in trouble with the police and authorities. He was forever in and out of Reform Schools and other criminal institutions. He also enjoyed boasting that he "was headed for the electric chair until he became involved with boxing." He didn't easily fit into any category of fighter but was an out-and-out slugger whose defence was his offence; he was described by one early report as "fighting as if the whole world was against him." After stopping top prospect Billy Arnold in 1945, he blitzed well-known fighters like Al (Bummy) Davis, world welterweight champions Freddie 'Red' Cochrane and Marty Servo and Harold Green. Rocky fought with a savagery ingrained in him as a product of the back alleys of the East Side of New York. He achieved fame outside the confines of the sport when he wrote a book, titled 'Somebody Up There Likes Me', which proved a best seller and was later made into an acclaimed film of the same name, which originally cast that other legendary rebel, James Dean, in the lead role. Dean was killed in a car crash before filming could commence and was replaced by a young, unknown actor called Paul Newman. The film made him a huge star. Graziano had been involved in three epic fights against 'The Man of Steel', Tony Zale, for the world middleweight championship, which further cemented his legend. They first met in September 1946, where after a bloody and vicious war Zale stopped him in six rounds. In July 1947, they met again and Zale continued his assault which he had started the previous year. For the first four rounds, Zale unloaded punishment which would never be tolerated in the sport today but in round six, with his face looking like he was wearing a horror mask, Graziano launched a ferocious and desperate onslaught which brought him the world middleweight crown. The rematch took place eleven months later and spectators feasted upon another pulsating battle where both warriors traded explosive punches before Graziano was knocked out in the third round. He took a year off from the sport before he embarked on his comeback, which included twenty one fights with twenty wins and a draw. Significantly, seventeen of these victories came inside the distance. The International Boxing Club was delighted to grant him his shot at Robinson.

A couple of days before the fight Robinson received a message which instructed him that a top Chicago gangster demanded a meeting with him "to discuss something very important." Robinson met with the mob boss, who was later revealed to be Tony Accardo, and was offered a million dollars if he agreed to allow Graziano to win the first fight. Under the terms of the agreement, he would then be allowed to win the second and the third fight would then be 'on the level' and the best man would win. Robinson point blank refused the deal and left Accardo in no doubt that he was not for sale. Later reports also suggested that the fight was nearly scuppered by Graziano's reluctance to go through with the fight. Nerves got the better of him and he attempted to flee Chicago. He only returned when Eddie Coco contacted him and insisted that he go through with the fight because he needed money to pay the lawyers defending him against the murder charge.

Despite all of the events leading up to the fight, both men entered the ring determined to put on a spectacle and from the opening bell, Graziano made it clear that he meant business as he moved after the champion with his fearsome right hand cocked and ready to explode. He was so pumped up that when they fell into a clinch, Graziano could be heard by ringsiders loudly cursing Robinson and insulting him with every filthy name he could think of. Graziano had told his handlers that he planned to look for a quick knockout but he later admitted that when he threw his first long right at Robinson, "it was like hitting a pillow; he was just so quick." Robinson was unrecognisable from the jaded boxer he had been against Olson and he was up on his toes, boxing beautifully behind his educated left jab, which repeatedly caught the former middleweight champion. Just before the round ended, Rocky said that Sugar Ray hit him with a left hook to the head and a right to his jaw and both hurt him enough to make his head "spin a little bit and I was forced to curse to try and spit out the pain." Graziano recovered and launched himself at Robinson, hoping to force an early ending. He later described the next few moments as "my kind of fight":

"We banged away. He hits me over the heart, in the stomach. I let him have it right back in the body and I can hear him go 'Ooof!' I'm swinging and laughing and cursing at the same time. This was my kind of fight now - no dancing, no weaving, just banging away, left, right, crack, crack. Every shot he hits makes me hit him back harder. Then, just as the round ends, he catches me a big one right in the middle. That one buckled my legs."

In his corner Irving Cohen sponged him down with cold water and tried to calm him down enough to aim for Robinson's head rather than looking for body punches, but he wasn't listening. In the second round, he stormed out of his corner and began throwing big looping right hands which Robinson evaded time and time again. The sell-out crowd of 22,264, a joint all-time record at the Chicago Stadium, were enthralled by the action. Graziano did manage to catch Robinson with one powerful left hook which he followed with a dynamic right, which the challenger suggested carried "more horsepower than any other punch" he could remember throwing. "That shot could have gone right through a prison wall," he recalled. The snarling Rocky continued to tear after the champion and he sensed victory, but Robinson held on, cleared his head and returned to his own plan of employing his left jab, which the eloquent Graziano remembered "left his shoulder like a trombone." However, with just a few seconds remaining before the bell to end the second round sounded, Graziano did find some success with a stinging right cross. He carried on his momentum and carried on throwing punches after the bell. The spectators began to boo and Graziano protested his innocence to the referee by claiming that he hadn't heard it. When he returned to his stool, he was incensed by the crowd's reaction and declared that "I'm gonna show those Chicago sonnavabitches just what a real fighter is. This next round is going to be the round."

True to his word, he opened the third round with a salvo which stunned the champion. A long right hand landed on the side of Robinson's neck and forced him to drop to one knee near the ropes and buy himself valuable seconds to regroup. Graziano later recalled: "I put everything I had left into that right hand. Everything I had left from over twenty years of fighting. Every lick of power I hadn't used up on the East Side streets, in reform school yards, in bootleg fight clubs, in the guardhouse, in eighty-two professional fights; every single ounce I had left was packed into my right fist and I let it fly. It seemed to me that the whole world was screaming: 'Come on, Rocky! Come on, Rocky.' All my life those three words were the sweetest music to me." Robinson was stunned by the ferociousness of the attack, but when the count reached one his pride forced him back into the fray.

The wall of sound generated by the spectators appeared to have no effect on Robinson, who used the brief cessation of hostilities to formulate his plan and he waited patiently for his opportunity to strike back. He moved gracefully around the ring and kept the aggressive New Yorker at the end of his potent left jab. He combined this with a couple of sharp left hooks which momentarily stunned Rocky. Robinson spotted this flicker of uncertainty and pounced with the speed of a cobra. He issued a dynamic right cross which landed with precision, right on the exposed jaw of Graziano. Before Robinson's forward momentum had carried him too far, Graziano was out. He landed in a heap and as he lay prostrate, his right leg began to twitch involuntarily while the fight official, Tommy Gilmore, counted him out.

When he was scooped up and placed on his stool, Graziano sat sobbing and it briefly appeared that he was going to continue fighting despite the fact the contest was declared over. He soon regained his composure and walked, unaided, over to congratulate Robinson. He told his conqueror that, "I saw the right hand coming and in that split second, I knew it was all over. The lights spun around in lopsided circles and the whole city of Chicago crashed in on top of me. It was like a radio that was fading, then blasting, fading then blasting. I heard the referee 'Two…six…seven…nine…Out.'"

Lenny Myers, writing in The Ring magazine, captured the feelings of all present when he declared, "The Robinson versus Graziano fight confirmed, once again, why Robinson is rated as the greatest pound for pound fighter in the world. Graziano really went after the Sugar boy with all the fury he could muster and even put the champion on the deck but after that, Robinson made Graziano look like a novice." When he spoke to the press afterwards, Robinson confirmed that he was booked to fight Paddy Young in New York on the 16th May and started to publicly muse on the end of his career. "I think two or maybe three more fights and I'll call it quits," he said.

At this time, Archie Moore was regarded as the legitimate number one contender for the world light-heavyweight title. Boxing pundits were unanimous in agreeing that he deserved his title chance against Joey Maxim. However, after the Graziano win, speculation soon began which suggested that Robinson's box office magnetism could prove a decisive factor in the division's events. Maxim was regarded as a decent boxer but a light hitter. He had captured the light-heavyweight crown through his extreme strength and durability and competent craftsmanship but this did not make him a box-office draw. Robinson's flamboyant reputation and height and reach advantages would make a confrontation between the middle and light heavy champions irresistible to both.

Robinson was intrigued by the opportunity to emulate his idol, the great Henry Armstrong and win three world championships at different weights. Maxim was eager to boost his public perception by taking on and beating the sport's leading man. Both men were enchanted by the huge sums of money which the television and film companies offered for the clash. Paddy Young, Robinson's next designated opponent, and Archie Moore, the legitimate challenger, were sidelined and less than two months after his scintillating victory over Graziano, Robinson began to prepare to meet Maxim at New York's Yankee Stadium, on the evening of the 23rd June to be precise.

On the day that the two champions were due to meet in the offices of the New York State Athletic Commission to formally sign the contracts for the fight, Maxim arrived early and was smartly attired in his suit. After an hour of waiting, Robinson had still not appeared. Eager to stoke up the clash, reporters enquired whether Maxim was offended at having to wait for the idol of Harlem. Sporting a huge grin, Maxim answered, "for the kind of money I'm getting I can afford to wait a long time." This was, by far, his biggest ever payday. He recalled that it had not been too long since he was fighting some extremely tough fighters "for a paltry two, three or four thousand dollars."

Eventually, when Robinson arrived with his son, Ray Junior, perched on his shoulder; he offered profuse apologies before outlining his strategy for victory. He said that although he was confident of winning, he didn't believe that he had any real hope of knocking out the heavier champion. He was adamant that he wasn't being defeatist. "I don't feel any different about facing Joey Maxim than I've done about the other fighters I've met. It's just that I know Joey can take a punch and so I'm going to be relying on speed; I'm faster than he is." Bob Christen Berry, the chair of the New York State Athletic Commission, told the press that "this will not just be the fight of the year; it will be the fight of the century."

Over the years Joey Maxim had become regarded as an enigma of a world champion. Many boxing followers often refer to him as a footnote of history, but this does not do justice to his achievements. He originated from Italian stock and his real name was Giuseppe Antonio Berardinelli. He was born in 1922 in Cleveland, Ohio. After an impressive amateur career, he turned professional under the guidance of Victor Rebersak, who convinced him to shorten his name to Maxim. He suggested the name after reading about the World War One Maxim machine gun and also pointed out that his name was too long for promoters to include it on their fight posters. Maxim was later managed by the legendary figure of Jack 'Doc' Kearns, who had successfully guided ten world champions, including Jack Dempsey and Mickey Walker, to honours. He began his professional career a year after Robinson, in January 1941, and during his 17-year and 115-fight career, he would meet the hardest middle, light-heavies and heavyweights of the forties and fifties. He had started as a promising middleweight and gradually moved up the divisions, maintaining the style of a consummate boxer. A few months before defending his title against Robinson he had defeated a fighter named Ted Lowry, who later was one of only five men who twice went the full distance with the awesome punching of Rocky Marciano.

The build up to the fight against Robinson set the pulses of fight fans racing. It seemed that everybody was discussing it on the buses, on the subways and in the cafés, bars and restaurants of New York and beyond; the fight created a tremendous ripple of excitement and was featured in the front and back pages of the papers. People were intrigued to discover whether Sugar Ray Robinson could go on to achieve boxing immortality by beating Maxim.

To the frustration of all involved, inclement weather forced the fight to be postponed for two days from the Monday until the Wednesday. This news did not do any favours to Jim Norris's ulcers as he had to pay back $10,000 in returned tickets. At the official weigh-in, which still took place on the original Monday date, George Gainford was less than happy. He was dissatisfied with the official scales and registered an official complaint that they were not accurate. He insisted that an official inspector of weights and measures was consulted and he came in to discover that the scales were 2½ ounces out of kilter. Vindicated by this news, Gainford still insisted that he was not happy and was unwilling to accept them. The Boxing Commission was, therefore, obliged to bring in a new set of scales. It was a distinct anti-climax for all attendees when both Robinson and Maxim claimed that the heat had helped them pass the required poundage easily.

It was a boiling hot night on the rearranged Wednesday and the 47,938 spectators who squeezed into the Yankee Stadium helped the ice drink vendors achieve a roaring trade. Meteorologist reports recorded it as the hottest night in New York history for fifty years as the temperature gauges hovered close to 92 degrees. The British correspondents, Peter Wilson and Frank Butler, were both sat at ringside and Wilson reported that "just bending down to fasten your shoelace brought forth beads of perspiration, which poured down your face as if someone had poured a jug full of water over the top of your head." The sweltering conditions seemed to fray the tempers of a number of fans and several skirmishes broke out around the venue between fans who attempted to move out of the three dollar cheap seats into the more expensive areas.

By the time both fighters entered the ring for the main event, the size of task facing Robinson became quite evident. Robinson entered the ring weighing 11 stones 3¼ pounds, whilst Maxim came in at 12 stones and 5 pounds, a 15½ pound weight advantage. This huge discrepancy was exacerbated on this particular night by the balmy conditions allied with the heat from the arc lights and the extra lighting for the film cameras, which raised the temperature to 105 degrees and made the inside of the ring feel like a furnace. After the introductions were concluded and the action began, Sugar Ray started by looking like the superstar he undoubtedly was. He got high on his toes and kept his distance by the use of his whip-like left jab. Maxim initially looked perplexed and unable to fathom out his opponent's strategy. A pattern was set where Maxim would move ponderously forwards towards the fleet-footed Robinson but before he could get within range to throw, Robinson would have scored points and moved away out of danger.

Each round seemed to follow this same pattern and the subsequent points gap between the two champions got increasingly bigger. The furrow on Maxim's brow also grew increasingly deeper as he looked more and more perplexed about how to bridge the chasm. Even his trainer, the usually abrasive Doc Kearns, seemed unable to inspire his charge to change the course of the fight. Their only hope was that the intense heat would eventually take its toll on the lighter man. This instinct would prove well founded as Maxim's slow style allowed him to eke out his energy reserves and maintain the same pace throughout. The heat became almost intolerable. Robinson, however, was slowly running out of petrol.

The British correspondent Frank Butler said he felt as if he had been locked in a sauna for a long period of time. "Nobody, fans or officials, had experienced this kind of weather situation before and everyone felt drained. So how were Sugar Ray and Joey Maxim feeling, having to keep moving around the ring and throwing and avoiding punches in these freak weather conditions?"

By the seventh round, the middleweight king was forging ahead as a clear winner. He caught Maxim with a peach of a left hook that surprised and hurt him and convinced the sweat-soaked spectators that a dramatic finish was about to take place. Robinson followed up his advantage with a vicious and spectacular bombardment that forced Maxim to cover up as Robinson tried, in vain, to end the contest. When the bell rang to halt his assault, he suddenly appeared completely drained. He looked crestfallen as he walked, on shaky legs, back to his corner where Gainford and Wiley doused him with a sponge of lukewarm water. As he slumped onto the stool, the two men issued their instructions but Robinson had a glazed look his eyes. Everybody in the venue looked drenched in sweat, it was pouring off them.

In contrast, Maxim had appeared to sense that the flame of fury which burnt inside his challenger had been extinguished and came out for the next round looking relaxed. For the next three rounds, Robinson continued to rack up the points with his crafty boxing, which included a few brisk uppercuts and whistling left hooks. Joey, however, seemed to be biding his time and he hardly threw a punch of note. Referee Rudy Goldstein also seemed to be affected by the temperatures and ring officials were becoming increasingly concerned about his welfare and brought Ray Miller, another top referee, to the ringside. In the tenth round, Goldstein began issuing incoherent instructions to the fighters and was helped out of the ring and replaced by Miller.

As the bell for the eleventh round rang, the whole picture of the fight was turned. Maxim attacked the Harlem fighter for the first time. Robinson, by now boxing from memory and with his energy reserves on empty, still commanded a healthy lead. The light-heavyweight champion, continuing to fight at his plodding, pedestrian pace began digging hurtful short punches into Robinson's weakening body, thus taking even more strength from him. In the thirteenth, despite his attempts to stay out of range, his eyes betrayed him and Maxim saw that he had nothing left. He was merciless as he moved forward throwing punches. Like a gambler with one last card, Sugar Ray tried to end the fight with one big punch and he aimed a right cross towards his oncoming target. It missed and as he scythed through the air, he fell face forwards towards the floor. The crowd believed that he had been knocked down but the new referee, Miller, did not score it that way. As he got back onto his uncertain feet, Robinson didn't have a clue what was happening to him. Maxim tore into his man, hoping to end the fight in spectacular fashion, but the bell stopped his attack before it could begin in earnest.

Robinson's legs had been reduced to jelly and he was forced to walk along the perimeter of the ring, holding the ropes to keep him upright. George Gainford bounded into the ring and helped his man back. As he dropped onto his stool, his head lolled forward like a rag doll onto his chest. Dr Alexander Schiff, the fight's medical officer rushed to the corner and although he could see that it was over he respected the warrior's spirit to allow him the opportunity to continue. Robinson responded in a hoarse whisper, "I can't get up to stand on my feet." Dr Schiff called the referee across and told him that Robinson was in no state to continue. Just as the bell sounded to signal the start of the fourteenth round, the fight was declared over. Dr Schiff later told the press that "Sugar Ray Robinson was the victim of extreme heat exhaustion. He was almost lifeless and absolutely unable to stand on his feet. I didn't stop the fight. Robinson stopped it when he said he couldn't get out of his corner."

So near and yet so far away from his third world title. Only six minutes separated him from being crowned the new world light-heavyweight champion. Judge Artie Aidale scored Robinson ahead by nine rounds to three with one even; Judge Harold Barnes scored it ten rounds to three in favour of Robinson, and Ruby Goldstein had marked his card with five rounds for Robinson, Maxim winning three and three rounds as even. His replacement, Ray Miller scored it two to one in favour in Robinson over the final three rounds. Back in the dressing room there was a tragic scene of sadness being played out as Sugar Ray, in his bemused state of mind, gradually came to realise that he had lost inside the distance. His mind and body were on fire and his rantings made no sense. His friend, Vince Impelliteri, the Mayor of New York, came in to try to console him but he had little success. He had lost eleven pounds in weight in the sweltering conditions and everyone tried to get him to get into the shower to cool down his overheated body, but he became hysterical and kept shouting that it was God who had decided that he would be beaten, not Joey Maxim. He eventually got into the shower and provided the only farcical moment of the night when he pulled the fully clothed Mayor in with him.

Robinson refused to go to the hospital and Edna Mae eventually took him back to their Riverdale home, but all through the night he sat awake vomiting. His petrified son, Ray Junior, later recounted that his dad was "near to death and his body was covered with blisters; he couldn't retain anything in his stomach for a couple of days and was ill for six months after the Maxim fight."

The press, however, were less forgiving of the fragility of the human condition. James P. Dawson of The New York Times questioned whether "the heat did affect Robinson or maybe he didn't have the stamina to go on or that he decided his strength was ebbing and he was afraid of serious injury. Only Robinson can supply the answer to that question, which will be a long time leaving the minds of those who witnessed this surrender by a champion who was only two rounds away from another title and a life's ambition." Nat Fleischer was more considered and paid homage to his fighting spirit, which had "the light-heavyweight crown all but clinched when the heat got to him. The defending title-holder could not possibly have retained his title except by a knockout as Robinson bossed the contest from the start to the thirteenth round. Up to the time of the collapse of the greatest all-around fighting machine in many years, the affair was too one-sided to give Maxim a chance. The first effective blows delivered by Joey didn't connect until the twelve when Ray began to show the effects of the powerful heat. It was the end for Robinson, but the fists of Maxim had not turned the trick. Physical exhaustion the doctors called it."

In 1961, Ruby Goldstein spoke for the first time about the night when Sugar Ray failed to last the distance. "It was so scorching under those ring lights. When I first walked out into that awful heat, it hit me harder than ever. After I collapsed, my mind was in a whirl and I told the doctor that I was worried about my scoring in the ninth and tenth rounds; I wasn't sure who was hitting who. He asked me why I was worrying and I explained that perhaps one of those two rounds had influenced the decision. He told me not to worry because the fight didn't go the distance. Then he pointed at a prone figure and said, 'that was Robinson who was just carried out by ambulancemen on a stretcher.'"

After a period of reflection, several criticisms were aired about the fight. Dave Anderson captured many of them in a later biography of Robinson. Many knowledgeable boxing people believed that he and his team had not given enough thought about the huge disparity in weight that he would be giving away to Maxim, especially in the period when there were only eight weight divisions from flyweight to heavyweight. Significantly, the weight difference between middleweight (11 stones 6 pounds) to light-heavyweight (12 stones 7 pounds) was the highest. The considered opinion was that he should have boxed a few lesser talented light-heavyweights to get a feel for the huge weight difference. However, in Thomas Myler's book, 'Sugar Ray Robinson - The Inside Story' he met Joey Maxim in 1989, when Maxim was working as a Las Vegas casino employee. He was aggrieved at the lack of respect afforded him, and talking about his fight with Sugar Ray, he asked: "Was my corner air-conditioned?" Joey claimed that from the start of round nine, his legs had begun to feel heavy and tired but if Robinson hadn't quit, he would have knocked him out.

16.

Retirement - The Song and Dance Entertainer

*Sing and Dance? The greatest prizefighter who ever lived took that chance.
That would be none other than Sugar Ray Robinson. I once asked Fred
Astaire what he thought of Sugar Ray's singing and dancing. Astaire smiled.
"He's a wonderful fighter," he said.* **Bill Gallo.**

DURING THE SIX months after the Maxim defeat, Robinson suffered a number of health problems. He was also distressed at the manner of his defeat and spent long hours quietly contemplating what the future held in store for him now that he had agreed with his close circle of confidants that his boxing career had ended. His medical adviser, Dr Nardiello, suggested that he take a long break away from the rigours of training and boxing, which increasingly bored him.

During this period of rumination, he met with Joe Glaser, one of the biggest agents in the showbusiness world, who handled Louis Armstrong and would later be involved with Barbra Streisand. He persuaded the champion that he could get him bookings, if he came into the world of sho business and on the 18th December 1952, six months after his defeat to Joey Maxim, Robinson officially announced his retirement from the ring. Smiling broadly, he told the press that he was embarking on a full time dancing career. He told reporters excitedly that he was looking forward to living "like a normal human being" and he confidently asserted that his career and his burgeoning business empire would mean that "he wouldn't miss boxing in the slightest". His agent, Joe Glaser, secured him bookings in the country's best theatres and nightclubs and boasted that "he was being paid more money than Fred Astaire and Gene Kelly received on their debuts on the boards."

Before officially making his debut, Edna Mae helped her husband to get a routine which he practiced religiously with Henry le Tang, a well-known Broadway choreographer and dancing coach, and Pete Nugent, a dancer who was a former member of the Peaches and Duke Dance team. His thoughts about an easy life were quickly squashed when this duo insisted that he complete five miles of running every morning before the endless hours of practise began. He had to learn how to deliver lines, tell jokes and sing popular songs, which he found a lot harder than he had anticipated. His biggest embarrassment, however, was having to wear make up.

His nightclub debut was scheduled for the French Casino at the famous Paramount Hotel, New York. Glaser secured a fee of $15,000 for this event, which every national newspaper eagerly sought to cover. Those journalists who were granted access to his rehearsals claimed to be "astonished at his graceful and sublime antics" and suggested that he had been dancing since he was nine years old. Robinson pointed out that he had never received any formal training as a singer or dancer before this one report gushed that "his natural rhythm suggests that he will be successful. He has traded in his boxing gloves for tap dancing shoes and a wardrobe of natty clothes and on stage, instead of feinting, punching and counter-punching, all he has to do is turn on his usual charm, dance with vigour and tell a few topical jokes to win an easy decision."

Over one hundred and fifty newspaper journalists from around the world attended his opening night, along with state and city officials, Broadway and Hollywood celebrities and several sportsmen. The French Casino reported that it was a sell-out for the opening ten nights and began the unprecedented step of accepting reservations for four weeks in advance. Robert W. Dana, a showbusiness reviewer for the World Telegram and Sun, wrote that "it is my guess that he will sweep across this country and through the continent as a dancing master-of-ceremonies. He may even set stage for similar experiments in showbusiness for other great figures of sports seem to have an affinity for Broadway and the footlights".

The French Casino show was presented by M. N. Martini and staged and directed by his wife, Helene Martini, and was billed as a show that had "the ability to combine the saucy, frothy qualities of Paris with sequences typically American, combining to make a generous, highly entertaining show." Robinson's entrance was delayed as long as possible to create suspense. Once he appeared, wearing a colourful sports jacket, he immediately broke into a dance routine with his partner, Joe Scott, who was the stooge to his jokes. He later made a change into white tie and tails and danced and sang a number of lively numbers. His act was supplemented by a number of other talented artists, including Dominique, a handsome young man, who was a magician and pick-pocket extraordinaire and Rudy Cardenas, a world famous juggler, along with the ballerina, Jane Laste.

The critics were kind in their appraisal of his stage debut. Typical examples included, "once a champion, always a champion, that's what Sugar Ray Robinson is ...A champion fighter in the ring and a champion entertainer in

**Robinson tap dances in Paris in the summer of 1951.
By the end of 1952 he was to be doing it for a living.**

**Robinson pictured with New York mayor Vincent Impellitteri,
Ray jnr. and Edna Mae.**

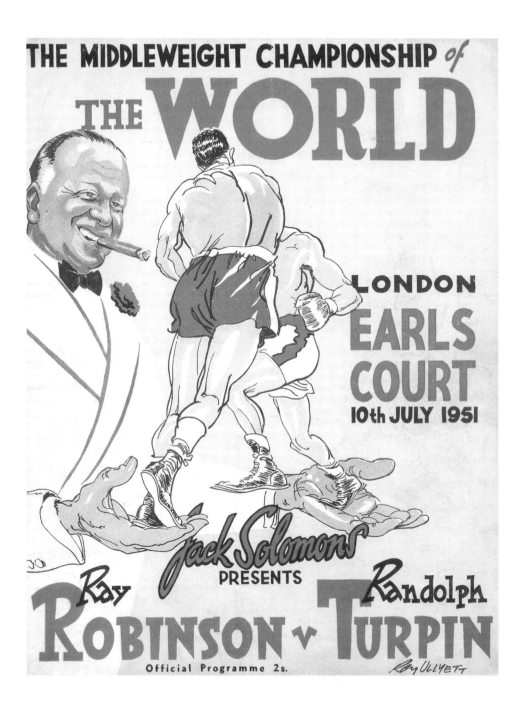

Jack Solomons' programme for the first Robinson v Turpin
fight at Earls' Court. Sugar Ray was to fall to a surprise defeat,
only the second of his career.

**Above: Robinson slips a Turpin left jab in their first fight in Earls
Court, which the Englishman won on points over 15 rounds.
Below: Robinson begins to take his revenge in the return
in New York City a few months later.**

Right: Randy Turpin lies flat on his back as Robinson heads for a neutral corner at the Polo Grounds .

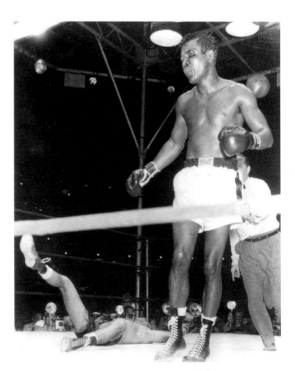

Below: Harlem welcomes home the champ after regaining his title.

Robinson attempted a hat-trick of world titles in the summer of 1952 when he took on Joey Maxim for the world light-heavyweight title in New York City. He was only beaten by the heat. It was a defeat that would lead to the announcement of his retirement.

An ageing Sugar Ray contemplates retirement.

Song and Dance Man.
Robinson attempted a career in musical entertainment after the
announcement of his retirement. Bill Gallo once asked Fred Astaire
what he thought of Sugar Ray's singing and dancing. Astaire smiled.
"He's a wonderful fighter," he said.

After an absence of more than two years, Sugar Ray returned to the ring. By the end of 1955 he had regained his world middleweight title when he sensationally knocked out Carl Bobo Olson in the second round of their fight in Chicago. To prove this was no fluke, he knocked out Olson in the fourth round of the return in the summer of 1956.

**In January 1957 Robinson lost his title on points to Gene Fullmer in
New York. However, he got it back in sensational fashion in Chicago a
few months later, knocking Fullmer out in the fifth round.**

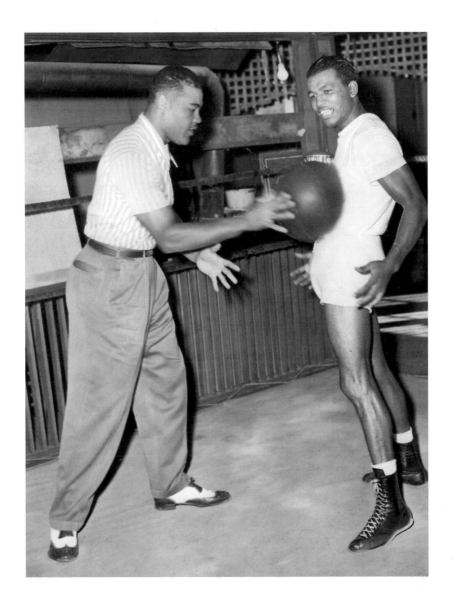

Joe Louis helps Sugar Ray prepare for the first of two awesome contests with Carmen Basilio.

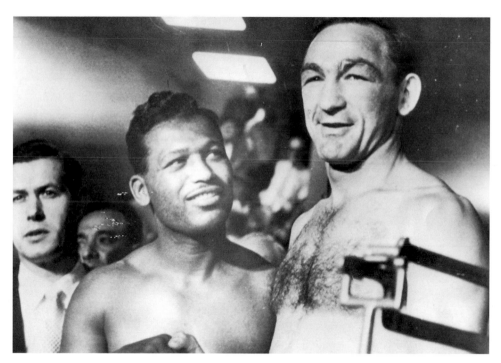

Above: Sugar Ray sizes up Basilio at the weigh-in and, below, lands a crunching right on the challenger. Basilio won the first encounter in New York in September 1957 but, remarkably, Robinson took it back the following March in Chicago, thus becoming the first person to win a world title six times.

Robinson and Basilio trade punch for punch.
The second Basilio fight was Robinson's only contest of 1958. He fought just once in 1959 too before losing the title to Paul Pender in January 1960. He failed to re-take the title from Pender and then tried twice in two closely-fought bouts with Gene Fullmer.

After the second Fullmer fight, Robinson was no longer offered any
world title fights and was forced to carry on boxing journeymen due to
his debts to the taxman. Above he spars with Otis Woodward before
taking on Terry Downes in London in September 1962. He lost.
Amazingly, he had twice fought in London and lost on both occasions.

Robinson in action in his 202nd and final fight, with Joey Archer in Pittsburgh on November 10th, 1965, more than 25 years after his first.

On the night of 10th December 1965, 12,146 fans gathered in
Madison Square Garden to bid farewell to Sugar Ray Robinson in a
special ceremony organised by the Madison Square Garden
Corporation. Organisers had arranged for four of the champions
who had fought Robinson for the world middleweight title to be
present and Turpin, Basillio, Olson and Fullmer lifted him onto their
shoulders and carried him around the ring apron.

nightclub and theatres. He blossoms as one of the truly vibrant personalities of our time, an entertainer par excellence and a champ, that's all!" Publicists Ralph Cayton and Leo Klemper worked overtime to ensure that his name featured in all of the newspapers, whilst three companies filmed him and seventeen special feature writers from magazines wrote detailed stories about him, including Life Magazine's front cover story heralding his nightclub debut. This article recounted how Joe Louis and 'Jersey' Joe Walcott had attended the first night and Louis looked on with disbelief and laughter when make-up was applied to his old friend's face. "Just put some Vaseline on," he urged.

While appearing in a nightclub in Vancouver, Canada, his mysterious army service record surfaced again. Apparently he had been asked to appear before the Congressional sub-committee concerning his army discharge and once again stories appeared in various newspapers about his military service and discharge. He was seething, and when questioned by Canadian reporters, he shouted: "I didn't have it easy while serving in the army." He went on to say he wasn't 'coddled' in the Air Corps. "I'd rather have taken my chances with bullets than do what I did," he declared in another interview. He then said that he was taken out of a military hospital in 1943 to go on tour with Joe Louis. "I was waiting to be discharged from active service because of a 'bad' left ear drum. Getting very angry, he shouted: "I'd like to know what privileges they gave me by letting me box." He went on to say: "I boxed exhibitions every day for eight months. Suffered two broken ribs." He then said he had been involved in four aeroplane 'crack-ups'. George Gainford told reporters that he would advise Robinson not to appear before the Congressional sub-committee. "Robinson would be crazy to go to Washington," he said. "Why should he prolong those hearings when it's the Generals in the army who are under investigation? The stories in the newspapers about Robinson's army service contradict themselves. They say he jumped ship, which means he was on a ship. But Ray was never on a ship."

He also branched out into making records and was encouraged by close friends, including Frank Sinatra, Nat King Cole and Billy Eckstine, but critics suggested that "his singing left a lot to be desired." As the show bookings continued to come in, Robinson discovered that he had to travel, which he didn't enjoy. He moved through the cities in the same bus which Count Basie used for his band and which the Dominoes singing group also utilised. It was while he was performing his show in Los Angeles that he met Millie Bruce, an attractive divorcee who had three children from her previous relationship. She had a credit for an appearance on the popular 'Amos'n'Andy' television show, due to her sister being married to Eddie Anderson, the actor who portrayed Rochester on the Jack Benny show. It was at this show where Robinson initiated the relationship which would lead to Bruce becoming the third Mrs Robinson.

Robinson was soon booked to return to Paris where the French people were eager to see their idol in his new career. He was crestfallen to receive mixed reviews for the opening shows and was instructed to include his rope-skipping routine from his boxing days into the act and one review urged him to remember that "the people want to see him do what he was famous for."

It was while he was in Paris that he received an urgent telegram instructing him to return home as quickly as possible. His business interests, Ray Robinson Enterprises, which consisted of the nightclub, Sugar Ray's Quality Cleaners, Edna Mae's Lingerie Shop and the George Gainford Golden Gloves Barber Shop, which were all valued at over $300,000 dollars, was in trouble. Before had left on his tour, he had left his business interests in the hands of the man he trusted implicitly and who he gave the title of business manager. By the time he had arrived back in Harlem and sat down in his office, he quickly calculated that $250,000 dollars had disappeared. Additionally, he was also made aware that he was being threatened with foreclosures on all his mortgages and the Internal Revenue Services (IRS) was demanding unpaid taxes. He sat with his head in his hands and fought the rising feeling of humiliation as he recalled his earlier boasts that he would be one of the very few fighters who would not go broke.

During the early months of his retirement, there was an incident which would have echoes in his future. In June 1953, Carmen Basilio was celebrating his victory over New York's Billy Graham to contest the New York state welterweight title. Whilst he took his wife shopping in the city, he spotted Sugar Ray on the opposite side of the street standing next to his pink Cadillac. He was at the centre of a large group. Film cameras and newspaper reporters were jostling each other to get closer to Robinson. Basilio's wife was intrigued by the well-attired Robinson - of course she had heard and read about his pretentiousness - and so, eager to impress her, Carmen made his way across to him. He had actually never spoken to Robinson before, and so he introduced himself. To his humiliation and embarrassment, Robinson never acknowledged him but turned his back and treated him with absolute disdain. Seething with anger, he walked back to his wife and promised her that: "one day that guy is going to make a comeback and I'll fight him and teach him a lesson." As Ray was forced to contemplate a reluctant return to the ring, Basilio's wish would come closer to reality.

******

In October 1954, Robinson made an announcement which delighted the majority of boxing followers as he revealed his intention to pull on the gloves and box again. The news had come as no surprise to those people close to him. Whilst his fledgling dancing career had been beginning, his business empire was crumbling due to the scale of embezzlement and stealing that was taking place within it. One example was that a bartender working for him had been on wages of $125 a week (the average wage was still only $50 a week). His associates had also neglected to pay the taxes owed and now the government came calling for its dues. His mother, Edna Mae and his sister Evelyn were all distraught as the full scale of financial mismanagement came to light. They pleaded with him not to box again and pointed to the example of Joe Louis. They reminded him that he had been blessed by not getting badly hurt during his career but now that he was older, the risks would increase.

He decided he needed help in order to get started in the boxing business again and he asked Joe Glaser and two other associates, Ernie Braca and Vic Marsillo, to help sort out his business affairs. He was too embarrassed to make it public that he was in trouble and he swore them to secrecy about his financial difficulties. He then began to arrange his fighting affairs and called George Gainford and asked him to organise a training routine and some sparring sessions. He soon began boxing in private exhibitions until he felt in shape to make a public appearance in November against his old opponent and sparring partner, Gene Burton, in Hamilton, Ontario. Of his new team only Vic Marsillio was involved with the boxing business. He had managed several fighters, including Charlie Fusari, who had fought Sugar Ray for the welterweight title in 1950. Marsillio was a lively character. He was small and chubby, a double for Lou Costello, the comedian of Bud Abbott and Lou Costello fame. His new team were like a corporation-sized board of managers and advisers.'

The first thing his new team did was check Robinson's business empire and go through the books. Braca and Glaser were designated to do this. When they visited Robinson's office and checked his books, they looked at each other and shook their heads in disbelief. They were shocked at the flagrant larceny they encountered. "There had been thieving on a large scale," said Glaser.

Jimmy Cannon said that Sugar Ray sold ten percent of himself to Ernie Braca for $10,000, besides the $10,000 he owed Braca he also owed Glaser $120,000 which he had loaned to Sugar Ray

On the 5th January 1955, he travelled to Detroit for the first of his comeback fights. Boston's Joe Rindone was selected as the sacrificial lamb, mainly because he had previously flattened Rindone in six rounds in Boston in 1950 and it would provide him with a good test of how much impact the lay-off had done to his form. His home city gave his comeback fight plenty of publicity and the promoters were delighted with an amazing turnout of 11,973 fans and the city's largest fight crowd in four years, who arrived at the Olympia to watch their old hometown favourite strut his stuff. Rindone, a tough ex-Marine, had not won a fight for over a year and the fight proved a walkover for Robinson, who stopped him in the sixth round.

Afterwards, when they analysed his performance, George Gainford and the other camp members struck a positive tone and agreed that it had been a satisfactory workout against a limited foe. Ernie Braca, however, was not so kind. He approached Robinson as he was taking his boxing boots off and he reminded him that he used to demolish the likes of Joe Rindone in a round. "Ray, you looked terrible," he barked in his gruff voice, "you've got a lot of sharpness to get back. Don't be fooled!" Robinson was hurt by these remarks and conceded that it wasn't one of his best fights but offered that "it's been thirty months since my last fight. That's a long time to be out of action. It takes time and more competition to regain your touch and sharpness."

Johnny Weber, the referee, suggested that "there is still a lot of the old Sugar Ray Robinson left, even at the age of 34." Rindone, however, was less impressed and suggested that "Robinson should never have knocked me out. I was silly to allow the guy to make me drop my plan and do something I had no right to do. Before round six, Bill Matney, secretary of the Michigan Boxing Commission, came to my corner and told me I had to speed up the fight. I did what he asked and got knocked out. Even so, I was up before the count of 10, but the referee grabbed me and insisted I had been counted out."

Robinson's purse of $8,503, a pittance against the huge sums he had been commanding, reminded him just how far he had to climb. He was eager to add to this fee and decided that he would box again a few weeks later in Chicago against much tougher opposition. A number of his friends, including Dr Arielle, urged him to rethink and be cautious. Dr Arielle, in particular, expressed his concern that this was too soon after the Rindone contest and that he would be better suited to get more training in before taking another fight. He steadfastly ignored the advice and agreed to another fight for Jim Norris's International Boxing Club.

By January 1955, the hunt was on to find the right type of opponent for his second comeback fight to face him on the headline for a Jim Norris-promoted televised bout at the Chicago Stadium on the 19th January, just over two weeks after the Rindone fight. Eyes turned to Philadelphia, where a young 21-year old middleweight with an impressive 27-2-1 record was being heralded by the city's old-time fighters as a future champion, if only he could only get the right breaks. As he was getting changed for his daily training session in Johnny Madison's Gym, the young man was told that George Gainford had phoned Herman Taylor, the wily Philadelphia promoter to ask if could supply an opponent for Robinson. Taylor had told Gainford that he had the ideal opponent. "Who is it?" Gainford eagerly enquired. When the name George Benton was mentioned, Gainford rejected it immediately on the grounds that he was too dangerous. Benton, who later enjoyed success as a world class trainer and guided ten world champions, remembered that, "Although Robinson was a great, great fighter, he wasn't averse to throwing an illegal punch; he was so quick that he got away with it. He would throw a left hook around the small of your back. Imagine a large screwdriver driven into the base of your spine. It used to paralyze anyone he caught with it. I suffered from the impact once when I was 15 and an amateur boxing in New York. I was matched with an older fighter from Sugar Ray's gym. This guy had sparred hundreds of rounds with Robinson and learned how to throw that left of by heart. In our fight he hit me with it and the pain was crucifying. My legs went numb. I lost but it was an education. I was sorry not to get the chance to meet the master in the ring."

The choice of opponent was finally agreed as Ralph Josiah Jones; also know to boxing fans as Ralph 'Tiger' Jones. He was born in Brooklyn in March 1928 as one of ten kids. He had spent a considerable part of his childhood moving in and out of children's homes. He had started boxing at 19 years of age and was coached by Gil Clancy. He had 55 amateur fights before he turned professional at the age of 21. He was a heavy-shouldered middleweight who told the press that he had never felt better in his life. "Robinson is the big name. I'm just a nobody, according to the experts, but I believe in myself emphatically." He explained that as an amateur he had fought several boxers from Sugar Ray's old amateur club and had never lost once. Quiet and unassuming outside the ring, once he stepped inside the ropes, he transformed himself into a busy and non-stop punching fighter who relied on his supreme fitness and a frightening determination. He was a television favourite and had already appeared regularly on the box. Gainford selected him because he was not a knockout puncher or a particularly skilled or technical boxer, but he was the ideal opponent for Robinson to have a workout with and get much needed rounds under his belt. Coming into the fight, he had lost the last five consecutive fights. And on paper it looked an absolute certainty for Robinson to gain his second victory; a fact the bookmakers concurred with as they made him a 6-1 favourite.

Over 7,000 fans braved the freezing winter night to cram inside the Chicago Stadium to see the latest leg of Robinson's return and watched as for the entire ten rounds, Jones, who was eight years younger than his legendary foe, gave him a torrid time. Robinson started off by employing his trusty left jab to find his range but Jones kept finding a way past it. This continued for the first couple of rounds until it became obvious to all that his seamless procession to victory was not assured and he had been drawn into a pitched battle for which he was not prepared for. Jones's style was crude but effective as he would drive the former world champion back against the ropes and then flail away with both hands driving forward like pistons. As he blocked and absorbed the blows, Robinson seemed to grow old before the eyes of the stunned audience as it became apparent that the perfect fighting machine of the forties was gone forever. The judges were unmoved by sentiment, however, and Ed Hintz scored Jones a unanimous points winner, scoring 100 points to Jones and only 88 for

Robinson. The other judge, Howard Walsh scored it 98 to 89 for Jones, while referee Frank Sikora made it 99 to 94 for Tiger.

Robinson presented a bold front to the reporters who clamoured for a reaction. He was adamant that the defeat would not spell the end of his comeback. "I never figured that I'd win them all and you've got to get beat somewhere along the way." He also accepted responsibility for not heeding the advice of his advisers. "George Gainford said that he was too tough for my second fight on a comeback." The press, however, were far less reflective and forgiving. "Literally beaten from pillar to post by an unranked, unruffled plodder named Tiger Jones, a sadder but wiser Sugar Ray Robinson should decide whether or not to hang up the red leather mittens for good," wrote reputed journalist Gene Ward in the New York Daily News. A month after the victory, Jones fought the world middleweight champion, Carl Olson, in a ten round non-title bout which gave a truer indication of his ability as a world class fighter - and a sadder indication of how far Sugar Ray had fallen - when he was thrashed out of sight and lost every round. To give an overall perception of Tiger Jones, he retired from boxing in 1962 having fought 88 times, with 51 victories, five draws and 32 defeats. He never fought for a world championship, which was something he always regretted.

Willie Pep, the former brilliant world featherweight champion who knew of Tiger Jones's capabilities, said that although Tiger was known as a 'Trial Horse,' he was a much better fighter than that. "He was one of the most popular fighters in the 1950's as his 63 appearances on national television testify. The boxing fans of the 1950s appreciated boxing skills, but he always seemed to get the wrong end of a close decisions. He was a very unlucky fighter because he fought every top welter and middleweight in America. After he beat Robinson there was talk of a return, but that never happened," he said. Tiger made only $150,000 in a 12-year career. Not much for a fighter who was constantly fighting the best fighters around. And entertaining millions of viewers. Tiger Jones was a great fighter and a lovely guy," concluded Pep.

Still, beset by the ever-growing financial troubles, which kept unveiling the extent to which he was being taken advantage of, Robinson's comeback continued. On the 29th March, he was paired off against Johnny Lombardo in Cincinnati Garden, where he once again looked completely lacklustre and devoid of ideas. In the opening rounds, he was out-jabbed by the limited Lombardo and throughout the full ten round duration, he kept falling into clinches and looking at the clock in desperation. He was awarded a close split decision but the 5,124 fans who attended didn't respond with any hostility but instead exited in a sombre, funeral-like atmosphere.

Later that same evening, back at the Netherland-Plaza Hotel which was their base for the fight, Robinson, George Gainford, Ernie Braca, Vic Marsillo and

Joe Glaser held a private conference to discuss Sugar Ray's future. Robinson was forced to hold an ice pack to his bruised face after taking shots which he would have sleep-walked through in his prime. Joe Glaser didn't mince his words and opened the meeting by telling him that he "had looked dreadful against Lombardo." As the other attendees held their breath, waiting for Robinson to explode in indignation, he simply looked at the floor. Glaser was unmoved and told him that he was "performing like he didn't want to fight anymore." Robinson tried to claim that he was slowly getting back on track and could feel his old rhythm and sharpness returning with each fight. Ernie Braca cut him off and brutally delivered his verdict; he said that, in his opinion, he was "finished as a fighter, all washed up." With this statement Robinson looked distraught. Braca told him to hang up his boxing gloves "so high that you would need a chair to stand on to even think about touching them. You're through," he said in a harsh tone. It was a stinging indictment and Sugar Ray dropped his head, and tears began to roll down his cheeks. He stuttered that he should be given another chance. He told them he just wanted to win the middleweight title again. "You're being unfair to me," said Robinson. At hearing this Braca shouted: "What are you on about, we are not being fair to you? We only want you to quit before you get seriously hurt. Let us get back to New York and try and sort your business affairs."

Vic Marsillo, who had experience of the fragile ego of a fighter after managing Charlie Fussari, stood up and told everyone, "Shut up, all of you. You guys listen to me." Then, looking directly at the hysterical former champion, bellowed: "Robinson, don't listen to these people. Listen to little Napoleon. I'm a fight manager, forget what these guys are saying, I'm telling you you're going to win the world title again." The room fell silent as Marsillo paced up and down the room, stopping objections with intimidating gestures. He then told Robinson he would make another fortune. Sugar Ray was relieved to hear these words of encouragement. "Your gifts have to be re-polished like neglected silver, more fights will make them shine again," he said. Ernie Braca finally relented and agreed that he would arrange one more fight in a couple of week's time in Milwaukee.

After the Tiger Jones defeat, George Gainford and Harry Wiley both told Ray that if he insisted on continuing boxing they would no longer train him or go in his corner. Robinson was distraught and accused them of "deserting the gravy train when it ran into trouble." He resolved that he didn't need them and vowed to continue and train himself. Edna Mae, however, sensed how wounded he was and she acted as the broker between the men and persuaded Gainford to call him and agree to resume their relationship. Initially, Robinson refused to allow it but his wife eventually convinced him to relent. Both Gainford and Wiley had made their point and sat hoping that the other men could change his mind.

During this period, Edna Mae continued to play an integral role to her hurt and confused husband. She asked him to think about how he had boxed during his brief comeback. "You are trying too hard," she told him. "You give the impression that you're trying to knock everybody out. Go back to what made you great. You were blessed with something special and you have to rediscover it by going back and practising until you are satisfied." Although he didn't tell her straight away, he knew that she was correct in her assessment of his inability to perform to the high levels of his glory years. Instead, he went back into the gym and practiced using his jab, hooks, uppercuts and two-handed combinations until slowly but surely, it started to come back to him. Years later, he acknowledged Edna Mae's counselling when he said, "I had trainers who had been with me from the beginning and they couldn't see what my problem was. It took my wife to put me on the right track and get back to using what brought me so much success." Edna Mae also convinced him to take Gainford and Wiley back as his trainers and cornermen. He agreed, but reluctantly.

On 14th April he travelled to Milwaukee to meet Ted Olla, a rugged journeyman fighter who was fighting in his hometown. He was regarded as being a class or two better than Johnny Lombardo, which convinced many in the press to speculate that Olla might be too much for the aged Sugar Ray. Prior to facing Robinson, Olla had fought a torrid battle with future Robinson opponent Paul Pender, before dropping a close points decision. He also drew with Jesse Turner and Walter Cartier, two top ten middleweight contenders. From the opening bell Sugar Ray was more focused and sharper and he speared Olla with constant left jabs and the occasional two-handed combination punches to mark his territory. In the third round, he walked out from his corner and took the spectators back down memory lane to deliver one of his right hand specials to send Olla sprawling against the ropes. Robinson then pounced like a cat and poured eight unanswered punches onto the unguarded head of the Milwaukee man. After an eight count, he proceeded to batter his outclassed opponent without mercy until referee, Dauber Jaeger, was compelled to stop the bout before the end of the third round.

Immediately after this fight, he asked the still-unconvinced trio of Braca, Glaser and Gainford to get him another contest as soon as possible. He stressed that he didn't want to enjoy a rest or endure a prolonged wait and so just four weeks after chinning Olla, he returned to his hometown of Detroit to take on tough Garth Panter, a crew-cut young middleweight from Salt Lake City. Panter had lost his previous six contests and in the first round he staggered Sugar Ray with a stinging right cross to the head. Ray's knees buckled, but he quickly recovered and Robinson still managed to impress all ringsiders with an imperious display of controlled boxing to herald the start of his 35th year and win a unanimous ten round points decision.

His management team were quietly pleased with his performance against Panter and his stamina in the ten round shellacking he dished out. It suddenly dawned on them that Sugar Ray just might possibly earn a couple of big pay-days and help pay back some of the money they had loaned him. It didn't take long for the offers to come rolling in.

The IBC watched this fight with interest and soon declared that they would make a match for Sugar Ray to face the world champion and old foe, Carl 'Bubo' Olson. Their reasoning was simple. Robinson still commanded a great deal of respect amongst the boxing public and television moguls had stated that they would be very interested in filming any fight which included Robinson's tilt at a world title. It was determined, however, that to give the fight added credibility Robinson would have to face a top ten contender. At the time, Charles Humez, a French fighter, was ranked number one with Holly Mims at number two; Robinson was rated at number three. Jim Norris didn't want Ray to box those two, so he matched him against Attilio Castellani, who boxed under the name 'Rocky' and hailed from Luzerne, Pennsylvania, in the Cow Palace, San Francisco with the prize on offer being a world title shot at Olson. Castellani lacked charisma and was regarded as 'colourless' by the boxing fraternity. He had fought his way through a series of formidable opponents, including Chico Varona, Holly Mims, Moses Ward, Kid Gavilan, Billy Graham, Ernie Durando and Gil Turner to earn a shot at the title. Less than a year earlier, Castellani had given Olson a torrid time in their fifteen round world championship fight and he had Olson down in the eleventh before he was decked in the following round. He was eager to avenge his loss. Sugar Ray was the 9-5 underdog in the betting and 8,230 fans paid to see if he could get past the sturdy-chinned, hard-punching Castellani. Robinson didn't particularly like the scrambling style which Castellani fought with and the press believed that this, combined with the greater strength of the Pennsylvanian fighter, would be too much for the veteran.

The opening three rounds saw Robinson stay in close and concentrate on his body punching, which appeared to have some effect. In the fourth, however, Castellani responded by jarring him with two solid left hooks to the head. In the following round he connected with a further two stunning right hands to Robinson's head and a paralysing left uppercut to the jaw. He followed this up in the sixth by clubbing Robinson to the canvas. Ray fell heavily on all fours before rising onto his knees and taking a count of nine. The referee, Jack Downey, studied him carefully and noted that Robinson looked tired and weary but Ray pleaded with him to be allowed to continue. Rocky flew at him like a dervish, eager to conclude the event and he forced Robinson backwards and against the ropes, where he blocked and avoided the punches and rallies which rained down on him; it looked like it was going to be an ignominious end until suddenly, without any warning, Robinson found a renewed zeal and started to claw his way back into the contest, putting on one of the greatest rallies of his long and distinguished career.

He started to box behind his whip-like jab and began throwing more powerful right hands and left hooks. Once or twice he stunned Castellani, who would fight back fiercely, but after the opening ten rounds Robinson was awarded a split points decision. Jack Downey voted for Robinson, as did one of the judges, Frankie Carter. The other official, Jack Silver, voted for Castellani by 56-54. It was an extremely close call and for those close to Robinson, it offered a potential happy ending to a fraught period; they hoped that he would now fight Olson and secure one last decent payday before retiring. Jim Norris and his cohorts were unconcerned by these matters but were simply delighted that he had won this eliminator because his charisma and box office personality would continue to ensure big money fights against Olson and the world welterweight champion, Carmen Basilio

The six comeback contests, however, had demonstrated quite clearly that Sugar Ray Robinson was, and would never again be capable of, scaling the great heights that he had done as the boxing phenomenon of the 1940s. Although his heart, courage and resolve were evident in every performance and allowed him to produce some epic performances, he was taking much more punishment than he had ever been forced to endure, which would have repercussions for him in later life. The great Ray Arcel watched Robinson's comeback with a deep sense of trepidation: "He had been great in the forties, but it was during this second phase of his career that he started taking those lickings and those fights can destroy you, just like the Muhammad Ali fights in Manila destroyed him. It's sad to watch greatness being extinguished but this was what was happening to Sugar Ray Robinson."

Unknown to the public, Sugar Ray trained and fought Castellani under a heavy personal cloud that would have forced most fighters to pull out of the fight. Edna Mae was pregnant and while he was training his wife was suffering dreadfully and having complications. She was rushed to hospital and Robinson broke training and sat at her bedside. He threatened to cancel the Castellani fight as his wife's condition worsened. Edna Mae, however, knowing this upcoming fight was his big opportunity, insisted he get back training and go through with the fight at all costs. The pregnancy proved troublesome and sadly Edna Mae eventually lost the child, although she kept this a secret until after Ray's victory over Rocky Castellani. Ray Junior, in his book 'Pound for Pound', said this was not the first child his mother had lost, nor was it the last.

17.

World Champion Again

EXHAUSTED BY the deep wells of reserves that the Castellani win had consumed, Robinson took almost five months to rest and contemplate his upcoming title challenge, which was scheduled to take place on 9th December at the Chicago Stadium. A month before the fight, he travelled back to his favourite training camp at Greenwood Lake, New York, to begin his preparations. During this camp, the journalist Jimmy Breslin was invited up to witness his comeback preparations. It was a cold, crisp November afternoon when he arrived and he had told friends that he was expecting to see Robinson looking like "a jaded former great champion looking for one last big payday before hanging up his gloves for good." Instead, he was pleasantly surprised to see Sugar Ray sparring like a young man; up on his toes throwing his left jab with a deadly combination of speed, accuracy and venom. Instead of throwing single punches, as he had done in virtually his entire comeback fights, Breslin saw him deliver bunches of five and six punches with rapier-like flashes of speed. Seeing the confused expression across the journalist's face, George Gainford quietly confided in him that, "You're now watching the real Robinson." He also revealed that they were not planning on winning the title through scraping a points decision but were preparing to deliver victory by a knockout! Breslin, who was on record as believing that Olson's mauling work inside and the extra zest and speed he possessed would wear Robinson down over the long, gruelling 15 round course, changed his mind and said that "Robinson will hammer Olson to defeat."

This optimism wasn't shared by the rest of the sportswriters, who readily recalled watching Robinson being mauled and pounded all over the ring by Tiger Jones only eleven months earlier. The consensus was that Olson, eight years younger, was far too fresh and tough to be threatened by the tired old warrior. The betting odds also reflected this view; Olson was a 4-1 favourite. Ernie Braca took an opportunity only a few days before the fight to watch Olson train in his hotel ballroom and, after studying the champion with care, reported back that he "was not impressed with Olson." He thought that "the champ's mind did not seem to be on the fight. I don't think he wants to fight and I think that Ray can stop him any time he wants to." Robinson, who maintained that Olson had never hurt him during their two previous encounters, was secretly pleased. He was pleased with how his camp had gone despite the difficulties. He had started to act increasingly like a recluse and had kept his emotional distance from his old trainers, Gainford and Wiley, whom he secretly referred to as hypocrites for their earlier abandonment.

What really irked him, however, was his treatment at the hands of Jim Norris and the International Boxing Club officials. "They treated me like a challenger," he complained, without any sense of irony or acknowledgement that this was his status. One incident which rankled related to Truman Gibson. Gibson was responsible for delegating tasks before the big title fights and had previously assigned Ben Bentley to Robinson to ensure the newspapers, television and radio reporters were granted access and interviews. Robinson took it as a personal affront when Olson had requested that Bentley handle things for him. He confronted Gibson and asked him for an explanation. Gibson bluntly explained that "the champion likes him and so he, Bentley, will work for him." Ray swallowed the slight and used it as a motivating force along with the knowledge that a victory would help to pay off his escalating debts. His purse would be in the region of $50,000 and a defeat would be the end of his claims to be 'the' drawing card. He was unhappy that he had been compelled to sign an exclusive contract with Norris and the IBC after they had secured his title opportunity and he stored it all up, ready to explode his frustration and anger out in the ring against Olson.

The preparations also included the emergence of a new addition to the Robinson entourage. Drew 'Boudini' Brown could best be described as a friendly, likeable 'con man' with a deep-throated voice. He was a heavily built man with a large round face upon which every expression possible would be displayed at will. He would explode in instant excitement or deep distress, depending on the situation. He was also an incessant talker who would happily hold court on any subject and declare himself an instant expert on it. He would do the miles of roadwork with Robinson and keep him distracted with his constant chatter. Robinson, who had grown distant from his old allies, George Gainford and Harry Wiley, began depending more and more on Brown, who would later earn his repute serving as the jester in the court of Muhammad Ali. Boudini joined the entourage that included Harold 'Killer' Johnson, Soldier Jones, June Clark, Pee Wee Beale, Honey 'Boy' Brewer, Wiley and Gainford.

A bitterly cold December evening didn't deter a crowd of 12,441 gathering in the Chicago Stadium to see if Sugar Ray Robinson would roll back the years and beat both Father Time and 'Bobo' Olson to regain his crown. Unswayed by sentiment, the bookmakers increased the odds to 8 to 1 against Robinson winning by a stoppage, just before the ring entrances. Olson had outlined his plan of action to the press before the fight and summed it up simply by suggesting that it was "move, move, move and then move some more." He was going to "tire out the older challenger and tie him up in the clinches" before stopping him in the later rounds. Olson had been far from impressed with Robinson's six comeback bouts and believed that he could avenge his previous losses because "Robinson is there for the taking." This bold talk helped to mask over Olson's own concerns about his difficulty in making the middleweight poundage.

When he entered the ring, Robinson's face was a mask of pure, intense concentration and when the fight started both men moved from their corners with some hesitancy. Robinson quickly found his groove though and started to box with fluency. They exchanged left jabs but he sensed that Olson looked a little cumbersome in his attempts to keep the fight at close range and he appeared to be confused by the hum of confidence radiated by Robinson. Olson did little to indicate that he was the world champion and Sugar Ray took full advantage to force him into making mistakes. He ended the round by snapping his left jab into the face of Olson repeatedly. And Robinson's jab really was a powerful weapon. He had cultivated it over the years. He didn't 'push' it out; he turned his left shoulder and snapped it out with venom. Over the years many opponents commented that his jab was like most fighters best 'right hand', it had terrific speed and awesome power.

In the second session, Olson showed his determination to get in close and a couple of close range confrontations took place before Robinson sensed that the time was right to execute the plans shared with the journalist Jimmy Breslin a few short weeks before. Olson scored with some hefty body punches in a close-quarter exchange before Robinson dug a left hook out from deep and landed it squarely on his exposed chin. Robinson was still close enough to look deep into his eyes and saw that they registered the hurt. He struck again, like a deadly cobra, when he saw the champion's hands drop to his sides and he instantaneously unleashed a torrent of punches which culminated with a tremendous right cross to the temple, followed by a grazing left hook which helped Olson fall backwards to the canvas. Olson seemed embarrassed as he groped in vain for the ropes and tried - in vain - to beat referee Frank Sikora's count, which tolled above him.

Sugar Ray Robinson was the new world champion after only two minutes and fifty two seconds of the second round. The whole stadium appeared to erupt in a tidal wave of undiluted adulation for one of boxing's greatest stars. Sportswriters sat ringside scratched their heads and smiled a "How did he manage that" expression on their faces. There was confusion amongst ringsiders, who were stunned by the dramatic turn of events; how many punches landed? The speed and accuracy had created the undoubted upset of the year to return him back to the top of the world. Gainford and Wiley jumped into the ring to embrace the new champion whilst Ray allowed the tears to cascade down his cheeks.

Robinson later recalled these moments in his book: "George Gainford and Harry Wiley were joyful. Laughing and shaking hands with everyone but I looked at them and thought, 'You bastards. You bastards told me I was through. You told me to quit.'"

After he was declared the winner and new champion Robinson broke down in tears. He was helped back to the dressing-room with hordes of fans slapping him on the back and trying to shake his hand. He was emotionally exhausted. He sat on a chair and wept uncontrollably. That old adage that 'They never come back' was knocked for six, with this sensational finish to the fight. "I had to cry," he told everyone in the room. "I'm just glad it's all over. This comeback has not been easy since Tiger Jones licked me here (in Chicago Stadium) nearly a year ago." His voice became louder and clear as he finished by saying: "Only a few people believed I should carry on this comeback after that defeat." He then thanked those who did believe in him, but emphasised there were many others who didn't have enough faith in him. "They said I didn't stand a chance of becoming champion again, and I should quit for good. It hurt me deeply, but made me more determined to continue."

He told the press that he now wanted to box a few exhibition bouts and engage in a few non-title fights, but the IBC were already working on their own plans and instructed him to defend his title against Olson again within ninety days. This was a similar contract to the one he had used when Randy Turpin had defeated him in 1951. Robinson made excuses and tried to delay the return until he felt that he had cashed in on his newly-won title but Jim Norris was unmoved and demanded that he should honour the return contract. His old wounds about not receiving his due respect from his countrymen were also reopened when the prestigious Neil trophy, awarded by the Boxing Writers' Association of New York to "the person who had done most for boxing during the year" was presented to Carmen Basilio. Robinson reacted with indignation and claimed that Basilio was "one of Jim Norris's favourites" and he admitted that he regretted getting tangled up with the IBC. He was further aggrieved when The Ring magazine published a poll of the boxing fans' top twenty favourite boxers. Carmen Basilio came first for the second successive year with Robinson a distant sixth. The same magazine also voted Basilio's return fight against Johnny Saxton, when he regained the welterweight title, as the 'Fight of the Year'. Robinson's knockout of Carl Olson was rated fourth but some consolation was gained by the final round being regarded as 'Round of the Year'. These perceived insults strengthened Robinson's growing enmity towards Carmen Basilio.

World Champion Again

After his sensational victory, Sugar Ray was in great demand. He was once again feted wherever he went. Newspaper and magazine articles appeared, he was asked to endorse several franchises and clothing lines, and made many personal appearances, including being nvited to top class nightclubs and appearing on television shows. He was a guest on the Ed Sullivan and What's My Line shows and at another televised show he looked resplendent and the host asked him to stand and take a bow - in a very embarrassing situation he was then told to get Edna Mae on her feet. However, the lady with him was not Edna Mae! He sang and danced. He and Edna Mae were treated like royalty, especially in Harlem. He lapped it all up

******

It was not until May 1956 that Robinson finally fought again in his return match against Bobo Olson. Both the International Boxing Club and the American Legion Stadium promoted the bout, which took place at the stadium of the Los Angeles Angels baseball team, Wrigley Field. When the wrangling had finally been resolved and the match was officially signed and sealed, Robinson immediately moved back to his training quarters in Greenwood Lake. He switched camps three weeks before the fight, and moved across country to Gilman's Training Camp, situated in San Jacinto about fifty miles from Los Angeles. Although he was plagued by government tax officials, who hounded him for the money he still owed, he took his usual coterie of friends and relatives to the training camp and paid for all of them to be transported from New York to Hot Springs. Among his group of sixteen were a cook, five managers and two sparring partners. He also arranged for a special ring to be transported from New York for his sparring sessions. Edna Mae chose not to stay at Gilman's but instead based herself in Los Angeles.

Robinson's training was hard and he looked sharp. George Gainford was concerned as there were still two weeks before the fight and he sensed that his charge needed to relax. He contacted Edna Mae and arranged for her to come to the training camp. Gainford took the unusual step of instructing him bluntly to "go to bed with Edna Mae." The combination of sex and boxing are traditionally frowned upon by most trainers, who believe that that having sex before a contest can weaken a fighter and can cause distractions. Gainford usually advocated an abstinence of six weeks before a fight and Sugar Ray was an advocate of this unwritten law. "If you're a fighter, you need your energy. You can't leave it with a woman," he often said. He also acknowledged the psychological benefits. "Abstaining from sex not only makes you stronger but you also think you are stronger. You're meaner because your nervous system is on edge." He would later cite this abstention as one of the major reasons for his marital problems. On this occasion, however, he was happy to comply with his trainer's demands.

In his training quarters based at Ocean Park Arena, Olson worked diligently on crowding Robinson and staying close to him to be able to hook to the body. He reasoned that he had not taken advantage of his youth in previous contests and so determined to make the fight a war of attrition and a battle of strength. He maintained that Robinson's victory in Chicago was something of an accident and that he had "run into a 'lucky' punch". The press agreed and dwelled upon the possibility that Olson would turn the tables on the veteran title-holder.

This time, 21,000 fight fans waited in the open air sunlit arena for the bell to ring and start the fight. The Hawaiian-born Californian began by boxing cautiously and burying his chin behind his arms and shoulders. Robinson later said that this tactic suited him because it spared him having to burn any excess energy. He appeared calm and banged out his left jab as a range finder. Olson would occasionally respond to connect with some telling body punches which made Ray wince. This mundane pattern continued for the first three rounds. At the start of fourth round, Olson seemed to have found his confidence and began ploughing forward, dispensing with his cautiousness to bob and weave, slip Robinson's leads and punish him with body shots. This raised his confidence further as Olson knew that he had hurt the title-holder earlier.

Within a split second it all changed dramatically. Robinson moved to his left, dropped his shoulder and drove a dynamic right cross under the heart of Olson. The breath gushed out of his body like a balloon being deflated and his defence was left in tatters; he dropped both his hands and Robinson's power-packed left hook smashed into the side of his exposed jaw with a sickening smack…What a pulverizing punch! Olson crashed to the canvas on his back, rolled over a couple of times, but was out to the world. The referee, Mushy Callahan, took up the count but Robinson's fighting instinct knew the conclusion. He looked down at the prone body and walked to a neutral corner and raised his hand as the winner and still champion. It was his 90th inside the distance victory in his 145 professional contests.

The fight was a tremendous financial success, achieving a new Californian record for boxing receipts of $228,500, with an additional $100,000 from television. Still, both fighters were unhappy with their purses. Olson's estranged wife, Dolores, claimed his share after a court hearing in California. The Internal Revenue Department confiscated $90,000 of unpaid income taxes out of Robinson's total $105,000 purse money, much to his chagrin. (It was later revealed that Olson lived a complicated existence. He was a bigamist, running between his wife Helen and their children and girlfriend Judy Crab and her children, plus having an affair with another lady named Dolores.)

After the fight with Olson Ray and Edna Mae stayed at a hotel and relaxed in the open air, dipping into the swimming pool. He was totally unmarked and accepted the congratulations of the hotel guests while posing for photographs. He was extremely vain and loved the glare of publicity and adulation. He also loved people pointing toward him and whispering: "That's Sugar Ray Robinson." He also did some deep thinking. A reporter had questioned him about the number of people that he had paid for while training for the second Olson fight. Pointing out that if he had all the problems with the IRS, why on earth was he footing the bill for so many people? George Gainford said Robinson was obsessed with having people around him. It eventually would cost him a great deal of money.

The critics were also unconvinced by Robinson's second consecutive victory. Joe DiMaggio, the baseball legend who was a keen fight fan, summed up the feelings of many when he suggested that Olson was an unconvincing opponent to judge Robinson against. He dismissively told the press, "This guy, Olson, doesn't get up when he gets knocked down, does he?" The general opinion was that Robinson would beat Olson every night of the week and twice on Sundays if he fought him again. A better indicator would come if he met a younger fighter like Tiger Jones or Gene Fullmer, who would wear Robinson down over the later rounds. Vic Marsillo opined that "Sugar Ray could not afford to be pressed for more than half a dozen rounds." He did caveat this view with the opinion that "equally, there are not many fighters who would stand up to Robinson's punches for six rounds either." Robinson didn't take much notice of these opinions but had a much more pragmatic approach; he just wanted money and plenty of it, "then we will find out if my legs can last those six rounds." The money he had earned so far in his eight comeback fights had not been great. In fact, after paying the government taxes, it had only covered his training camp expenses.

He was greatly upset when Johnny Saxton defeated Carmen Basilio for the world welterweight title because the proposed fight between him and Basilio would have attracted a huge outdoor gate and resulted in a huge payday for him. His mood was improved by rumours emanating from Hollywood that his friend Frank Sinatra was planning to make a film based on Sugar Ray's life. 'Ole Blue Eyes' had said that he planned to produce the picture himself as part of his contract, which stated that he could produce an independent film. Robinson declared that "he had always fancied himself as an actor." Eventually, the rumours came to nothing but were reignited again many years later.

Jim Norris started negations for Ray to defend his world crown against a fighter named Gene Fullmer. These talks seemed to go on forever, with Robinson holding out for the money he wanted. In November, Robinson fought a warm-up fight because he had become frustrated that the discussions to defend his crown against Gene Fullmer had started to stall. He travelled to the New Haven Arena, Connecticut, where he coasted through ten rounds against the former Golden Gloves and light-heavyweight champion of the Atlantic Fleet, Bob Provizzi from Freeland, Philadelphia. He weighed in at five pounds over the middleweight limit and was conscious of the stamina of the 23-year old challenger and so paced himself throughout the ten rounds and didn't open up until the final round, when he dropped Provizzi twice with neat, lightning-fast combination punches. He concentrated on improving his defence and Provizzi never looked like troubling him unduly. This was the first time in sixteen months that he had to travel the distance and he declared himself satisfied with the easy ten rounder.

******

On the 25th May 1956, Gene Fullmer outpointed the European middleweight champion Charles Humez over ten brutal rounds in New York. This victory had elevated Fullmer to the position of number one contender for Sugar Ray's newly-acquired world title and talks quickly commenced to match Gene against Robinson. The two men shared some common foes, which convinced many onlookers that Gene would present a formidable test for Robinson. Fullmer had beaten Rocky Castellani before outpointing Gil Turner over ten rounds and then followed up with another ten round victory over Ralph 'Tiger' Jones. After beating Humez he destroyed the cagey Moses Ward inside three rounds, and then he began to wait patiently for Robinson to sign the contract for their meeting. Robinson was in no rush to put pen to paper and he was happy to fuel the heated debate about the fight's outcome whilst stalling. Fullmer, who was used to fighting at regular intervals, soon became frustrated by the seemingly unnecessary delay and became angry. He told enquiring journalists that "Sugar Ray is messing me about" and fatally undermined his own negotiations by claiming that he was "so keen to get Robinson into the ring that I'll fight him for a mere pittance." Robinson looked to take this claim literally in his own negotiations.

Jim Norris and his International Boxing Club were especially anxious to promote the fight because their proposed vacant world heavyweight championship battle between Archie Moore and Floyd Patterson, which had been booked for the 18th September in New York's Yankee Stadium, had been postponed and they needed a replacement showcase event. It was to be the first title fight seen in New York since Rocky Marciano and Archie Moore had fought for Marciano's world crown. Norris offered Robinson $50,000 from the proceeds of the closed circuit television income. Additionally, The Ring magazine reported that Fullmer had offered to forgo his own share of the television money and would even accept a meagre 12½ % of the money in order to get the fight signed and sealed. But still Robinson kept putting obstacles in the way. He told the press that he "was fed up being told what he had to do." He made vague references to the possibility of "fighting elsewhere in the world," which was actually legally impossible because of the strict stipulations he had agreed in his commitments to the IBC. He also briefed some selected reporters that he wanted to fight Art Aragon, who was a huge draw in Los Angeles. Robinson privately believed that he could earn over $100,000. The newspapers fuelled the interminable delay by recounting the numerous other postponements he had been involved in during his career. A number of dates were set and broken before the official date of 12th December was announced. The Fullmer camp was outraged when Robinson withdrew only a few weeks before, blaming a virus. Robinson wanted the bulk of the money on offer and Norris, exasperated by the debate, finally relented and gave in to his demands. The critics blasted Robinson for his undignified stance and cited it as "a rather greedy deal". Robinson, however, did well for both him and Fullmer. He successfully argued that he should pocket a further $100,000 guarantee plus both of them share a further $100,000 from the sponsors and television rights.

While the negotiations were being conducted, Robinson met the former world welter and middleweight champion 'Toy Bulldog' Mickey Walker at his training camp back at Greenwood Lake. After they posed for the routine press photographs, Walker sat down with just Robinson and George Gainford in attendance. "Try for a quick knockout," he advised. "I've watched this kid (Fullmer) and he's like a bull rather than a bulldog. He's got ten years on you and if you don't nail him in the first six rounds, you lose."

After the December date was postponed and the final negotiations concluded to his satisfaction, Robinson trained diligently through the Christmas and New Year period. He agreed to face the Mormon who hailed from West Jordon, Utah, on the 2nd January 1957at his favourite Madison Square Garden venue. During the festivities, he whipped himself into top physical and mental shape as he knew that Fullmer's record of 40 fights, with 37 wins and three losses only told part of the story. He was a tough, rough-house fighter who was well used to employing any measures to overwhelm his opponents, including a liberal use of his head. He was also well-known for fouling while working inside. Although he had stopped twenty of his opponents he couldn't be described as a genuine knockout puncher. He was born in July of 1931 and was a schoolboy when his interest in boxing surfaced. He was helped by the man who later became his manager, a successful businessman named Marvin (Marv) Jensen, who was also a mink rancher. He was a well-respected man in West Jordan and he was also the Mayor of Utah were both men lived. Both Fullmer and Jensen were strict Mormons who rigorously adhered by the codes of their religion. He had his first pro fight in June 1951 when he knocked out Glen Peck in one round after an undistinguished amateur career. He had bulldozed his way to the shot at Robinson's title. It was not an opportunity he intended to let bypass him.

While training over the festive season, Robinson was sparring with Gil Turner, a top class welterweight who fought the best in both the welter and middleweight divisions, when Turner caught Ray with a solid punch to the ribs. The punch doubled him up and numbed his right side. That night the pain got worse and George Gainford decided he needed to travel into New York for medical treatment. Normally Dr. Nardiello would have been summoned, but he was ill and unavailable. Robinson refused to seek the help of the State Athletic Commission medical officer, Dr. Alexander Schiff, who had diagnosed his virus which led to the first postponement. (Robinson told Gainford and Braca, he wouldn't let Dr. Schiff call off the fight a second time because the press had crucified him for the first postponement. Thus, Sugar's pride dictated he go through with the fight in violation of one of his own cardinal rules, that he never go into a ring unless in top physical condition. It was decided that he would seek the help of a doctor he knew from Harlem. The doctor examined Ray and diagnosed a rib separation. He gave Robinson treatment and prescribed rest, which was the reason a group of newspaper reporters who arrived at his camp to watch his workout but were disappointed to learn he wasn't training and didn't even see him. On that day and for three further days he was confined to his bed, his torso swathed in adhesive and bandage. When he resumed training Sugar Ray restricted himself to light drills but never sparred again, his excuse to reporters was he didn't want to leave his fight in the gym. However, he still couldn't sleep and in desperation the Harlem doctor was contacted again for something to ease the pain. He prescribed Miltown tablets, which he took each night.

12,000 spectators squeezed into the Garden, the best attendance since 1953, and they saw in the opening round that Fullmer's raw energy and all out brawling style was not best suited to the champion's own approach. For the fifteen rounds Robinson could not get into any kind of rhythm and was forced backwards throughout the whole fight; he struggled to put his usual majestic moves together and found himself constantly on the defensive. He wasn't given time to gulp a lungful of air, let alone fight such was the force of the Utah whirlwind. Fullmer later admitted that he was motivated by anger at the champion's financial demands. He had finally been forced to accept a lousy $21,000 against Robinson's $138,000 purse and he fought with a fury that looked, at times, like it would consume Robinson. The ten year age gap soon told; there was a great deal of holding by Sugar Ray but Fullmer was so strong that even whilst he held on, Fullmer continued to flay away to his head and body, which hurt and annoyed him. His best rounds were the fourth and fifth but just as he looked to be getting into a rhythm, in the seventh round Fullmer sent Robinson through the ropes for a count of six. George Gainford complained loudly to the referee, Ruby Goldstein, that the challenger was repeatedly using 'rabbit punches', but Marvin Jenson countered by suggesting that Goldstein should deduct points from Robinson for 'constant holding'. Both fighters appeared oblivious to this debate and the swarming Fullmer cut Robinson's left eyebrow and the blood dripped down his face and onto his chest. As the bell for the final round sounded Ray realised that he was way behind and he summoned up old reserves of power and spee,d but it was much too late. Goldstein scored it to Fullmer by eight rounds to five; Judge Frank Forbes had it ten to five and Harold Barnes scored it nine rounds to six, all for the new champion. It had been an anti-climax as far as Robinson was concerned. It had been fifteen torturous rounds.

The majority of sportswriters held the same opinion that Robinson had lost clearly. His close friends and fans believed that the defeat should herald his retirement. Robinson was unmoved by the well-meaning sentiments and told the press that he had a contract for a return contest, which he fully intended to honour. He complained about Fullmer's illegal punches but was magnanimous enough to concede that the better man had won. although he pointedly declined to praise his conqueror. Fullmer fully embraced his new status as champion and began appearing on television chat shows and radio as well as lending his name to numerous endorsements and newspaper and magazine articles. He was still feeling raw at his treatment at the hands of the deposed champ during their protracted negotiations, and by the "pittance" he had felt forced to accept, and so he never failed to take every opportunity to rubbish Robinson. Marvin Jenson also eagerly embraced the opportunities to speak with derision about Robinson's stalling tactics and his lack of grace when discussing money matters.

Robinson maintained that he would offer his response in the return. "Just wait until then," he said. "Then you'll see the real Sugar Ray Robinson." Because the IRS hadn't taken any of his purse money, he was happier. The defeat didn't stop him making high profile appearances around Harlem and Broadway in his pink Cadillac, like the king of Harlem. His sexual appetite was also undimmed and his many indiscretions and infidelities were common knowledge throughout Harlem.

A few days after the loss of his title, Gene Ward, a reputable sports journalist, wrote that Robinson was strangely ineffective and lacklustre in the Fullmer fight. He said that it had baffled experts and boxing fans alike.

"Those who were nonplussed by Robinson's lack of fire and his failure to call on the ring cunning which had been his trademark either blamed Sugar Ray's age or his business instincts for a lucrative return match. Some went so far as to hint he'd bet against himself. Others gave credit to the strong boy tactics of his youthful and orthodox adversary, and let it go at that. But," said Mr Ward. "There was much more to that defeat than was ever revealed, and the full truth of it remained, until now, one of sport's best kept secrets." Ward went on to reveal the training injury Ray suffered against Gil Turner. He said Ray had had an X-ray which disclosed the rib injury on Robinson's right side. The tranquilizers and Miltown were also mentioned. He said Robinson continued taking them through the night before the fight so as he could get some sleep, which he had not been able to do because of the discomfort of his injury. "The drug was the same general type which General Maxwell D. Taylor, the Army Chief of Staff, and the Air Force Surgeon General's office, in an order made public, banned its use by pilots because 'it just doesn't mix with flying'. Robinson said that the reaction from taking the pills once in the ring was that he felt contented, "Just plain contented to let things go along. Nothing Fullmer did seem to hurt me."

The film star, Gene Kelly, of 'Singing in the Rain' fame, was a great fan of Robinson's and thought it would boost ratings for his television show by featuring him. Delighted at the opportunity, Robinson drove to Kelly's offices to discuss the requirements for the show. The dancing legend and the boxing superstar agreed on the format and the script. Finally, Ray enquired about his fee and outlined his demands. Kelly, well versed in Hollywood pay demands, was shocked at the inordinate amount being demanded and told Robinson that "it would be virtually impossible for him to ask his television bosses for this amount" and advised him to reduce his demands. Suddenly the atmosphere cooled and Robinson refused to compromise; he walked out and refused to appear. When he returned home, he explained to his wife the day's events. To his surprise, Edna Mae went ballistic and told him, in no uncertain terms, that he had made a mistake to turn down the opportunity of appearing with one of world's best known and loved dancers. She listed the opportunities he was missing, including the publicity and boost to his public relations. She then took the bull by the horns and phoned Kelly directly. The final result was that Robinson lowered his asking price and agreed to appear on the show. Edna Mae then spent hours practicing routines and dance steps with him. The show was a huge success and Sugar Ray received brilliant reviews from the normally acerbic television critics.

18.

Sugar Ray, the Miracle Man

OVER THE YEARS boxing fans had been astounded at a number of Robinson's amazing feats in the boxing ring, but none more so than when he miraculously rose, like Lazarus, to deliver a most unexpected and sensational knockout victory - to paraphrase the great Al Jolson's famous words: 'You Aint Seen Nothing Yet'.

The return was signed and sealed for the Chicago Stadium on the 1st May 1957. Sugar Ray told the press his pride had been stung by the loss of his crown to Gene Fullmer, who he described as 'a strong, awkward boy.' Shaking his head and with a slight smile he went on to say he couldn't understand how he had lost to him. "I've watched the film of the fight over and over again," he said, before adding, "I still can't understand some of the things I did or didn't do." He claimed the real Sugar Ray was missing in the championship encounter with the tough guy from West Jordan. "Just wait until the return," he told them. "Then you'll see the real Sugar Ray Robinson."

Robinson trained for a while in Joe Louis' gym in Chicago. Leading up to the bout Jim Norris and his associates sent Joe Louis to talk to Sugar Ray and soften him up with his financial demands. At this period the great former heavyweight king was an IBC employee. Robinson lost his temper with his friend. "You should be on my side," he told a startled Louis, "not the IBC. Do you want the same thing to happen to me that happened to you?" They argued but later Robinson claimed reporters blew everything out of proportion.

Murray Goodman was working in New York City as a Public Relations adviser when, prior to Sugar Ray's second fight with Fullmer, he was approached and asked if he would consider handling the publicity work for Robinson. Murray was extremely reluctant to take on the challenge after having some previous experience of dealing with the egotistical champion at the 1948 Tournament of Champions. After much persuading, he agreed on the proviso that Robinson gave him his personal approval because of his involvement with a number of his old opponents. He was surprised when Robinson invited him to his camp and welcomed him warmly. Their first disagreement, however, was not long in coming when Robinson told Murray that he didn't want to belittle Fullmer or make predictions about the fight's outcome. This was part of Robinson's own plan to improve his public persona from being regarded as prima donna.

Before the Fullmer encounter, Robinson would rest in his room at the Conrad Hilton Hotel in Chicago, dressed in his silk pyjamas and with a bandana wrapped around his head. The telephone was constantly ringing, which was something that annoyed him and so he asked to divert calls to his trainers' room and asked them to intercept all calls, except for his mother who he would speak to for over an hour every day. She would call and read the Scriptures to him while he sat listening quietly. George Gainford noticed that although Robinson had always been religious, he was even more observant since he had embarked on his comeback. Murray Goodman was also pleasantly surprised by the changes he observed in the previously arrogant champion. "I was once very critical about him but I am convinced this is a different Ray Robinson," he said. He cited examples such as old Soldier Jones, who had been with Robinson from his early teens but was now an old man crippled by arthritis; Sugar Ray still allowed him to be a paid member of his coterie and reduced his duties to merely rubbing his legs after training. He also acted as the unpaid chief coach of one his old neighbour's children, the Richardson family's youngest son, Jimmy, who worshipped him. He did this on condition that that the boy kept up his education.

1st May 1957 is a date that will be eternally special for all followers of Sugar Ray Robinson, for this was the day when he met Gene Fullmer, determined to avenge his loss in January. Many boxing fans had a love-hate relationship with the new world kingpin; his style of fighting was described by some as being awkward, clumsy, sloppy, mauling and brawling and he was often cited as a dirty fighter. His fans argued that not all boxers could be like Willie Pep, Joe Louis, or even Sugar Ray Robinson, but he utilised his natural strengths and used them to their optimum advantage. The Philadelphia promoter, J. Russell Peltz, best summed up the rugged effectiveness of the Utah man by creating the term 'winning ugly' for him. Robinson had trained diligently and had repeatedly studied the film of his first fight against Fullmer in an effort to get to grips with his aesthetically displeasing style.

The crowd of 14,757 were tingling with anticipation of watching an exciting encounter between two completely different fighters. Robinson was the underdog in the betting and a confident world champion predicted he would hound the older man like he had done in their first fight. The first round of the contest was disappointing and lacked any drama as both men sought to gain an early advantage. The champion just waited for Robinson to attack and when he did, he would venture from his defensive shell and repel him with brisk left hooks to the body. The majority of the crowd watched Fullmer scrape the first two rounds with his greater work rate, but at the start of the third, Robinson switched his tactics and instead of taking the lead, he stood back and forced Fullmer to do the leading which he countered. He feinted Fullmer into coming straight at him and he offered a beautiful counter with a flash left jab which connected right on the champion's face. Fullmer lost his composure and earned a stern rebuke from Frank Sikora, the fight official, for hitting low. Robinson confused his foe again at the start of the fourth round by getting on his front foot and banging two hurtful right hands to his unguarded jaw. When Fullmer attempted an attack to the body, Robinson willingly mixed it up with him and both men stood toe to toe and slugged it out at close quarters; the crowd, who sensed a classic encounter taking shape before them, responded and began a roar which hardly abate throughout the rest of the round and the interval.

The fifth round started at a slightly less furious pace, but Fullmer was first to the punch and scored with a couple of effective lefts to the body. Robinson refused to retreat and the crowd jeered Fullmer when he hit Robinson after Sikora had clearly ordered them to break. Robinson seemed to see a glimmer of opportunity in this action and felt that Fullmer was losing his composure. He was lunging towards him with a desperation that had not been evident in their first match, and when he did Robinson employed all of his wiles to hook to the body and then stepped back to wait for another lunge. When Fullmer made it, expecting to catch Sugar Ray with a body punch, he left his jaw fatally exposed. In a split second, Robinson calculated the lunge to perfection, dipped his shoulder to his left, bent his left knee inwards and with meticulous precision, fired his lightning left hook on to its designated target and swivelled the champion's head around. The crack could be heard around the ringside and all watched as Gene lurched forward face first, as if shot by a sniper's rifle, to the welcoming canvas. He made a vain attempt to get up but fell forward again, where he lay prone until Frank Sikora counted him out for the first time in his 44-fight career. Thirty seven year old Sugar Ray Robinson had made history by winning the same championship four times.

The left hook with which Sugar Ray knocked out Gene Fullmer has, over the following years, been described as 'the best left hook ever thrown'. It was such a perfect punch sportswriters said it should be preserved on film for prosperity. The World Book Encyclopaedia has a photograph of Robinson executing the 'perfect left hook' punch. Over the years Robinson's stunning inside-the-distance victories against the likes of Jake LaMotta, Randolph Turpin, Rocky Graziano, the two Carl 'Bobo' Olson fights, and this latest one were seen as masterpieces of boxing history and are still discussed all these years later. It was these championship triumphs that put Robinson on a much higher pedestal than many other champions before or since his reign.

The devastating impact of the punch was later described by Gene Fullmer: "He hit me with a left hook I didn't see, hear or even feel. I actually asked Marv Jenson, my manager, why Robinson was doing exercises between rounds as I saw him jumping up and down! It was only later it became clear to me that he had won and was celebrating. I missed the fact that they had counted to ten!" When he was back in his dressing room, an ecstatic Robinson was asked to describe the punch; one reporter asked him how far the left hook had travelled, and he replied, "I can't say but I think he got the message." He then offered his thanks to "everybody who had kept their faith in me" and singled out Edna Mae and Father Lang for special mentions. Gene Fullmer and Marvin Jenson both came to shake the hand of the new champion and offered their congratulations on the perfect punch. Robinson thanked them both and told the press that "in boxing, once the fight's over, that is usually the last you see of your opponent. Gene Fullmer and Marvin Jenson are different, they are gentlemen."

Not all of the press were prepared to be contrite in admitting that they had been wrong to dismiss the irrepressible Sugar Ray. Harold Weissman, a respected journalist, wrote one report which was dripping with vitriol for the champion and chose to reflect on his previous behaviours. He wrote, "In Ray Robinson's book, contracts were made to be signed but not honoured. What would this man, who has spent as much time in a courtroom as Clarence Darrow, know about obligations? He has more suits in his desk than Beau Brummel had in his closet and his skeletons are another matter. This is the man who ran out on a troopship, he is not a veteran of the foreign wars because he missed the boat," referring to the incident in April 1944 when Robinson didn't join Joe Louis in heading to Europe. "Sgt. Robinson wound up in a Military Police pokey at Fort Jay and was charged with being AWOL. In addition to his extraordinary talents as the best piece of fighting machinery this generation has ever seen, Sgt. Robinson also possesses keen foresight; he checked into a hospital, where the beds are secure and was not subject to the see-sawing whims of the Atlantic Ocean." Robinson, through his press attaché Murray Goodman, was a model of understatement. "How could I have jumped ship, when I wasn't even on it?"

More trouble and bad publicity regarding Sugar Ray came on the 19th July when the headlines in the newspapers read: 'Managerial Tangle - Braca Threatens To Sue Robinson for A Million'. What happened was after the Fullmer fights Robinson amicably severed relations with Ernie Braca, who acted as one of his advisors when he made his comeback in 1955. Braca threatened him with a prospective million-dollar lawsuit. The complex and often controversial fistic affairs of Sugar Ray were aired at a hearing before Julius Helfand, the chairman of the New York State Boxing Commission. By mutual agreement, Robinson and Harold 'Killer' Johnson, who was described as a Chicago tavern keeper and a close friend of the world champion's, terminated their one-year boxer-manager contract, which still had four months to run. Braca, the manager of Robinson from February 1955, when Robinson commenced his comeback campaign, and 'assignee (which was the commission term for a co-manager,) refused to sign the release of the Robinson/Johnson contract. Braca apparently had a 50 percent interest in Johnson's managerial end, which amounted to one-third of Sugar Ray's fistic earnings. Helfand was sceptical of the reasons why Johnson willingly gave up his manager's contract with a million-dollar fight scheduled. (This referred to a possible Robinson v Carmen Basilio fight.) The chairman questioned Johnson as to this matter and was told by Johnson he was doing so because he was a personal fried of the world champion and it was at Robinson's request. Johnson testified that he was not receiving anything then, nor was he promised any future payment for releasing Sugar Ray from the contract. "Even though Braca had a financial interest with Johnson in the contract under state law the commission had no recourse but to grant the release requested by Johnson and Robinson," said Mr Helfand.

Braca later filed a suit for damages, and in March 1958 Robinson, appearing at the Bronx Supreme Court before Justice Sidney A. Fine, was ordered to pay Braca $18,000. This represented settlement brought by Braca against Sugar Ray and Harold Johnson. Braca contended he was entitled to a share of Robinson's earnings over the previous three years. The earnings were estimated at close to $200,000.

19.

The Two Brutal Wars With The Onion Farmer

"HE WAS IN LOVE with himself! He thought he was better than anyone else. He was arrogant a real egotist and he expected everybody to get down on their hands and knees for him. I'm a stubborn SOB too, and I was getting down on my hands and knees for anybody. I remember in 1953, I took my wife to New York City and we were walking down Broadway when we saw Robinson near his pink Cadillac, and my wife wanted to meet him. He gave me the 'brush off' I never forgot that. Now I have my chance to kick his ass," said Carmen Basilio before his first fight with Sugar Ray Robinson.

Just four months after his epic victory over Fullmer, Ray Robinson defended his crown against the popular and exciting world welterweight champion, Carmen Basilio, on 23rd September. When the fight was announced, it caused a great deal of bitterness for Gene Fullmer and his manager Marv Jenson, who had believed that it was a done deal that he would meet Robinson in a third rubber match. Instead, he felt that he had been shafted by the authorities. Years later, Robinson verified his old foe's instincts were correct when he recounted to Dave Anderson, his co-biographer, that the night before he fought Fullmer for the second time, Jim Norris had visited him and explained that if he beat Fullmer, he "had something bigger for me - a meeting with Carmen Basilio outdoors." Robinson claimed that he had asked Norris, "Doesn't Fullmer have an agreement for a third fight if I beat him?" But Norris had smiled and told him not to concern himself with that problem. He reassured him that "the commissioner really wants the Basilio fight."

There was certainly no love lost between Robinson and Basilio when they eventually fought each other in the ring. These legends would have two brutal confrontations that are still part of boxing folklore. Carmen respected Sugar Ray's ability inside the ring but couldn't care less about his antics outside.

Before the Carmen Basilio fight could be officially ratified, Robinson engaged Norris in his, by now customary, quarrel for the lion's share of the purse. Norris had argued that this wasn't possible because Basilio was also bringing a world championship belt to the ring. Robinson dismissed this argument by claiming that "in this fight, he's the challenger for my title." The debate became increasingly heated and the deadlock was only broken when Norris suddenly became ill and had to be rushed to hospital suffering from a suspected heart attack. For many of the critics in the press, they quickly blamed Robinson's abrasive attitude and negotiating style for this. When it was later revealed that the illness was actually acute food poisoning, due to a corned beef sandwich, this accusation was later dropped.

The argument between Robinson and the IBC raged on with Sugar Ray still refusing to sign a contract with Jim Norris. Carmen was getting fed up and sent word to Robinson: "I'll give you a few more days to sign the contract to fight me, or else I will consider other offers for fights I have received." Carmen told reporters he tired of waiting for Robinson to make up his mind. He wanted to fight in the summer, whether it was against the middleweight champion or somebody else. He had offers to defend his welterweight crown against Gasper Ortega in Los Angeles or in Boston against Tony DeMarco again. Good money fights, but nowhere near the kind of money he would receive by crossing gloves with Robinson. Significantly for Ray, he would receive the purse fee he had been demanding.

Carmen Basilio was born in February 1927 in Canastota, New York but was based in Chittenango. He was a 5 feet 6 inches tall block of concrete, and a throwback to the brine-skinned old-timers who were as tough as old boots; he seemed to care little about who he fought and even less about their reputation. He told the journalists that he "had a score to settle with the champion for the brush-off" he had received in 1953 and stated that "he is arrogant and needs bringing down a few pegs." He had served his apprenticeship to gain the position he now found himself in and the fans loved his style of fighting. He had beaten the former lightweight king, Ike Williams, before losing a fifteen round decision to Kid Gavilan and then beating Tony DeMarco for the world welterweight title. Robinson claimed that Basilio was a favourite of Jim Norris, and that Norris hoped Basilio could beat Sugar Ray and become a double champion.

He was astutely managed by John DeJohn and Joe Netro. The two managers, Norris and his IBC officials met to discus the Robinson situation. The champion was demanding 47-and-a-half percent of all the net receipts, plus back payments he maintained the IBC owed him for European and Latin American showings of the film of his first fight with Gene Fullmer in January 1957. Everyone present at the meeting knew Robinson v Basilio would be a huge money-spinner for all concerned (The fight was expected to draw a gate of over a million dollars) but Basilio would have to drop his demand for 30 percent. It was pointed out that even if Norris could get Robinson to accept 40 percent, the IBC would still be paying out 65 percent of the receipts, an unprecedented amount. Norris phoned Sugar Ray and asked if he would meet at the IBC's office to discus the new terms. After agreeing, he failed to show up. When reporters heard the news they tried to contact Robinson but couldn't, so they spoke to Joe Glaser instead. He told reporters that Robinson would meet Norris within 48 hours and hoped to put pen to paper and sign the contract. However, more bitterness and controversy was in store.

Robinson eventually met Jim Norris in his office on the second floor in Madison Square Garden. He told Norris he could get more money from another Theatre Network company than the one the IBC were using. Of course news of this new argument reached the newspapers and journalists were not slow to fill their columns with the bitter conflict. Ray was perceived as a 'Prima Donna' out of control. In an effort to try and save the fight and bring the bitter wrangling to a conclusion, Commissioner Julius Helfand was summoned both Robinson and the IBC to a meeting. Sugar Ray then announced that he would like the meeting to be 'open' so that the press could attend. The meeting took place on the 28th June and it was reported by journalists that Robinson's speech and the way he presented his case would have 'brought forth cries of admiration from the floor of the Wall Street Stock Exchange. "He certainly showed how to market his product," recalled one journalist, which of course was himself! Norris told the hearing that Basilio had voluntary given up a further five percent of the 25 percent that he had originally signed for. Robinson ended up getting the best deal of his career. $228,666 as his 45 percent of the live attendance, $255,000 from the theatre and television, plus $30,000 from the radio and film rights. It was also revealed that Norris had advanced Robinson $30,000 on the strength of the proposed match.

"Ray will beat Basilio quite easily," said George Gainford a few hours before the fight. "Ray will jab him, feint, dodge, stick and move, stick and move."

When the famed ring announcer Johnny Addie bellowed out his introductions there was a distinct tingle of excited anticipation around the huge Yankee Stadium, which contained 38,000 expectant spectators, which was dwarfed by the 174 theatres in 131 US cities which allowed a further half million people to watch the proceedings. As Addie announced Sugar Ray the vast crowd cheered lustily. Carmen, heavily unshaven, received muted roars as he entered the ring wearing a plain white cotton dressing gown, unlike Robinson's glitzy velvet gown. Referee Al Berl called them both together and issued his final instructions, and as he finished, the beetle-browed Basilio looked like a desperado straight out of a spaghetti western; his resentment and undiluted hatred for Robinson was almost palpable as he strained at the leash to begin his furious assault. Journalist Peter Wilson later wrote that Basilio's whole body language gave the message that "you can best me but only if you take my heart out of my body, and then you'll have to trample on it before it will stop beating."

Up until the day before the fight, Basilio was the heavy betting favourite, but his odds were reduced to even money on the actual day of the fight. Most of the betting, however, was based on the expectation of a knockout being the deciding factor. Basilio's backers believed that Carmen would eventually wear the aged Robinson down with his non-stop attacks, whilst those who championed Robinson thought that he would win the fight with one telling punch. Nobody anticipated that it would go the full distance and when the fight began, these calculations looked accurate as both men threw themselves into the fray immediately. The challenger won the opening two rounds as he consistently beat Robinson to the punch. As the bell signalled the end of the second round, Basilio aimed a late shot at Robinson which sparked heated protests from both camps. Early in the fourth, Sugar Ray, who was absorbing Basilio's shots with surprising resilience, opened up on Basilio and when they emerged from their close-quarter confrontation, Basilio sported an ugly gash over his left eye. After a bout of in-fighting Sugar Ray caught Carmen with a foul body punch. The champion shouted: "Did that hurt you?" The onion farmer smiled, and sneered, "Naw, do it again and I'll show you what happens!" Basilio was enraged when the Harlem flash did land another low punch and attempted to butt Robinson in revenge; he settled down to win the fifth by some distance and looked like he might edge ahead on the scorecards, but in the thrilling see-sawing battle, Robinson rallied in the next round and thrilled the crowd with a wonderful exhibition of flawless boxing which drew him back into the fight. There was no quarter asked for or received throughout the whole fight as both men mixed some savage fouls in amongst their repertoire.

A curious rhythm seemed to emerge from the frenetic pace where both men appeared to take it in turns to inflict damage on the other. Robinson blasted away with hooks to the kidneys from either fist and he caused Basilio to hold on a couple of occasions when he wobbled him. The iron-willed Basilio would just not be subdued and he would then surge forward with an awesome strength as he mixed his attacks between Robinson's slender body and his head. Despite his age, Robinson's durability surprised Basilio and many ringside observers. In the ninth, Basilio attempted to rough up his opponent by pushing his head into his face, and so Robinson retaliated with low kidney punching which finally forced referee Berl to intervene and issue a stern warning to both. Robinson held out his hands in a theatrical token of apology but Basilio knocked them away with a withering contempt.

The eleventh and twelfth rounds were two of the finest rounds ever witnessed in the history of the sport as both continued to take turns to rock each other. Basilio had blood dripping from his gashed left eye but ploughed on in a relentless metronomic fashion and Robinson continued to snap out repellent jabs from his hands which had started to dangle lower, as if he had weights in both of his gloves. But they produced an exhibition of box-fighting not seen for quite some time. In the twelfth, Robinson dredged up his full reserves and delivered a series of right uppercuts that possessed power and deadly accuracy. Basilio ducked low down to try and avoid them, but he gave signs that he was tired and weary for the first time. At the end of these six absorbing minutes, both fighters had Basilio's blood smothered all over them. Despite his injuries and fatigue threatening to overwhelm him, Basilio drove forward relentlessly. Robinson caught him with one left hook which almost dropped the former Marine and a further right hand piledriver to his body hurt him visibly and it finally looked as if he was going down, but he resisted and fought back like a wounded tiger. When the bell rang out to end the fifteen round X-rated thriller, it was difficult to hear it such was the din made the crowd, who sensed that they had witnessed something truly remarkable unfold before them.

The swinging action of the fight and the trading of momentum between both warriors made it a tough battle to score and the judges were as split as the huge audience which had witnessed it. Judges Artie Aidala and Bill Retch both voted for Basilio; Aidala thought he had won it by nine rounds to five but Retch believed that Basilio had won eight rounds to six. Referee Al Berl, who was closer to the action, thought that Robinson had won nine rounds to Basilio's six. These scores ensured the coronation of a new middleweight champion of the world. Angelo Dundee hoisted Carmen up as the winner was officially announced, as George Gainford was shouting "Robbery!" and complained to the referee Al Berl that an illegal substance had been put in the Vaseline.

"It was rough...It Was tough...It was Brutal," said Peter Wilson. "In all my life, so much of which has been spent at the ringsides of the world, I can't recall a better fight than this one, where Carmen Basilio took the world middleweight title from Sugar Ray Robinson. This was an 'X' certificate fight. If the two men had been armed with knuckledusters or razors or sharpened bicycle chains instead of leather boxing gloves, one of them would have been killed... I Think It Would Have Been Robinson. Because Basilio fought the kind of fight which a man is born to fight just once."

Robinson was dejected. He thought that he had won the fight and feared that his status as a challenger would weaken his position in future negotiations with Jim Norris and the IBC. Furthermore, the Internal Revenue Service quickly confiscated all of his money directly from the IBC and both Ernie

Braca and Joe Glaser announced that they were filing lawsuits against him for their financial dues. Basilio confirmed that there was an agreement for a return bout between them to be organised within ninety days. He was still bitter about his treatment during the negotiations and declared that he planned to wait for a while before making any firm decisions. He said that he felt that this fight had vindicated him and British reporter Peter Wilson agreed: "In the hour he spent in the glimmering oasis of canvas, clutched by the dark shadows of this mighty stadium, Carmen Basilio justified his birth, his marriage, and his thirty years on earth. If he had dropped dead when he walked down the ring steps, and don't think that couldn't have happened, he would have left a memorial more lasting than those they put up in concrete or metal. A memorial in the hearts of all those thousands privileged enough to see him."

******

Robinson's tax problems continued to cause him considerable worry as he could see no obvious and immediate way out of his predicament and had heard other rumours that the income tax authorities were also planning to confiscate his purse money from the upcoming Basilio fight. He appeared to be constantly on edge and would often fly into a wild rage at the slightest provocation and he began to direct his rage towards Edna Mae. He employed the services of one of the country's leading lawyers, Edward Bennett Williams. He grimly accepted that the legal help would not come cheaply, but he felt that he had no other option but to seek his services.

He also discovered that his beloved sister, Marie, was suffering with terminal cancer. He rushed to the hospital and spoke to her doctor, who calmly informed him that she had only four or five months to live. He was absolutely heartbroken; she was his big sister, who had given him her share of food when they were kids when they didn't have enough money to buy sufficient supplies; the sister who had fought his battles against older and bigger kids when he was an infant; she had been like a mother to him.

As Marie's condition deteriorated, Ray phoned his father in Detroit and arranged for him to come to Harlem and stay with Edna Mae and himself. One morning during his visit, his father reported hearing slapping noises and screams emanating from the room next door. It was Sugar Ray slapping his wife, and Walker Smith hurried into the room and tried to stop his son from hitting his wife, who was hysterical. When he grabbed hold of him, Edna Mae dashed downstairs and called the police, who arrived within minutes. They were visibly shocked to find out that the perpetrator was Sugar Ray Robinson. Ray immediately turned on his famous charm and offered them drinks and hospitality before signing photographs for them and persuading them not to press charges.

Ray Junior later suggested that his mother had suffered five miscarriages because of the abuse which she was forced to suffer. The abuse claims were a shock to those close to the couple. Whenever the couple were out in public they appeared to be in a loving, caring relationship. It later emerged that Edna Mae would go to great lengths to hide the bruises with make-up to ensure that the trouble between them very rarely reached the newspapers and remained strictly under wraps.

Despite Basilio's initial hesitancy to commit to a return, he was legally obliged to fight on the 25th March 1958 in one of Robinson's favourite venues, the Chicago Stadium. Negotiations had been far less fraught without Robinson in the driving seat and Basilio agreed to accept a 30% share of the purse. He was niggled that Robinson, despite being the challenger, still managed to get an equal share because of a clause he had inserted in the contracts for the original fight that ensured he was on the same guarantee as Basilio for any rematch.

Despite scoring some of his greatest victories in Chicago, Robinson was a little more circumspect when he considered his chances of repeating one of his epic nights. "This is my 156th fight in over eighteen years of boxing," he clarified. "I'm almost 38 and my legs are just a little bit slower but my fists are still as fast as ever they were." The betting money didn't think he could do it, but this didn't appear to faze Robinson. "The only time I haven't been an underdog since I came back was against Tiger Jones and that guy gave me a licking," he said. Basilio weighed at a lean 10 stones 13 pounds for the fight whilst Robinson was nearly half a stone heavier at 11 stones 5¾ pounds. Robinson explained that "he would rather give away nine pounds than nine years" to beat Basilio, whose own strategy was centred on attacking his opponent's body because he believed that Robinson had been struggling to make the middleweight limit. Indeed, Basilio's instinct was correct and Sugar Ray had been forced to forego eating any food for almost twenty hours before the final weigh-in. At the final press conference, the esteemed British reporter Reg Gutteridge managed to get a few words with Basilio and asked him where he planned to get away and rest after the contest. His words were a chilling premonition of the war he planned to wage. "At the nearest hospital," he answered. "Because that son of a bitch Robinson will be fighting rough and so will I. There's no way I am getting out of there without being badly cut up."

On the Saturday afternoon prior to the fight, Sugar Ray was supposed to be relaxing in the Conrad Hilton Hotel. At the same time, Truman Gibson, Jim Norris's right hand man, was allowing himself a few hours private time where he could forget about the preparations for the fight. He and Norris had declared themselves pleased with the smooth running of the event. His phone rang and Truman answered the call from Robinson, who instructed the IBC official that he wished to collect his $200,000 purse in cash within the next 24 hours. Gibson later admitted that he was staggered by this incredible demand. He explained to the fight legend that even if he had the necessary authority to get that amount of money, the practicalities of obtaining it were more difficult because all banks were closed for the weekend. Robinson, however, appeared nonplussed and answered, "Your own bank isn't closed." Sugar Ray had done some investigating of his own and discovered that Norris and his business partner, Arthur Wirtz, actually controlled a Chicago bank. Robinson demanded that Norris issue authority to open the bank and have the cash delivered to his hotel room. Gibson attempted to placate him and begged him tom wait until Monday, but he was adamant that his demands were complied with or he would call off the fight. Several minutes of frantic phone calls later, Gibson phoned Robinson and confirmed that he would bring the money to his room the following day but explained that Robinson would have to make his own security arrangements. "Thank you, Truman," said a clearly delighted Sugar Ray, "I'm proud of you."

A short time after he had finished counting the money, Frank Sinatra called his room and asked whether the fight would be going ahead. He had heard rumours in Las Vegas that he had withdrawn suffering from a virus and Sinatra wanted to know whether his custmary bet on Robinson was safe. Sugar Ray assured him that he was fine. He neglected to mention that the information was disturbingly correct as he was suffering with a virus and was required to have a couple of penicillin injections from Dr. Nardiello.

The day before the fight, the opinionated broadcaster, Howard Cosell, a self-professed expert on anything and everything, was doing a preview for the television. Cosell had a distinctive, whining, nasally - some would say, irritating - voice and wore a badly-fitting toupee, and he managed to obtain an interview with Basilio. He pulled the fighter in towards him and, with a condescending smirk on his face and microphone in his hand, said, "Carmen, I have polled ten newspaper reporters for their opinions on who they think will win, and they all pick Robinson. What have you got to say about that?" Basilio looked unfazed and quickly replied that "ten of them are wrong". He turned away.

There was a late winter chill to the night when 18,000 fans made their way to their seats in the Chicago Stadium, which glared down onto the scarlet-roped ring which was surrounded by over one hundred blazing arc lights. A straw polling of thirty four sportswriters situated around the ring revealed that twenty one of them believed that Basilio would emerge victorious once again. Sugar Ray jigged down to the ring swathed in his dressing gown. He looked immaculate, prompting one report to compare him to "a black Clark Gable". In contrast, the champion made his entrance by marching purposefully towards the ring flanked by a posse of men looking like policemen. His stumpy frame and his battle-scared face were a contrast to the smooth Robinson. What was unmistakable, however, was the determined look both men wore, which made their intentions obvious to even the most disinterested observer: they had come to fight. Ben Bentley was the evening's announcer and when he handed over to Frank Sikora, the silver-haired referee, to issue the mandatory commands, neither man acknowledged him but fixed each other with scowls. Sikora had to repeat his demand that they touch gloves before returning to their respective corners.

The chimes of the opening bell were barely audible as the crowd, sensing the mutual antipathy which existed between the two men, had started their guttural roaring before it had even sounded. The sole intention for both was to hammer the other into abject submission and walk away victorious, and there was no attempt to ease their way into the fight as they immediately began to hit each other with punches to the head, body, kidneys and even below the belt; they locked their gloves around each others necks, tried to butt each other and transgressed every rule in the book in what was described as "a real 'Pier Six' brawl of undiluted violence." Even after the bell to end the round was rung, they carried on brawling until separated by the fight official. Chaos erupted outside the ring too. Honey Brewer, one of Robinson's cornermen, who had been delegated to watch that there was no underhand or foul play by Basilio's seconds, began to scream that Basilio was repeatedly fouling until Joe Netro, Basilio's rotund manager, physically threw him out of the corner. Reg Gutteridge captured the mayhem perfectly in his analysis. "Basilio, a fighter with the crude insistence of Rocky Marciano, hated Robinson because the ring's black prince had forced him to compete for comparative pittance pay. The first round was the most spiteful I can ever recall. Both unloaded their nurtured hate. Basilio, who seemed to resent the inhibiting presence of a referee, tore at Robinson like a wild dog that had been let off the lead. Rule books had been parked at the front gate because Basilio's blows landed in forbidden parts, his head bore into Sugar Ray's face and chest. Robinson looked appealingly at the referee who merely waved play on, so Sugar departed from his text-book style and contributed his share of butting, elbowing, and added rabbit-punching. They fought furiously, and deliberately, long after the first round had ended and had to be prised apart."

Carmen Basilio began the second session in his usual manner of creating all-out mayhem for Robinson. It was clear that his fight plan was to hustle and attempt to wear down the older man by continually crowding him and hooking to Robinson's head and body with all of the power from his sturdy frame packed into each thumping punch in the hope that just one would stop the challenger. Up until the fourth, the fight ebbed and flowed in a similar manner to the first fight as each man tried to gain the advantage. Robinson was the first to seize the initiative when he flayed away with a catalogue of bolo punches and numerous uppercuts and one of these punches caught Basilio straight over his left eye, causing the eye to instantly begin to close and a huge swelling to appear. This forced Basilio to change his strategy. In order to get a clearer view of his enigmatic opponent, he was forced to stand square on, which was fatal against such a sharp puncher. Robinson did not need a second invitation to grasp this advantage and he exploited it fully by standing side-on and employing his left jab to remain in the face of Basilio.

Basilio was courage personified as by the seventh round he was fighting with just one eye as his other was closed tightly. Robinson's thoughts of a quick victory were dismissed by the lion-hearted Basilio, who gave notice of his devastating capabilities by absorbing all of the punishment and then occasionally lashing out with left hooks to the head and body. His grotesque eye injury and the forced change of approach negated his own equalising punch, the left hook, which allowed Robinson to focus instead on catching him with whiplash combinations. He would use lightning fast left jabs and then suddenly switch the jab into a left hook to the right side of Basilio's body. Time after time, the champion was clearly hurt and his knees seemed to turn to jelly but he would spring back at Robinson like a wounded tiger. From the halfway stage, Robinson started to feel the pace and started to hold on at every opportunity and would gulp down a lungful of air. He knew that he was winning this contest and realised that keeping his head would ensure that he would make boxing history by being a world champion again.

In the tenth round, Basilio seemed to sense that the dark shroud of defeat was about to envelope him and so threw all caution to the wind. He launched one left hook which Robinson anticipated and countered with his own response, a fast right cross which connected on Carmen's jaw, followed by two sizzling left hooks which sent Basilio reeling across the ring. Just when it seemed that a knockout was imminent, the brave little fighter bit down on his gumshield and tore back into Robinson with a combination of two-handed punches firing out like machine gun bullets. Amazingly, Robinson didn't go down but instead showed his own remarkable resilience, catching the champion with two vicious right hand punches followed by an awesome left hook and two more right hand smashes that all hit their intended target, leaving Basilio's left eye horribly discoloured, like a piece of raw liver. Robinson looked stunned that he still hadn't ended the fight and George Gainford had to work hard to maintain his morale at the break.

For the last four rounds, neither man conceded an inch in their quest for victory. Robinson caught Basilio once with such a thudding right cross on the edge of his jaw it saw him shudder and walk straight into another right hand which would have felled a horse, yet he continued plodding forward. Basilio, the former onion farmer, responded in the next round by cocking his right hand and unleashing it straight at Robinson with a thunderous crack, which caused the spectators to jump out of their seats in anticipation of a knockdown which never materialised. Sugar Ray soon got back on his toes and started delivering his punches in combinations again. Carmen tried to burrow underneath them, to avoid further damage to his eye and the mask of swelling which his face had become, by bobbing and weaving but Robinson changed tack and started bringing his punches upwards; one tremendous uppercut hit Basilio on the chin and straightened him up immediately. Still, the former American Marine would not surrender; he was going out with his pride.

The venue was a wall of sound when the fifteenth and final round began. Robinson left his corner with George Gainford's reminder ringing in his ears that he was three minutes away from becoming the world champion for a record fifth time, and he carried on from before, punishing the proud champion who only had minutes to go before he would surrender his reign as the middleweight champion of the world. A lightning fast right hand almost separated Basilio's head from his shoulders and brought howls from the fans, who now wanted to see the champion finish the thrilling encounter upright and on his feet. Robinson showed no such mercy and, within seconds, connected with a whistling left hook special straight into the solar-plexus, which sent Basilio jack-knifing upwards. When the bell sounded to bring an end to one of the finest fights in the entire history of boxing, the whole arena, knowing that it had witnessed something remarkable unveil itself before them, stood and paid homage to two unforgettable champions. Both warriors looked consumed by fatigue and had to be helped by their cornermen.

There was dismay when the scores were finally announced as the referee, Frank Sikora, had somehow given the fight to Basilio by nine rounds to five with just one round classed as even. Booing and whistling were heard throughout as this scoring was declared. Judge John Bray offered a wildly different perspective by awarding Robinson the fight by eleven rounds to four, while fellow judge, Frank McAdams, had it for Robinson by ten rounds to four with one round even. When Ben Bentley declared the decision in favour of the new champion and lifted Sugar Ray Robinson's left hand in victory, the crowded arena cheered in agreement. Basilio left the ring with help from his loyal followers and was quickly escorted back to the sanctity of his changing rooms where he could be treated. Equally, as he left the ring to return to his dressing room, Robinson was feted every step of the way and he tried to walk, to no avail without the assistance of his seconds. His chin was sagging, his legs were like jelly and his face was distorted in a grim mixture of pain and exhaustion. It was an hour before he was capable of speaking to anyone.

In the changing room, Robinson was besieged by reporters who wanted to hear his views. Lying on a table and having his legs rubbed to restore life to them, he was finally able to speak to them and told them that "Carmen had given me the hardest fight of my life since I won the title from Jake LaMotta." In contrast, Basilio sat in his dressing room with his head bowed and an ice pack held against his injured left eye with tears trickling down his lumpy face as he answered questions. He told the press that "Robinson never hurt me once." His opinion was that if it had not been for the injury to his eye he would have repeated his first victory over Sugar Ray. "I know I'll beat him again if he will fight me for a third time," he said. He was then whisked away to spend several days in a Chicago hospital to recuperate.

'Amazing! Marvellous!' wrote Ring editor Nat Fleischer, who went on to say it was a great accomplishment by Robinson, but he was certain neither Sugar Ray nor Carmen Basilio would ever appear in a fight again. He said Basilio had been examined by several doctors who predicted that for the preservation of his eyesight, it would be best if Carmen hung up his gloves. "Robinson challenged a much younger fighter and ring precedent and he triumphed over each. No other world champion ever won a world crown more than three times." He said Basilio was favoured to repeat his first victory because of his age advantage and because he was rougher and more rugged, but determination, the will to reach a goal never before attained and faith in his ability enabled Sugar Ray to turn the tables. "Sugar Ray Robinson is the Wonder of the Roped Square," he concluded.

The British journalist, Peter Wilson, who was held in respect by Robinson, was one of the few reporters granted access to the reposed champion's hotel bedroom a few hours after the fight. Robinson was in a reflective mood when he said, "I don't know whether I'll ever fight again." He acknowledged, however, that it was too soon to decide. He revealed that he "felt as if ten men had attacked me; every bone in my body is aching and I'm sore all over, even my feet." He told Wilson that he didn't want to make a final decision about his future plans for a few days or possibly weeks. The only issue about the fight which roused him to anger was when he spoke about Frank Sikora's scoring for the fight. Peter Wilson's reporting of these thoughts only included the line that they were unprintable! Robinson, however, paid tribute to the tenacity of Basilio and claimed that the only stage of the fight when he had felt certain that he was winning was when 'the man said - the winner and new champion.'"

Reg Gutteridge's view was that when champions like Robinson and Basilio fought, there was more at stake than money. They fought for pride, he said. He believed that Carmen and Ray genuinely disliked each other and fought to hurt each other. He said they might even have fought each other for nothing, except for interfering managers. Carmen Basilio wanted a vast audience to witness him beating up a man who he described as being "despised by other fighters". He said that Basilio, a fighter with the crude insistence of a Rocky Marciano, hated Robinson because the ring's 'black prince' forced him to accept pittance money. In his opinion the first round was the most spiteful he could recall. "Both unloaded nurtured hate," he said. Basilio disregarded the referee and tore after Sugar Ray like a wild dog that had been let off the lead. "Rule books had been parked at the front gate because Basilio's punches landed in forbidden parts, his head into Robinson's face and chest. Robinson looked appealingly at the referee who merely waved play on, so Sugar Ray departed from his text-book style and contributed his share of butting, elbowing, and rabbit-punching." He finished by saying it was a great fight and he had Robinson the winner.

Towards the end of 1958 Jim Norris became increasingly desperate to get Sugar Ray to agree to a third meeting with Carmen Basilio. Deep down Robinson didn't want another gruelling physical confrontation with the irrepressible former onion farmer; he was also aware that Norris's IBC Empire was beginning to crumble and so he was reluctant to commit himself. He started the negotiations by demanding a ridiculous purse and stalled for time in refusing to compromise. Norris became increasingly agitated because they were under investigation by the government for the practises and the way they maintained their monopoly of the sport until finally, on the 12th January 1959, The International Boxing Club was dissolved and Norris and his business partner, Arthur Wirtz, were forced to sell their interest in Madison Square Garden. This decision privately thrilled Robinson, especially as the new owners quickly appointed Harry Markson as the managing director of the newly-named Madison Square Garden Boxing Club. Markson was respected and known throughout boxing as a straight and honest operator. Markson immediately declared that if he could clinch a third Robinson versus Basilio fight "it would be a feather in the cap for Madison Square Garden."

In later life, Robinson claimed that he attended a meeting in Harlem with Madison Square matchmaker Teddy Brenner, Harry Markson, Ned Irish, who was the new president of Madison Square Garden and Admiral John H. Bergen, the esteemed chairman of the Garden's board. The meeting took place in Ray's Seventh Avenue office and before the discussions began, Admiral Bergen made a show of presenting Robinson with a new set golf clubs; the Admiral was an admirer of the fighter and had even played a few rounds of golf with him. When the negotiations began, the MSG team offered Sugar Ray $500,000 dollars to fight the rubber match with Basilio, which was the most money they had ever offered outside of the heavyweight division. Robinson sat poker-faced and casually told them this wasn't enough. He told them that he believed he could get $750,000 for the fight. Eventually, when they realised that he was not prepared to compromise, Admiral Bergen broke off negotiations and told Robinson, "The only thing you have to sell is Sugar Ray Robinson. If you can get more than $500,000 for a fight, then go right ahead." Robinson was not bluffing. Irving Kahn, a smooth operator who had close ties with close-circuit television, had been in contact and had, indeed, been mentioning such astronomical fees, which had dazzled Sugar Ray. This would later prove to be a very costly mistake for him. At the same time, General Melvin Krulewitch, the newly-elected chairman of the New York State Athletic Commission, began to threaten to strip Robinson of his title because he had made no plans to defend it. Robinson was forced to produce certified documents and a cheque, made out to Carmen Basilio, as his share of his purse for the proposed third meeting between them.

Also during this period, he started to hatch an audacious plan to fight Archie Moore, the light-heavyweight champion of the world. He invited Moore and his wife to dinner and to talk boxing business. Being a natural showman, he told Moore that he had a proposition which would "make him (Moore) more money than he had ever earned before." Curious, Moore asked how much and almost fell of his chair when the figure of $250,000 was suggested. Hooked by now, Archie asked who he would fight for this purse and nearly fell again when he heard the answer. "We will fight each other," declared a beaming Robinson; he went on to explain his plan to beam the fight into America's cinemas. The light heavyweight champion listened intently before he asked Robinson what his purse would be; Robinson, sporting a melon-sized grin, answered that he himself would take a cool $750,000. The negotiations ended as suddenly as they had begun. Moore was indignant that he, the champion, was only receiving a quarter of the purse. He left immediately and shortly afterwards signed to fight a return with the Canadian, Yvon Durelle, for the same amount Robinson had offered.

It wasn't just Archie Moore who was offended by Robinson's parsimony. Both Carmen Basilio and Gene Fullmer were frustrated and highly critical of him, too. Both men believed that he ruined their plans for return fights which would have earned them their biggest ever paydays and set them up financially for the remainder of their lives. They both blamed his greed and egocentricity for ruining the plans and so Basilio and Fullmer arranged to fight each other instead. The persistent rumours remained about a third showdown fight but Robinson knew that they would both be finished if they completed forty five rounds. In fact, Basilio only fought eight more times after his final encounter with Robinson.

******

As he heralded in the new year of 1959, he allowed himself a pause for reflection. He had appeared as a guest singer on a few television shows and he had started to think of pursuing a career as a crooner in the style of Billy Echstine or Nat King Cole. He had even been rehearsing with a voice coach and talked at length about returning to showbusiness. He realised, however, that the serious money for him was still in boxing. He hadn't fought since winning back his title from Carmen Basilio nine months earlier in March and he was unsure about which direction to take.

Undeterred by his earlier aborted meeting and negotiations, after Archie Moore had successfully defended his light-heavyweight title against the Canadian fisherman, Yvon Durelle, in the Montreal Forum in a memorable fight in which Moore had been knocked down three times in the first round and again in the fifth before rising from almost certain defeat and knocking out the brave Canadian in the eleventh round, Robinson decided to try a different tack. Moore was subsequently honoured by the Boxing Writers' Association at a dinner in the Waldorf Astoria, New York and Truman Gibson approached him to ask if he would fight Robinson. "I beat Durelle and I'm ready for Robinson. We'll make a lot of dollars," answered Moore. Despite this, negotiations could not entice both men to meet. Interestingly, Robinson's desire to fight the heavier champion caused some bemusement from his inner circle. They asked whether he had not learned his lesson after coming unstuck against Joey Maxim in 1952. Robinson believed that in the Maxim fight, he was winning quite comfortably until the intense heat had weakened him and so felt that he was now ready to try for his third world title. Others reminded him of his previous reluctance to face heavier men. When Ezzard Charles was heavyweight champion of the world, George Gainford had fancied Robinson to beat him but had been met with the response, "Are you trying to get me killed?" Gainford had also thought the same about Floyd Patterson but one day, after hearing George challenging Patterson to reporters, he had shouted, "Hey George, you fight him."

The first half of 1959 involved a great deal of political wrangling. Basilio, still seeking revenge, began petitioning the New York State Athletic Commission to either force Robinson to fight him or to strip him of the title. The Commission, however, ruled that the champion had made an honest effort to afford Basilio the return bout but blamed Basilio for failing to accept the terms. The National Boxing Association did not agree and, after failing to contact Robinson to discover his plans, declared that the world middleweight title was immediately vacant. Former Robinson foes Gene Fullmer and Carmen Basilio fought each other on 28th August and Fullmer was awarded the NBA title after winning by a technical knockout in the fourteenth round.

Basilio's bitterness towards his great rival lost nothing in the passing of the years. He told Peter Heller that he wanted a third fight with Robinson, "but he'd never fight me again." He also suggested that "a third fight would probably be one of the biggest fights in the history of the middleweight division from the perspective of drawing a massive crowd response and from the money angle. There was a huge public demand for a third fight." He believed that Robinson also regretted not going through with it. "He would have got twice as much money as I would have received," said Carmen.

20.

A Prophet without honour in Harlem

A NUMBER OF newspaper journalists were regularly briefed by those who attempted to enter negotiations with Robinson and began to be openly contemptuous about the manner in which he conducted his negotiations, especially regarding the proposed third fight against Carmen Basilio. They focused upon his indifferent treatment of his opponents by insisting that they accept the lowest possible terms before he would agree to fight them; they criticized him for being greedy and arrogant, for the incessant bickering which took place before every fight, for his cantankerous approach to the press on occasions when he was not afforded his own way, the postponements on spurious reasons, all behaviour providing ammunition for the press to aim at him during this period of inactivity. One reporter from the Amsterdam News even interviewed a number of black residents from Harlem, where Robinson still lived and delighted in his reputation as being "the Prince of Harlem", and where the local residents were said to worship him. The article dismissed this as a fabrication and suggested that many local residents believed that their esteemed neighbour was "far too vain" and often "walked about the area with desperation to be recognized and adored." The Amsterdam News report was a damning and devastating dismissal of the respect which Robinson had craved and which he felt was assured amongst his own people. It concluded with the summary that "the folks of Harlem will tell you that as a boxer, he is great. As a person, however, there is something superficial about him which falls way below the public acclaim."

This criticism was reported to have privately wounded Robinson. In public, however, he disguised this and argued, "I have no control over what people think about me." His admitted that his "only concern is for Sugar Ray Robinson and my family." It was, however, an issue which caused him some consternation. He knew that he was admired and respected for his ring prowess, but that there was something in his aloof and superior manner which seemed to prevent that respect spilling over into his personal life, unlike what had been afforded the old champions, such as Jack Dempsey and his friend Joe Louis, years after their retirements.

A Prophet without honour in Harlem

On the 14th December, a full twenty-one months after the torrid encounter against Basilio, Robinson finally returned to the square circle in a scheduled ten-round non-title contest held at the Boston Garden against Bob Young of Providence, Rhode Island. He had finally agreed to defend his crown against Massachusetts's Paul Pender on 22nd January 1960, and accepted that he needed a warm-up fight to regain his rhythm. The idea was for Pender to also fight on the same Boston bill in order to help build up the anticipation and the gate receipts for when they met.

At the weigh-in for the Young fight, Robinson arrived looking resplendent in a stylish camel-hair overcoat and sporting a groomed moustache and beard. He greeted Young with a warmth and cordiality usually reserved for close friends. He wished the Providence fighter good luck for their meeting and left Young in awe at meeting a living legend. The 28-year old was the light-heavyweight champion of New England and was coming in on the back of a loss to Tony Anthony and was expected to extend Robinson into the later rounds. In the press conference, he revealed that he had merely been "pleased to meet the champ."

Pender fulfilled his obligations by easily outpointing Gene Hamilton from the Bronx, but it was Robinson whom the 6,633 crowd had come to see. The fight began at a leisurely pace and Young displayed some composure to test his illustrious opponent and caught him with his long, looping left jab and the occasional left hook. During the first interval, Robinson expressed his annoyance at letting himself get tagged so easily and came out with a grim resolve. He carefully measured the tall figure of Young before letting fly with a chilling left hook, which deposited his man on the canvas for a count of nine. Young's instinct forced him back up but he knew that it was a matter of time as Sugar Ray returned back to the ring apron a further two times before the referee, Eddie Bradley, signalled that the fight was over. "When I missed with all those punches in the first round, I realized that I was rusty," he explained immediately after the conclusion. "I didn't want to take any more chances when I knew I could be reached so easily, and that's why I decided to end it in the second." He admitted that his training had consisted of a "lot of roadwork but only twenty five rounds of sparring in preparation for this fight." He acknowledged that he would have to improve when he met Paul Pender.

******

Paul Pender was born in Brookline, Massachusetts on the 20th June 1930. By the time he had earned his opportunity to fight for the world middleweight championship, he had been boxing professionally for nearly eleven years. His journey had been an eventful one after he had been spotted by a former professional fighter, named Red Priest, boxing on a bootleg tournament. Priest had told his old and experienced manager Johnny Buckley that he had seen a genuine prospect and both men convinced him to box legitimately. Pender had made no secret of his deep loathing for professional boxing and openly admitted that he was in the sport for one reason only, to make as much money as possible. He told reporters that he "despised boxing with a passion" and confessed that "if I could have found another way to make a living, I would never have laced on the gloves." At the beginning of his career he had been plagued by brittle bones in his hands and had broken his right hand four times and his left, three. These injuries had forced his retirement on four different occasions, but he returned each time when he needed to earn some money to support his childhood sweetheart, Rose, and his two children, Paul and Joyce. He had also worked as a fireman for the Brookline Fire Department and just before he fought Robinson, he had passed his exams to become a policeman in his local town.

He was vocal about the dubious business practises he saw within the sport and suggested that "no manager should take a big percentage of a purse" (this was an era when managers regularly claimed up to 50% of a purse) and he suggested that "the worst thing that has ever happened to managers was the day when boxers started to learn how to read and write." He believed that the sport should have been suspended for a five-year period to purge it of the unscrupulous characters which inhabited it and then started afresh. In one frank interview with Bud Collins of the Boston Herald, before the Robinson fight, he stated that it was a sport "infested by gangsters and thieves which the public has lost all confidence in." He was ordered to appear before the Massachusetts State Boxing Commission to explain his comments and was subsequently reprimanded. He later claimed that he had spoken out to try and make a difference, and "not for any kind of glory, because all the other fighters can have that as much as they want." When he heard that the Tennessee senator, Estes Kefauver, was to chair a committee which would investigate boxing and its malpractices, he expressed his delight.

His sporadic fighting career had involved a number of respected opponents, including a loss and a draw against Joe Rindone, the fighter Sugar Ray had made his comeback against in 1955. He had also been knocked out by Eugene Harrison in three rounds and had also been flattened by Jimmy Beau, which left him so disgusted that he made his first retirement decision. He came back to lose to Gene Fullmer on points after he had injured his left hand and broken his right during the fight. He retired again to become a fireman and resisted the overtures from the veteran manager Johnny Buckley to return. It was an unusual incident which changed his mind. One night, Pender was out with his wife when three men began to cause trouble. Pender ended up pasting the three troublemakers and was amazed that his fragile hands hadn't caused him any distress. He, therefore, decided to embark on the comeback that would lead him into facing Sugar Ray Robinson for the world crown. He was not regarded as a crowd pleaser as his style was careful and calculating as he used what resources he had to the very best of his ability. The pre-fight betting, therefore, had the twenty-nine year old Pender as a 6-1 underdog, which didn't appear to bother him in the slightest; he even backed himself to win with a $2,000 bet. He even declared that if he failed to take the middleweight crown away from Robinson, he would retire from boxing for good.

A couple of days before boxing Paul Pender, Jimmy Cannon headlined his article in the New York Journal as 'The Greatest Comeback': "Jazz should be the language used to describe the pilgrimage Ray Robinson, the greatest fighter of modern times, made from retirement to the middleweight championship of the world. It is the most thrilling and profitable comeback in all the seasons of sports. Only Massachusetts and New York still recognized him as world champion. When Robinson was young, he was the perfect fighter. He had a variety of punches, stamina, speed, courage, agility, zeal, and knowledge of his trade, savagery, durability, toughness, meanness, serenity, coldness, rhythm, grace and controlled competitive fury. He could box or slug and knock a man out with either hand, put combinations of punches together and protect himself with a variety of defences."

He then mentioned Sugar Ray's private life. When Robinson retired in 1953, Joe Glaser booked the former champion into nightclubs for a fee of $15,000 a week, and he was eventually pushed out. "Glaser threatened to foreclose on Robinson's real-estate before a scheduled of payment was arranged. Although Braca estimated his ten percent entitled him to $120,000, he eventually settled for $18,000 when Robinson abruptly informed him he was no longer a shareholder in the profits of his comeback." Cannon said he was speaking to Braca a few days before the Pender fight: "'I hear Ray is friendly with Glaser again.' But Glaser said he wanted no part of Robinson. 'I wouldn't take a piece of him (Robinson) for nothing. But what a great fighter he is.' It seemed even those who detested Sugar Ray agree on that point," said Cannon. The columnist mentioned the time Jim Norris suffered his heart attack, which many believed was due to Robinson's aggravation. "Sugar Ray paid the wealthy tycoon a visit. After exchanging pleasantries Robinson looking concerned and said: 'Jim, I want you to get well.' 'I will,' Norris replied, 'If you let me.' On another occasion Robinson vilified Norris, whose wealth was estimated at $250 million dollars with a series of insults. 'How can you stand for that?' a member of his staff asked Norris after Sugar Ray left.

Smiling, the handsome millionaire replied: 'He's such a great fighter.'" Cannon added that it was normal for people to resent imperfection in a man who does something better than anyone else alive. "That," said Cannon, "was why Robinson rarely measured up to the image created by his public performance."

In Jimmy Cannon's opinion Paul Pender was a "pug of minor ability with hands that broke easily." He agreed that Pender at 29 moved swiftly and easily around the ring, but added, "It will be Robinson's failure or triumph. I know as much about Sugar Ray as most people and a lot more than many. But he's still a guy I can't write off with a positive identification. He's the most complicated and fascinating guy I've come upon in sports. And no matter what happens in Boston, Ray Robinson will be the greatest fighter I've ever seen."

The fight attracted 10,680 spectators and there was a palpable buzz in the atmosphere as the New England boxing fans came in the hope of seeing their man claim an unlikely victory. They knew, however, that the champion had selected to meet Paul Pender because he believed that it would offer an easy defence of his crown, and from the opening bell Robinson boxed with a confidence that he was going to be in complete control. He floated around the ring whilst snapping out his famed left jab and watching for an opportunity to bring about an early finish. Pender, meanwhile, stuck firmly to his own fight plan, which was to wear down the thirty-nine year old champion and take him into the later rounds, where he hoped that his youthful energy would tell.

The champion won the early rounds with an almost contemptuous ease but was frustrated by Pender's refusal to fight toe-to-toe with him. Whenever Robinson delivered breathtaking combinations, Pender would break off the rhythm and fall back on his plan. It soon started to become apparent in the middle and later rounds that this could reap dividends for the underdog as Robinson started to increasingly miss the target with his wayward punches and began to lose his strength. After the tenth round, Pender began to pull away and assert himself. He was the busier fighter and his jab was finding its target with greater frequency for the whole of the final five rounds. When the final bell sounded, Robinson instinctively knew the result and walked dejectedly back to his corner to await the official confirmation. The referee, Joe Zapustas, scored it in his favour by 148 points to 142, whilst in a complete reversal, the two judges, Joe Santoro and John Norton, scored it to Pender by 148 to 142. The sportswriters were similarly split in their assessments and those seated on one side of the ring scored it for Pender while those on the opposite side had Robinson as a clear winner. Paul Pender cared little for this as he was acclaimed as the new world middleweight champion.

A Prophet without honour in Harlem

Back in his dressing room, Robinson sat looking dejected with tears flowing freely down his cheeks. He wistfully reflected on the half a million dollars which he had turned down for a third encounter with Carmen Basilio and the same amount of money he had attempted to make to fight Archie Moore. When he eventually faced the reporters, he regained his composure and claimed that he had won the fight but was determined to maintain his career-long reluctance to argue with the official's decision. He instead turned his attentions to the future and insisted that he had no intention of retiring but instead wanted to take advantage of the 90-day return clause which he had insisted be included in the contract with Pender. He suggested that the return would not be staged in Boston but would more than likely take place in Madison Square Garden.

Pender's manager, the 78-year old Johnny Buckley, laughed when he heard Robinson's views. He cheerfully recounted the problems which he had endured in negotiations to get Robinson's name on to a contract and now declared that, "We are doing the dictating, no matter what any contract states." He revealed that Robinson had earned a purse of $30,874 with a further $57,437 coming from radio and television fees, whilst Pender had been forced to accept a modest $14,529 plus $9,406 from the media coverage. He agreed that Robinson would be granted a return, but that it would be staged in the Boston Garden and offered the damning indictment of the former champion by suggesting, "He's washed up and doesn't yet know it."

A few weeks after the defeat, Ray travelled to Baltimore to face the state's local hero, Tony Balcony. The Baltimore Coliseum was a complete sell out for this first time in its fifteen year history with 4,500 being crammed inside and another 2,000 fans having to be reluctantly turned away outside, which delayed the fight for over twenty minutes. Robinson stated that he was using the bout as a warm-up for his proposed return contest with Pender, but his intentions to get in some hard rounds was never realised. He opened up by hitting Baldoni with a wicked right cross that landed around the kidney area, which he followed up with a sickening punch to the midriff which was like a red-hot poker. Balcony tried to regain his feet but wished he hadn't as seconds later, a right hand hit him on the jaw and forced referee Benny Goldstein to count him out after just a minute and forty seconds. Afterwards, while getting changed, Robinson admitted that, "I had wanted to get ten rounds under my belt because I needed the work in the ring but after I realised that he wasn't going to cause me too much trouble, I couldn't carry him any longer." The local promoter, Al Flora, expressed his disappointment; he had hoped that the fight would have gone a few rounds in order to give the crowd a view of the great Robinson.

Immediately after the fight, Robinson embarked on his usual round of visiting the night spots and indulging his own celebrity. When he was about to enter his own Harlem nightclub, he had noticed a big, handsome young man waiting outside. Subsequent enquiries revealed that it was a fighter from Louisville, Kentucky, named Cassius Marcellus Clay. The youngster was regarded as a top class amateur and had been selected to represent the United States as a light-heavyweight in the imminent 1960 Olympic Games in Rome. Clay had actually waited for hours to meet his idol and when Sugar Ray drove up in his flamingo pink Cadillac, Clay hurried over to the car and immediately began to hit Robinson with a blast of his famous rhetoric about how great he was and how he intended to win a gold medal in the Olympics before winning the world heavyweight title. Robinson was off-handed and dismissive of the kid, and when Clay asked Robinson if he would become his manager, Robinson curtly explained that he was still fighting and couldn't manage him. Unperturbed, Clay said that he wanted Ray to train him and teach him all his tricks because, "Mr. Robinson, you are the best boxer ever!" Robinson laughed at the youngster's enthusiasm and fast talk and he merely wished him luck in the Olympic Games. This encounter between two of the sport's greatest exponents was recalled by Ali's own daughter, Hana Ali, in 2001. She claimed that her father had told her that "he had worshipped Sugar Ray Robinson and had waited outside a Harlem club for a whole day and night to get his autograph. When Robinson came out, he told my father that he was too busy and didn't give him the autograph."

A few weeks before the return engagement against the new champion, Paul Pender, Sugar Ray appeared before the Maryland State Athletic Commission in Baltimore to answer the charge as to why he failed to appear a few days previously for a scheduled ten round contest in the Municipal Stadium against a journeyman middleweight named Pedro Gonzales, from Rankin, Pennsylvania. This was supposed to be a tune-up fight before boxing Pender again. Before the hearing was over Robinson was in a raging temper; snarling and cursing he pushed a reporter and verbally attacked the promoter, Al Flora, owner of a local tavern and who it was claimed had lost a substantial amount of money as a result of Sugar Ray's non-appearance for the match against Gonzales. He then attempted to punch Mr Flora, then brawled with members of his own entourage and exploded an incomprehensible diatribe from the witness chair on racial bias and the Russians, showing a completely disrespectful display of bad temper. Mind you, the hearing started on a humorous note when Chairman Charles H. Rosenbaun introduced the young assistant state attorney who was to conduct a portion of the interrogations…His name? Jim Norris!

A Prophet without honour in Harlem

When Robinson was called to the witness stand, he was annoyed and straightaway launched into a long, involved explanation for his failure to return to Baltimore and go through with the contest. His main argument was he thought the proposed fight, which was postponed from the Saturday because of rain, had been cancelled a second time. "I was going to come back to honour this as I honour everything," he shouted. Then, raising his voice even higher, his persecution complex getting the best of him, he broke into a tirade of blame, mentioning racial bias and the Russians for all his problems. George Gainford followed Robinson into the witness stand to testify that he wasn't Robinson's official manager, merely his advisor. "An advisor," said 'Emperor' Gainford in that precise, imperious way of his, "is the one the fighter asks what to do and what not to do. A manager contracts for the fights and makes sure the fighter shows up. I'm Robinson's advisor." Sugar Ray was asked to return to the witness stand and Mr Norris asked him if he had ever been in trouble before for failing to turn up for fights? This touched off a further outburst. Just as Robinson was about to tell the hearing about the wonderful things he had done, he was stopped in his tracks. "Some other time," the young assistant state attorney said softly, and for the first time in this two-hour session Robinson appeared cowed.

Promoter Flora entered the witness stand and Sugar Ray insisted he be allowed to interrogate the witness. Shouting questions and brow-beating the promoter, he assumed the role of prosecuting attorney and the whole hearing became a farce. Suddenly tempers boiled over and the two men were rushing at each other. "For two cents I'd knock you out," screamed Robinson. "I don't care if you were a champion," shouted Flora, attempting to throw a punch at Robinson over the shoulder of Gainford, who had grabbed Robinson and was pinning his arms. "What a sad and sorry night," remarked Gene Ward. "This disintegration of a once great champion, who not only has lost his rare great talent but is unable to face up to the fact it is gone forever." He said he could only think with what dignity Joe Louis had made his exit from the fistic scene. When the hearing was finally over, one of Robinson's entourage took the journalist to one side and attempted to explain Sugar Ray's behaviour. "He even took a punch at me," he said, adding: "You might have behaved that way, too, if you had taken as many punches around the head as he has taken over the years." This was a sad indictment indeed!

The return with Paul Pender finally took place on the 10th June in the venue which Johnny Buckley had insisted it would, the Boston Garden. The promoter, Sam Silverman, was disappointed that only 8,422 paying punters turned out for the return, with Robinson made a 9 to 5 favourite. This was partly because it was documented that his training had gone well. Buoyed by this, Sugar Ray opened the fight by trying desperately for a knockout and in the second round he opened up a cut above the champion's left eye. Pender, however, appeared unconcerned and seemed to be boxing to his pre-determined plan, which seemed to be similar to his first fight. After the sixth session Robinson began to tire and looked to end it with one punch, but Pender anticipated most of his lunges and remained on the move and didn't allow his challenger to ever get set to land his shots. Pender was at his most effective when he pulled the tiring Robinson into the clinches, where he banged away at Robinson's face and marked him up. From the tenth round onwards, the pattern from the earlier fight was repeated. The champion forced the pace and caught his rival with stiff jabs and straight rights, while Robinson only fought in short bursts before attempting to rest in the clinches. Sugar Ray made one last desperate throw of the dice in the penultimate round when he rocked Pender with a combination to the head and body which appeared to be dredged up from his past. Pender managed to evade the more damaging punches and the effort appeared to drain Robinson, who was unable to stop the champion taking the final round with consummate ease. The scoring of the fight reflected the split nature of the contest. Referee Jimmy McCarron seemed to remember Robinson's early dominance and awarded him the fight. Judge Johnny Savko disagreed and voted for Pender. Judge Jimmy Carrig concurred and made Pender the winner on a split decision.

After getting showered and changed, a crestfallen Robinson asked for another crack at the title. "I've given Pender two chances in Boston and now I would like to fight him in New York," he requested. He disagreed with the assertion that he was outclassed and highlighted that he had Pender in trouble in the 5th and 15th rounds before also claiming that "Pender never really hurt me" and complaining that Pender had used illegal 'rabbit-punches' in the clinches throughout the fight, which the referee should have dealt with. When he was asked about retirement, he was adamant that he would only retire when he couldn't defend himself. The only thing that pleased Sugar Ray was the money he had negotiated before the first fight. Each boxer received $20,000 from the live gate, however Robinson ended up making $105,000 from the television and radio rights, while champion Pender got only $26,000. There was no doubt about it, Robinson came out a clear winner financially in his two fights with Pender.

Pender continued to be pragmatic in the manner in which he viewed his victory. He explained that he planned to take a month's rest before preparing to challenge Archie Moore for his light-heavyweight title. He dismissed Robinson's claims that he had been a threat by insisting that "he fought exactly as I thought he would and I was ready for him." He claimed that "I knew from the fifth round that I had him where I wanted when he began breathing hard and missing his punches. Robinson kept holding and clutching and I asked the referee to stop him but he didn't have any strength to break us in the clinches." He suggested that he had nothing to prove by meeting Robinson for a third time. "I'm the champion of the world," shouted Pender. "So now I'll do the dictating."

It seemed like everything was turning sour for Sugar Ray. His defeats by Paul Pender upset him and on top of this he and Edna Mae parted company.

21.

The Uncrowned Champion

IT WAS ANOTHER six months before he climbed back into the ring and, to the boxing public's surprise, it was against his arch-rival Gene Fullmer for his National Boxing Association's version of the world middleweight title; the same title which Robinson had been stripped of and which Fullmer had subsequently gone on to beat Carmen Basilio for. The fight was fixed for December 3rd at the Los Angles Sports Arena.

Since their second fight, three and a half years earlier, the 29-year-old Fullmer had remained active by fighting ten times without defeat. His victims included Tiger Jones, Milo Savage, Spider Webb, Joe Miceli and Wilf Greaves, who were all respected and highly ranked fighters. It was his fight against Carmen Basilio in San Francisco's Cow Palace, however, which was most memorable. It was a battle royal between two like-minded sluggers who took and distributed immense punishment, like two Billy goats colliding in the way they tore into each other. After fourteen ferocious rounds, the referee stopped the battle in favour of the bigger man, Fullmer. He successfully defended his crown with a points decision over Spider Webb before engaging in a fully fledged war against Joey Giardello. Fight reports suggested that both men left the rule book in the commission offices and decided to set about each other as if their very lives depended on it. They butted, elbowed, pushed, shoved, hit below the belt and broke every rule in the book before the fight was concluded as a draw. After this, he gave Basilio another tilt at his title and, on this occasion, he stopped his old foe in twelve rounds.

13,465 Los Angeles spectators crammed into the salubrious arena in anticipation of watching a slugfest between two bitter rivals. Neither man had attempted to hide the fact that there was no love lost between them. Robinson had trained with dedication because he knew that he was fortunate to get another chance to become a six-time world title holder and he left no stone unturned in his preparations. He had also maintained his customary problems in the fight negotiations when agreeing his terms, but he put all of this behind him when he danced down the aisle and slipped through the ring ropes, determined to dig into his memory bank and produce another one of his stunning performances. Many critics, however, thought that this was now beyond him. They joked that Fullmer, who had donated 10% of his earnings to the Mormon Church, had the greater entitlement to expect a miracle.

When referee Tommy Hart called both men together to issue his instructions, it was difficult to identify who was the older man. Forty-year old Sugar Ray still looked fresh-faced when compared to the chalk white current champion, who possessed a squashed nose and carried substantial scar tissue over and under each of his eyes. Robinson certainly looked up for a fight whereas Fullmer appeared complacent and uninterested. This initial impression was sustained after the opening bell as Robinson took the fight to Fullmer. Fullmer's crude response was to bulldoze forward and try to trap Robinson on the ropes, where he would blast away at his body, but to his amazement, Robinson could not be pinned down. He was up on his toes, moving like a man twenty years younger than he was; his textbook left jab was a constant source of irritation as he bore little resemblance to the apparent weary old man who had staggered to two decision losses against Paul Pender earlier that year.

Fullmer didn't panic despite losing the early rounds; he reasoned that fatigue would slow Robinson down and make him a more viable target in the later rounds, when he planned to increase the pace. He did start to connect more frequently with his crushing body punches but looked shocked when Robinson failed to wilt and began to box his way out of trouble. Instead, Sugar Ray opened the eleventh round by hitting the Ohio man with a dazzling combination of punches that left the champion standing on unsteady legs. This would have been the instant when the Sugar Ray Robinson of an earlier vintage would have dispatched his foe without compassion, but this time he couldn't find the punch with which to administer the final connection to seal victory. As the fight entered the home straight, Marvin Jenson, the champion's manager, became increasingly desperate in his commands. He could be heard bellowing numerical signals which were designed to keep his man from receiving a lethal blast. "Two-Plus and Five-Plus" were the pre-arranged signals which indicated that Fullmer should adopt a shell-like posture with his arms held up high.

Fullmer did score points for his relentless aggression but the Harlem fighter was deemed to have been the classier and more effective combatant. Nat Fleischer described it as "Sugar Ray's finest performance over the past four years." He also went on to say that it "was a performance that definitely should see him declared the victor and new champion." The majority of spectators believed that he had done well enough to win the contest by some distance. This was echoed by a straw poll of ringside journalists who had Sugar winning by a ratio of 3:1.

As the bell rang for the end of the final round of what had proved to be an absorbing, if not thrilling contest, hordes of fans stood and applauded what they considered to be an acknowledgement of witnessing Sugar Ray Robinson marking his name in history for winning the world middleweight crown for a record sixth time. The timekeeper's bell brought a hush to the arena as the Master of Ceremonies cleared his throat and announced the official scores. Californian fights were scored under the simplified five point system where each ring official awarded a score of between one and five points, depending on their dominance, to the winner of each round and no points to the loser. If the round was deemed as being even, neither fighter is awarded a point. Referee Hart scored it for Robinson by a wide margin of eleven points to four; Judge Lee Grossman voted in favour of Fullmer by nine points to five, while the deciding judge awarded eight points to each man, meaning that the final result was a draw and Fullmer retained his title.

"The crowd rose almost as one and gave the agile Sugar Ray a deserved ovation when he left the ring," enthused Eddie Muller, a well-respected journalist for the San Francisco Examiner. "Robinson made a superb showing in the face of the 1-3 odds against him. Many people, for days, will argue Sugar Ray should have been awarded the verdict. I had Robinson the winner by a 10-7 margin. But none of the spectators left the arena claiming they hadn't got value for their entrance fee. At times during the fight it looked as if the 39-year-old Robinson, the guy with 'nine lives', would achieve what he did to Fullmer in Chicago - flatten him for the full count. This was the third fight between the pair, who hated each other, and it was the best of the series."

Boxing fans who watched the fight via their television sets were incensed by the diabolical decision. "I'm disgusted," wrote Richard Van Houten from Elmira in New York, who went on to say when the fight was declared a draw he nearly lost interest in boxing, "Robinson was a clear winner" Earle Sorenson from Fairfield in California wrote to Boxing Illustrated: "How could they call it a draw? I personally think Robinson was robbed." Charles Ippolito, writing from New Rochelle in New York, concurred: "Of all the fights I have ever seen, I never before saw such a disgraceful decision as the one given in the Fullmer - Robinson fight."

Nat Fleischer spoke for most observers when he expressed his confusion at the newly-adopted points system and at the wide variance in their marking of each official's scorecards, but added: "It was a performance that definitely should have seen Robinson declared the victor and new champion if the officials had done their jobs properly."

In his dressing room, Robinson could only manage a wan smile and attempted to be gracious despite his disappointment. George Gainford, however, struggled to contain his fury and suggested that there had been foul play in the scoring. The reporters converged upon his dressing room and told him that he had won the fight in their eyes. Robinson wearily thanked them for their words but reminded them that "Fullmer is still the champion and that's all that counts in this business." When they pressed him on whether he would now retire, he shocked them by revealing that he had received an offer from the famous Italian film director, Dr. Felice Zappulla, to star in his latest film opposite the beautiful blonde screen siren Rita Giannuzzi in Rome. He suggested that he would accept this offer and would then tour Europe as the world champion because, he argued, that after being stripped of his title by the National Boxing Association and then drawing with Fullmer, he had never lost his title in the ring and could, therefore, legitimately consider himself a world champion as well as Fullmer. When he heard this argument, Marvin Jenson was indignant and dismissed the idea of a final return ever being staged. "There is no way that guy will ever be considered for another title fight," he screeched.

Jenson and Fullmer were unprepared for the outpouring of disbelief and hostility which followed the announcement of the result. Many fans who had watched the fight on television were incensed by the decision. Stanley Weston, the editor of Boxing Illustrated magazine, captured the mood of many by suggesting that "in the event of a drawn decision, when the point-rounds system is used, we agree that the points total should decide the issue. Robinson would, therefore, have won had the fight been judged on that basis." He believed that Sugar Ray had won every round except for the first couple and declared that Fullmer was the luckiest champion in the history of boxing.

"I'll fight Ray Robinson on a street corner, in my manager Marvin Jenson's gym or anywhere else he chooses, except in a boxing ring. What's more, I'll even fight him for nothing. Somebody should open up a local gym and invite all the kids of the neighbourhood in to watch and Robinson and I can fight each other again. That's the only way I will ever fight him again. I will never give him another chance to make a nickel fighting me," declared Gene Fullmer a few months after the Las Vegas draw. Fullmer was incensed by the public outcry to the draw and decided to issue a public response. He also chose to offer an amazing insight into the drawn-out tactics employed by the notorious negotiator, Robinson.

"For all of our fights, the actual fighting has started from the first day of training right up until the final minute of the fight. The real fight with Robinson takes place before you ever step into the ring with him." Fullmer believed that "if Sugar Ray spent more time in planning the actual fight as he did in scheming, conniving and taxing the patience of everybody beforehand, he'd be a much better fighter." He argued that these tactics are actually designed to belittle his opponent and the State Athletic Commissions, the promoters and everybody else connected with staging the fight and was the reason why many promoters ignored him. He agreed that Robinson was still a drawing card but felt that his demands meant that promoters were beginning to speculate whether the headaches which he also brought were worth it.

Fullmer offered the general boxing public a fascinating insight into the world of a fighter who was preparing to face Robinson. "His demands were outlandish," he recalled. "Hours before the last fight, one national wire service sent a story across the country that the fight was called off after Robinson had said that he would not climb into the ring against me unless the ring size was increased from 16 to 18 feet inside the ropes." He also explained that Robinson had complained about the referee, the gloves, and even the colour of the boxing trunks. "Whenever a champion defends his title, the procedure is that he can choose what colour trunks he is going to wear and as the champion, I wanted to wear white trunks but he insisted that he was wearing white trunks as well." Despite the pleadings of the promoter and the boxing commission for him to change the colour of his trunks, Robinson refused to concede and so both fighters came out wearing white trunks. Fullmer also articulated the events surrounding Robinson's argument about the boxing gloves he wanted to use. "He wanted a glove made up primarily of foam rubber and looked like the gloves which most gym boxers use to punch the heavy punch bag." This type of glove was banned in New York and in California because when the gloves became wet, the rubber set like cement. "Marv Jenson knew about this and he informed Jim Deskin, the Chairman of the Nevada State Athletic Commission," Fullmer recalled. "Mr Deskin immediately banned the gloves and brought in the standard horse-hair type of glove. This set Robinson off and he shouted and bawled but eventually had to abide by the Commission's decision." Fullmer later complained that because of Robinson's antagonistic manner, one of the State Athletic Commissioners suffered a heart attack.

Fullmer was also critical of Robinson's approach to training and wondered aloud how he could be ready in time for a fight. He clarified that he didn't believe that this approach was conducive to elite boxing and he suggested that was one of the reasons he asked for so many postponements. Fullmer believed that Robinson's approach was "unprofessional and left a lot to be desired." He recounted the characters that made his gym appear more like a Hollywood film set, including the jazz musicians and dancers who would perform while Robinson trained. Eleanor Powell, a well-know musical and film star was a regular visitor to his daily sessions and Robinson would insist on concluding his training sessions by going through a dance routine on a small stage outside the ring. To a puritanical fighter like himself, Fullmer believed that these antics "were sheer arrogance and no way to get physically fit for a fight." He concluded his character assassination of the fallen idol by accusing him of selfishness and crass insensitivity. "He has little time for anybody but himself and he has caused considerable inconvenience to everybody he has dealt with in boxing. With him, his attitude is all about 'me, me, me'. His disregard for the other fellow is notorious in boxing. When a fighter is in training to fight Robinson he sits on a hot seat waiting for the first postponement."

Despite all Fullmer and Jenson's criticisms regarding Robinson, the fourth and final match was made for the 4th March 1961 in Las Vegas. Norman Rothschild, Jack Doyle and Mel Greb organized this fourth meeting along with Madison Square Garden. As usual there had been long drawn out meetings between Sugar Ray and the promoters. Ray threatened to pull out of the fight when he checked a clause in his contract concerning the world -wide rights of the fight to the promoters and Sugar Ray demanded his share of that money. He also insisted that Madison Square Garden, whom he owed $10,000, drop that demand. A meeting between Robinson, Rothschild, Greb, and Doyle and the promoters and officials from Madison Square Garden, Admiral John Bergen, Harry Markson, attorney Bob Carlson and Teddy Brenner was held and a deal was struck with the former five-time world middleweight champion and the fight was on.

Sugar Ray stayed at the same log cabin in San Jacinto where he had prepared for his last fight against Gene Fullmer, but a week before the fight he moved to the plush Dunes Hotel on the glittering neon strip in Las Vegas. This was his first fight in the gambling city, although he had performed here during his showbusiness career. While in Vegas he was fascinated watching various showbusiness entertainers appearing there. His friend Nat 'King' Cole was appearing there and Ray was delighted. He fancied himself as a Nat Cole type of ballad singer. He had in the past employed a vocal coach to teach him how to sing opera. One night before he fought Fullmer, Robinson surprised Nat Cole when he put on a private party in his hotel room. Cole was astonished when Sugar Ray took the microphone and burst out with an aria with comical solemnity. One guest said, scathingly: "He was like a guy who was making people forget the great Caruso." Another guest blurted out: "Jesus, this guy's as vain as Liberace."

Sugar Ray started fast, knowing this was his best chance. The champion though stuck to his task of wearing the older man down with clubbing punches. Fullmer used his jab to good effect and had Robinson going to the wrong corner. Fullmer was getting stronger while Robinson looked as if he was becoming weaker. Both fighters were warned by referee Frankie Carter for fouling. Fans and older reporters were saddened at the lacing Sugar Ray was taking. His left eye was cut, while the champion's eye was also seeping blood.

The final chapter of the Robinson vs. Fullmer series was an anti-climax as far as Sugar Ray's supporters were concerned. It was a fight to forget! He was out-fought, and out-hustled by the stronger champion. He never looked as if he could capture the form of their previous encounter and although he tried he could not contain the more rugged and robust Mormon. The 7,410 spectators in the Convention Centre were disappointed. But Fullmer was a clear winner. Referee Carter voted 70-66 Fullmer. Judge David Zenoff had it 70-64 Fullmer and Judge John Tihe had it 70-67 Fullmer. The newspaper reporters had the champion winning by a wide margin, 73-60.

Afterwards Robinson was highly critical of the Nevada Commission; he blamed them for the size of the ring. "The ring they supplied was supposed to be eighteen feet, but it wasn't eighteen foot, it was much smaller. I couldn't move around as I'm used to doing and that's why Fullmer was able to corner me so often. If the ring had been the size we agreed I believe he would never have mauled me about like he did."

22.

The Unmourned Departure

"RAY ROBINSON has a split personality," said Jimmy Cannon. Obviously one was a superb boxer, graceful and recklessly poised, precise and harmfully furious with a controlled anger, a thrilling man who was practically perfect at his trade, he said. Then, speaking about the other side of Sugar Ray, he said Ray was like a stranger to the man who on five occasions won the world middleweight championship. "He was like a vandal that disfigured his public image, like an envious fellow scheming to defame a brother he despised. As a boxer, Robinson had a kind of majesty and, in the years of his prime, his style endowed him with an exhilarating dignity which all men who had toiled at hazardous tasks assume when they are contemptuous of pain. But he diminished as a man once he took off his boxing trunks and put on his street clothes," said Cannon. He said that in public Sugar Ray put on a performance, but was petty and spiteful and treated Carmen Basilio and Gene Fullmer with utter contempt during negotiations for their fights. "It ended last Saturday when Fullmer punched him around the ring for fifteen rounds." He also said Robinson might fight on but promoters would only pay him a little money. "This is the way they all go. Promoters will still want him on their promotions because his name was still an attraction, but he warned they would match him against up-and-coming young stars. These youngsters can make their reputations by beating him because all he has got is his name....Sugar Ray Robinson!" He concluded by saying that Ray turned down a guaranteed $500,000 to box Carmen Basilio a third time. And George Parnassus of Los Angeles was willing to pay Sugar Ray $20,000 to box someone named John Smith. Cannon said this was a very generous offer when you realize Robinson hadn't been great in his last few fights. "Robinson doesn't seem to understand he isn't a champion. He refuses to respect a guy like Gene Fullmer, who is a world champion. He has never learned how to accept defeat, as Joe Louis could."

The sands of time had finally run dry for Sugar Ray; he would never again box for a world championship. This brutal and withering assessment of Robinson seemed to capture the feelings of many people within the sport and his demands for a re-match fell on deaf ears. He was forced to endure a six month sabbatical and he used it to indulge in a great deal of soul-searching about his future. He knew that he had squandered over four million dollars of ring earnings and was now broke.

His marriage to Edna Mae had ended, but although he was no longer part of Edna Mae's life, he still took his paternal duties seriously and would call on a regular basis to see Ray Junior. Edna Mae later revealed that on these visits, when she confronted her erstwhile husband about his behaviour he admitted that he had started smoking marijuana. Edna Mae confessed that she was surprised, given that he had hardly drank alcohol or smoked before. Ray vowed to her that he would never smoke in front of his son but he conceded that he had started to smoke to cope with the immense pressure and emotional turmoil he was under. The contemptuous words which he had uttered about never ending up penniless, like his friend Joe Louis, came back to haunt him over and over again during this time. His attempts to meet with America's power-brokers and promoters were rebuffed. He only knew fighting and resigned himself to a bleak future of travelling to the small towns and venues to look for a fight.

His first such destination was a meeting with Wilf Greaves from Ontario, Canada, at the Convention Arena, Detroit. He won an uninspired ten round points decision amid a chorus of boos as most observers believed that his visit to the canvas in the eighth round was enough for Greaves to be awarded the spoils. Greaves a 5ft 8 tough, aggressive fighter had a victory over Dick Tiger for the British Empire title, although Tiger beat him in a return. A few weeks later, he made a poignant return to Madison Square Garden in front of a meagre 7,200 crowd to face the eager twenty-two year old Denny Moyer from Portland, Oregon, who was keen to add the legendary scalp to his record The Oregon fighter had victories over Emile Griffith and the late Benny Kid Paret. In 1962, he would beat classy Joey Giambra for the World Boxing Association light-middleweight title. Moyer had him in real trouble in the third, fifth, ninth and tenth rounds after setting a blistering pace, which Robinson struggled to live with. The referee, Arthur Mercante, kept a close eye on the Harlem boxer and was vigilant in his concern. After ten rounds, however, the disbelieving crowd watched in a stunned silence as Robinson was somehow declared the winner.

His next outing was to the Auditorium in Providence, where his limited opponent, Al Houser, came into the fight on the back of six losses. Robinson had enough to dominate all six rounds and the referee stopped the fight. He closed his year by meeting Wilf Greaves in a return after Greaves had continued to complain bitterly that he had been robbed three months earlier. The fight was held in the Civic Arena in Pittsburgh. It was a fast and open contest and the aggressive Greaves attacked for all he was worth and enjoyed success in the second round when he decked Sugar Ray. Robinson was forced to dig deep into his memory and put together some of his old moves, including some two-handed combination punches, which knocked Greaves out in the eighth round.

******

Whilst Robinson was beating Greaves in the month of December, the world heavyweight champion, Floyd Patterson, knocked out Tom McNeeley in a defence of his world crown. Patterson was on record as stating that he was a great admirer of Robinson and claimed to study films of his technique and Robinson was well disposed to him because of this. After the McNeeley victory, the press turned their attention to who he would meet next and heaped criticism upon his manager, Cus D'Amato. Robinson read the newspaper reports which labelled D'Amato a crank, an oddball and a plethora of other insults for his jealous protection of the champion and the heavyweight crown, including allowing Patterson to fight Pete Rademacher, a youngster having his first professional fight and being pitched in for a world title. Robinson spoke out in favour of both champion and his manager in the press and pointed out that D'Amato's job was to get the easiest opposition for as much money as he could. He contrasted this with his own career and the demands to fight opposition such as Artie Levine, Jake LaMotta, Georgie Abrams and Kid Gavilan.

He began his own fighting year in February by returning to Madison Square Garden to attempt to silence the complaints of Denny Moyer, who had asserted that he had been robbed in their last fight of a clear and conclusive victory. He was unable to summon up his old magic and in a sad episode, the once-peerless Sugar Ray was soundly beaten on points over ten rounds. A few days after this dismal showing, Robinson returned to the Garden and was summoned into the office of Harry Markson, who had the unwelcome task of administering the death knell for his career in the hallowed Madison Square Garden. Markson recounted how he had gulped and explained that "the Garden couldn't be held responsible for allowing him to risk injury by continuing fighting. He recalled: "Ray got up from the chair and put on his coat and walked out without uttering another word. He was obviously hurt and I noticed how tears welled up inside him."

Around this time, Joe Glaser, who had first secured him bookings during his short showbusiness career and then acted as an advisor when he made his first ring comeback, announced that he was suing him for money which he claimed Sugar Ray owed him. This was in addition to fighting Ernie Braca in court, who was also suing him for money owed. He tried to forget his woes by flying to Port of Spain in Trinidad, where he won in two rounds against Bobby Lee in April. In a depressing July contest, he fought in Los Angeles against Phil Moyer, the brother of his conqueror Danny, who replicated his brother's success and beat him on points over ten rounds. The twilight was quickly drawing in on one of the sport's greatest career. Unfortunately, Sugar Ray seemed incapable of recognising it.

In the late summer, he left New York on the luxury liner The Queen Elizabeth and headed to London to meet London's crashing, bashing all-action Terry Downes. Robinson was still regarded as a huge attraction in the British Isles and this was his first visit to the country since he had lost to Randolph Turpin eleven years earlier, and this was reflected in the fact that all 12,000 tickets for the fight at the Wembley Pool were sold with thousands more left disappointed. The promoter, Mickey Duff, expressed his disappointment at not hiring a bigger venue. Robinson was happy to comply with the press requests and posed for publicity photographs, wearing a black bowler hat and carrying an umbrella like a real city gent. He also appeared on a wide variety of radio and television programmes and answered questions about his perilous financial situation. When asked whether he was boxing just for the money, he claimed that everybody needs extra money but his real motivation "was to end my career as the world middleweight champion again." He did speak about his tax bills and explained that "Uncle Sam has been taking 91% of my money, so you figure it out how much I have left." He told them that the American government was holding $514,000 of his money from the first Carmen Basilio fight.

He received a warm reception from the fight crowd, but after giving a good account of himself he was unable to summon up his old magic and lost a clear ten round points decision. "Without hesitation Sugar Ray Robinson was the greatest fighter I've ever seen," said Downes after his victory. "Yes, I beat Robinson without a doubt, but it would be a liberty to say I beat the Sugar Ray Robinson. The name was the same, but I beat a forty-one year old man who was going through the motions from memory."

Whilst in Europe, he travelled to Vienna to cross gloves with Diego Infantes. The Swiss boxing fans fondly recounted his last visit to the continent and gave him a tremendous welcome. He obliged by knocking out Infantes in two rounds before he closed his year in Lyon in November, where he scored a six round technical knockout over Georges Estatoff.

On the 2nd October, another period of his life came to a sad end when Edna Mae, fed up with the increasing ill-treatment at the hands of the man she still professed to adore, travelled to Mexico to file for a divorce. She had read that some of Hollywood's leading stars were granted a quick divorce in the country and as her estranged husband was currently in Europe and knew nothing of the divorce proceedings, she wanted to resolve it quickly. The end of the relationship was no surprise to those close to the couple. Only a year before, Edna Mae had been granted a legal separation from her husband and given uncontested custody of their son, Raymond. Sugar Ray was ordered to pay his wife $200 a week plus a percentage of his overall earnings. He was also required to pay her legal costs, which were estimated to be $2,500. Over the next twelve months, and with no hint of any payments, she was forced to take her husband to court and was awarded a $30,000 judgment against him. It was a futile gesture, however, as he had no means of paying her. She even arrived home on one occasion to find that her home had been ransacked and all of her jewellery, ermines and minks were stolen. She tried to claim on her insurance policy with Lloyd's of London and found out that Sugar Ray had not renewed it. It was a depressing state of affairs for Harlem's once golden couple.

She maintained in later years that she always held great love and affection for her wayward husband and she always refused to contemplate marrying anyone else. Her Manhattan apartment continued to display photographs of happier times with him, but she also painfully recounted his sudden displays of terrifying violence she was forced to endure at his hands. Sometimes, he would leave her battered and bruised without any apparent motive and these bouts of rage only seemed to increase when his troubles with the income tax authorities became more prevalent and his business empire collapsed around him. She also suggested that the worse element of these attacks was the fact that their son had witnessed the violence on several occasions.

******

He began the next year by still feeling forced to fight in order to pay his tax arrears. His first fight was against Ralph Dupas, who was a highly respected foe. In May 1958, Dupas had lost in eight rounds against the reigning world lightweight champion, Joe 'Old Bones' Brown. In July 1962, he had fought Emile Griffith, the world welterweight title holder, and travelled the full fifteen rounds before losing on points. The Robinson fight was staged in the magnificent Miami Beach Auditorium in front of a crowd of 6,232. Robinson was on the right end of a razor-thin ten round decision after the referee, Billy Regan, and Judge Barry Pearlman made him a split-decision winner. He ignored the widespread disagreement by the crowd and declared that "this was a very important victory for me. I'm going to keep going." For the first time, he had Ferdie Pacheco assisting in his corner. Pacheco would later earn his repute as Muhammad Ali's fight doctor. Pacheco, however, was upset at watching the former great champion, whom he had hugely admired in years gone by, look so ponderous. He privately told friends that "although Robinson physically looked immaculate, it was obvious that he was merely going through the motions." This was an assertion he repeated in his own memoirs many years later. Four months after losing the decision to Sugar Ray, Dupas defeated Denny Moyer for the world light-middleweight title.

His next match was against the top middleweight contender, the tough experienced 33-year-old Joey Giardello, and he was given the added incentive by Dick Tiger, the world champion, promising that he would put his title on the line against the winner. Giardello cynically recounted that "when I was the number one contender, from 1953 through to 1960, I never got close to being granted a title fight against Sugar Ray" because when he was the middleweight champion, Robinson contemptuously dismissed his challenge. Suddenly, once Tiger had made his promise to fight the winner, "Robinson announced that he would fight me." Giardello said that Teddy Brenner had clinched the Robinson fight for him because Brenner had assured Robinson that Giardello was a shot fighter.

Robinson was forty-three years old when he stepped through the ropes of Philadelphia's Convention Hall on the 24th June in front of a crowd of 8,598. The promoters hyped up the meeting between the ring legend and a man ten years younger than him by suggesting that a potential thriller was in the offing. Robinson had won his last six contests while Giardello, who had been boxing professionally since 1948, had fought a draw against Gene Fullmer in a foul-filled fifteen round encounter for Fullmer's world title and was a feared operator on the world scene.

When the first bell rang, both men quickly left their corners, but it was Giardello, who had sparred more than 150 rounds in preparation, who looked the more determined. Robinson, meanwhile, looked fleshy in the face and it was obvious that his physical conditioning would be no match against his hungry foe, who immediately settled to his task and began to pummel away at Robinson, who quite honestly, looked awful. Giardello used his left jab to telling effect and although Sugar Ray tried to get his own jab working, his once finely-honed reflexes appeared to have deserted him. Many fans shook their heads in a mournful recognition of the terminal decline which had set in as Giardello simply brushed Robinson's feeble attacks aside. Ray delved into his memory bank and dredge up those sublime skills of his glory years. But it wasn't to be. Joey was too fit, faster and stronger.

As the rounds wore on with a grim predictability, Giardello continued to get stronger and in the fourth round, he gained his first noteworthy success by landing with a thumping roundhouse left hook and dropping Robinson backwards onto his rump. His pride ensured that he got up after a count of eight but he soon found himself in difficulties in the sixth, when he was hurt by a left hook and fell into the ropes where he was hit by a ferocious right uppercut before struggling to ride out the frenzied storm whipped up by is younger opponent. The final result was never in any serious doubt when the referee, Buck McTiernan, separated both fighters at the final bell and awarded the fight to Giardello by 49 points to 43. Judges Bob Polis and Lou Tress both agreed with scores of 47-43 and 48-45 respectively and recorded an undisputed unanimous victory for Giardello. Less than five months later, Giardello beat Dick Tiger for the world middleweight title.

The Robinson-Giardello fight was also noticeable for the entertainment which was unwittingly provided by the then Cassius Clay, who stood up from his ringside seat to lead the cheering for his idol whenever Robinson put together a good flurry of punches. Clay later told reporters that, "next to me, Sugar Ray Robinson is still the greatest."

After this latest loss, Robinson chose not to enter the ring again until the 14th October, when he elected to return to Europe and, more specifically, his favourite city, Paris. He met Armand Vanucci, an uninspiring twenty-eight year old prospect in the city's Palace de Sports. Vanucci was a part-time professional fighter, having only twenty six contests in over seven years and winning seventeen. His fights punctuated his permanent employment as a security guard at the Louvre Museum. Robinson easily outpointed the limited Vanucci over ten rounds. He then travelled to Lyon to fight an Italian middleweight called Fabio Bettini, who celebrated wildly when it was announced that he had managed to hold Robinson to a draw after ten dull and insipid rounds. A few days later, he crossed into Belgium to knock out the Bruges-based Emile Sarens in eight rounds. He followed this up by claiming a ten round points victory over Andre Davier in Grenoble. His final contest of the year, and the last fight in his five fight agreement, was a return bout against Armand Vannucci back in Paris. Once again, he beat Vannucci on points over ten rounds, but the trip was tainted with sadness for him. Everywhere he went served as a reminder of his halcyon days, when he had been feted as a French hero and thousands flocked to see him wherever he travelled.

23.

The Blueprint of Victory for Cassius Clay

AFTER THIS European sojourn, Robinson was inactive for five months as he found himself caught up in the tangled mess of complications which his business and personal affairs represented. On the 25th February, however, the boxing world which was so familiar to him changed irrevocably and Robinson had an influence in it. Ever since he had turned professional, Cassius Clay had asked Robinson to join his team in some capacity, more specifically as his manager or coach, and his tactics involved showering his hero with fulsome praise.

Before he challenged the fearsome Sonny Liston for his heavyweight crown, Clay's wooing of Robinson stepped up a gear and he bombarded Robinson with repeated phone calls beseeching him to travel to Miami and help him complete his preparations for the fight. Robinson enjoyed talking to the cocky but vulnerable Clay, seeing a number of parallels and similarities with himself, and he secretly enjoyed being praised as "the greatest". Eventually he conceded and travelled to Florida where he would spend hours sitting with the heavyweight prospect watching Robinson's own 1951 victory over Jake LaMotta. Robinson would then highlight certain tactics to the sponge-like Clay, such as the manner in which he would spin LaMotta around before delivering a left hook to the exposed part of the body and how to fully utilise his effective left jab, which he believed were tactics which could be equally employed against Liston. Clay would sit in an uncustomary silence and would be spellbound as his idol spelt out his battle plan. Angelo Dundee, Ali's official trainer, was asked by some reporters whether he was upset and felt undermined by having the presence of Sugar Ray Robinson in the camp. "Not in the least," he replied, "I've been asked that question many times but it was never a problem. Ali loved boxing trainers and being around boxing people and it was great to have such a great presence like Sugar Ray around to relax and focus him."

Robinson enjoyed the trip and the distractions from his own mounting problems, but he felt uncomfortable being in the presence of Malcolm X, who

228

was staying with Clay, and Sugar Ray tended to distance himself whenever the charismatic Malcolm began outlining his beliefs. It was after Clay defeated Liston in a huge upset that he changed his name to Muhammad Ali and pledged his allegiance to the nation of Islam.

******

'Who is Gaylord Barnes?' was a question being asked by many fight fans when Robinson announced that he would face the New York middleweight as his first opponent in 1964. Known by only those members of the boxing fraternity that possessed encyclopaedic memories, Barnes had lost his previous six bouts before he faced Robinson in Portland. It was a sad reminder of how far his powers had waned that he outpointed the overawed New Yorker in ten stagnant rounds. He continued on with a weary resignation and his next opponent was of a similar vintage to Barnes. Clarence Riley from Detroit had a number of impressive names on his track record, including George Benton, Wilbert McClure and the future world heavyweight champion, Jimmy Ellis, who all handed him comprehensive defeats. He was able to add the name of Sugar Ray Robinson alongside that litany as he was stopped inside six rounds. Ray next travelled across country to Omaha, where he found the local boy, Art Hernandez, to be tougher opposition. Hernandez was building a decent record, which consisted of fifteen consecutive victories, before they met and he overcame his nerves to gain a creditable draw in the City Auditorium. Bill Engel, the referee, thought it was a great ten round fight and said he was honoured to be in the same ring as the great man, Robinson.

In September, he, once again, crossed the Atlantic and travelled to Scotland to meet the British middleweight champion Mick Leahy, who hailed from Cork but boxed out of Coventry. Leahy was a rough and tough scrapper who had captured the British title by beating George Aldridge and was a respected boxer. At the weigh-in, Robinson was three and a half pounds above the official weight limit agreed by both camps. George Middleton, the former manager of Randy Turpin was also Leahy's manager and he was vociferous about not allowing the fight to continue because of the weight discrepancy, but Leahy begged him to allow it to go ahead and was vindicated by beating a cowed Robinson on points. Many shrewd judges thought Robinson had done enough to win, but it wasn't to be. George Gainford was angry and said the decision was robbery. He then returned to Paris and met the European title challenger, Yolande 'Yves' Leveque from St Quentin. Leveque had quietly built an impressive twenty-two fight record with his only blemish coming in his first tilt at the European crown. Robinson had just enough in his quickly emptying tank to snatch a tight points victory.

He then headed back to London and gained his only career victory in the British Isles by handing defeat to the tough Nigerian, Gabriel Dada, but fighting under the name of Johnny Angel, inside six rounds. He hopped back across the Channel to fight Jackie Cailleau from San Quentin, in Nice, just twelve days later and outpointed him over ten rounds before heading to Caen to notch another points win against local lad, Jean Baptiste Rolland in the city's Helitas Stadium. He then continued his journey south to Marseilles to score another uninspiring points win over Jean Beltritti. He remained in the city for an extra week and his final bout of the year was a return against the Roman, Fabio Bettini. Since their previous drawn contest a year before, Bettini had remained active and had fought six times and had won twice, lost three times and drawn once. Robinson was unable to improve on his previous lacklustre showing against the determined Beltritti and could only grimly hold on to salvage another draw to close his year in the flat manner which it had been conducted in. The end was drawing close but Sugar Ray was both unwilling and unable to accept the dying of the light, which had once burned so brightly.

******

Although he was not aware of it, 1965 was to be Sugar Ray's last as an active professional boxer. The range of his once expansive ambition was such that he was buoyed by not being defeated in his last five fights and so eagerly took on three fights in quick succession. In March, he headed to Kingston, Jamaica and beat Jimmy Beecham in two rounds, followed a month later in Savannah with East Basting being hammered in the opening round, and then three weeks later, he demolished Rocky Randal in three rounds. Not sated by this, he immediately challenged Randal to a return and just over a week later, he beat him on points over eight rounds. His winning streak was abruptly ended when he lost a ten round bout to Memo Ayon in Tijuana before dropping another ten rounder to the unsophisticated and unpretentious Stan Harrington in Honolulu. Next up, he beat 'Young' Joe Walcott in Richmond, Virginia over ten rounds before he maintained his hectic pace by heading to Las Vegas, where he lost on points to Ferd Hernandez. He then boxed a return with Walcott and repeated his ten round points victory from three months earlier. He then fought another return with Stan Harrington but fared no better than the first outing and lost on points again in Honolulu.

When he visited Jamaica to box Jimmy Beecham he was accompanied by the world heavyweight champion, the then Cassius Clay (AKA Muhammad Ali) and his wife Sonji. There were dozens of reporters, photographers, radio and television cameras and fans waiting at the airport. Clay was in his element and as soon as the party stepped off the aircraft he shouted: "The Greatest cornerman has arrived to look after Sugar Ray." Everyone was laughing. "He (pointing to Sugar Ray) is the King, the Master, and my Idol. He is the Greatest (well next to me)." After the fight a reception was laid on by officials to honour the two distinguished Americans. It was on this occasion that the two men would go their separate ways. Clay had told Robinson that Elijah Muhammad said he would give him seven-hundred thousand dollars if he became a Muslim!

Although he was struggling financially, Sugar Ray explained that he could not do that because he had his own religious beliefs of as a Christian. Also, while in Jamaica Clay was feuding with his wife and there was a great deal of friction because Sonji wouldn't adhere to her husband's request on eating certain foods and her code of dress. Sugar Ray tried to intervene when he thought matters were getting out of hand between man and wife, but this only caused more unpleasantness. Clay told him to mind his own business. Ray was anxious to get away from this by now unpleasant atmosphere. Once back on American soil they parted and each went to their own homes. Over the proceeding years they would keep in touch by phone. Clay changed his name to Muhammad Ali and became the legend he is today. Talking about Robinson, he said: "That man was beautifull. The way he moved in the ring, his poise and the way he could punch was something only someone special could get away with. I have to say, yes, he was the greatest."

On 15th September, the official entry in his own record shows that he fought a bout against Neil Morrison in Norfolk, Virginia. The International Boxing Hall of Fame's official record book, however, details the opponent as being Bill Henderson. This is substantiated by the report in The Ring magazine by the referee of the fight, Jack Levinson, where Bill Henderson was the named foe. The truth, however, is more complex. The fight was staged in the Norfolk Arena in front of a mere 838 spectators. Midway through the first round, Robinson delivered a deft but innocuous left hook which caught Henderson on the arm. Henderson, who was fearful of meeting such a ring legend, immediately fell to the canvas as if he had been pole-axed. Fight official Levinson ordered him to get up and continue fighting, which he did after receiving an eight count. When the bell rang soon afterwards, Levinson followed Henderson back to his corner and told him, in no uncertain terms, that if he failed to put some effort into the fight and improve his dismal showing he would have no hesitation in stopping the fight and his purse.

When the second round bell tolled, and within the opening twenty-five seconds, Robinson landed another tame left hook which grazed Henderson's right glove and saw him sink to the canvas for another eight count. When Levinson ordered him back into action, the petrified Henderson dropped to the floor again before a punch could even be thrown. Levinson didn't even bother to start a count but walked out of the ring in disgust after declaring the fight a 'mismatch'. He told The Ring magazine that, "I wanted no part of the fiasco." He absolved Robinson of blame by suggesting that "He was trying to make a fight of it but it takes two to do that. I was disgusted with Henderson's showing."

A few days after this bizarre episode, he headed to Philadelphia and outpointed 'Young' Joe Walcott for the third and final time. In October, he beat Peter Schmidt on points in Johnstown and then three weeks later, knocked out Rudolf Bent in three rounds in Steubenville.

24.

A Sad Farewell

JOEY ARCHER was a proud Irish New Yorker, hailing from the Bronx. Standing at 5 feet 10 inches tall, he was a rangy middleweight whose ring prowess had earned him a huge following amongst the city's Irish fight fans. He was managed by his older brother, Jimmy, and trained by Bill Gore, who had trained the great Willie Pep and guided him to victories over Dick Tiger, Holly Mims, the ferocious Rubin 'Hurricane' Carter, Blair Richardson, Denny Moyer and Mick Leahy to name but a few. Archer was a clean-living athlete who had declared that his goal was to become a world champion before turning his considerable talents towards a career in business. First, however, he was focused on succeeding in his initial target: beating Sugar Ray Robinson.

The setting for their fight was the Civic Arena in Pittsburgh, which was filled with many of Archer's boisterous fans amongst the 9,023 crowd, a crowd which also contained a mixture of older fans, who fondly remembered Sugar Ray's brilliance and came to see a mere glimpse of that magic, and younger patrons, many of whom had been reared on tales of this great man and came with intrigue and curiosity.

The pug-nosed Joey Archer, eighteen years younger than Robinson, was eager to commence the most important fight of his career, and when the fight began he was the first to attack. His left jab was his main weapon and he threw his whole shoulder behind it. Robinson, who looked remarkably fit, belying his forty-four years, attempted to counter but found that his punches were falling short and he was missing his target repeatedly. The fans were enjoying the confrontation and they applauded the valiant Robinson whenever he managed to display a fleeting glimpse of his old majestic moves. Then, at the start of the fourth round, quite unexpectedly, Father Time entered the arena and presented Robinson with damning evidence that the journey was all but over.

Archer approached warily and then suddenly sprang into life and caught his foe with a right hand which bounced off his chin and dropped him. In the corner, George Gainford finally knew that the end had arrived and his soulful face was a mask of sadness. He closed his eyes and thought of the wonderful thrills which he had experienced from this position. Robinson, however, summoned up the last vestige of his warrior's soul and determined to go out on his own two feet. He struggled to his feet after a count of nine before asking the referee, Buck McTiernan, to allow him to continue. He then managed to evade the stalking left jab which Archer pursued him with for the rest of the contest. There was no doubt at the end that Robinson had lost for the nineteenth time in his remarkable 202 fights. There was an eerie silence as the judges scores were announced, which were all heavily in favour of the younger fighter.

Back in the solemnity of his dressing room, he quietly confirmed to George Gainford that he was retiring for good. He was nearing his forty-sixth birthday and had been a five-time world champion and a professional for twenty-five years, and yet he clearly heard the hands of time chiming for him to stop. His close friend, the musician Miles Davis, came in with tears streaming down his face and bent over Ray and captured the moment by telling him, in his famous gravel-gargled voice, "Sugar, it's time, man."

The press were waiting outside when Gainford emerged to tell them that Sugar Ray Robinson had, indeed, decided to quit. He explained that he was not contracted for any further fights and had been offered an opportunity to appear in two Hollywood films and so would pursue his new career. He asked the press to consider the facts of a remarkable career, which will never be equalled, let alone beaten. 202 bouts, 175 victories, six draws, one no decision, one no contest and 19 defeats. From his amazing total of 175 wins, he scored a phenomenal 109 knockouts. Joey Archer, unwittingly cast in the role of executioner after handing him his final defeat, attempted to offer some perspective. He expressed the opinion that despite being forty-five, he had offered him enough problems to think "how great Robinson must have been when he was in his prime, during the 1940s and '50s." He mused that if he had been matched against Robinson when he was tackling the likes of LaMotta, Gavilan, Turpin, Graziano and Olson, he "would have remained in my dressing room."

A few days after the Archer contest, Robinson received a phone call from John Condon, who did the publicity for events at Madison Square Garden. He told Ray he had an idea and a proposition to put before him and asked Ray to call and see him to discus things. Robinson had always respected Condon so agreed to a meeting. Condon outlined his plan to make Ray's retirement official. He was told it would be a wonderful send-off for him with fans and officials paying their respects and both Sugar Ray and boxing would benefit. "You shouldn't be allowed to end your career without an official ceremony," said Mr Condon. Sugar Ray was thrilled. The ceremony was to take place as a prelude to the world welterweight championship match in the Garden

234

between Emile Griffith, the champion, and his challenger Manny Gonzalez. Condon casually mentioned that R.K.O. General Television would film the event. Robinson smiled, and asked how much he was being paid. The MSG official was shocked and said nothing. "We thought you would be thrilled," said Condon. Robinson got on his high horse and said no fee, no coverage. Harry Markson and other officials smiled and said nothing had changed regarding Sugar Ray when it came to money. So his official exit was not shown live on television.

On the night of 10th December 1965, 12,146 fans gathered in Madison Garden. The main attraction was the world welterweight title fight between Emile Griffith and his challenger, Manny Gonzalez. The newspapers, however, spoke for many when they stated that "the large turnout was mainly to bid farewell to Sugar Ray Robinson in a special ceremony organized by the Madison Square Garden Corporation." Organisers had arranged for four of the champions who had fought Robinson for the world middleweight title to be present. Randolph Turpin attended, along with Carmen Basillio, Carl 'Bobo' Olson and Gene Fullmer. The only one missing was Jake LaMotta, who was embroiled in giving his testimony before the Kefauver Senate investigation into boxing after admitting that he had thrown a fight against Billy Fox.

The three former champions were introduced first and each of them was dressed in their old boxing trunks, boots and dressing gowns. Although they looked old and a little heavy, they each received a tremendous ovation when they entered the ring. When it was time for Sugar Ray's entrance, the whole arena fell into a hushed silence. The spotlight searched for him as he entered the arena, wearing his boxing shorts, a three-quarter length white terry cloth robe and with not a hair out of place. The arena spontaneously erupted with a tingling, never-to-be-forgotten ovation which was seldom heard before from a hardened boxing crowd. During his walk down the aisle towards the ring, he was feted in a staggering crescendo of affectionate noise which increased in intensity when he finally stepped through the ropes.

Turpin, Basillio, Olson and Fullmer lifted him onto their shoulders and carried him around the ring apron. The former Mayor of New York, Vincent Impelleteri, then entered and presented him with 18-inch trophy on behalf of the Madison Square Garden Corporation. The trophy was simply inscribed, 'To Sugar Ray Robinson - the World's greatest fighter - from the Madison Garden Corporation and his legion of friends throughout the world.' Impelleteri offered him the microphone and invited him to say a few words. "I don't know whether to be happy or sad," he stammered with emotion threatening to choke him, "but I Thank God for this and all the other blessings I've received" before he thanked the boxing commissions and the press. Hollywood star Gordon McCrea concluded the event by singing a haunting rendition of 'Auld Lang Syne'.

Back in his dressing room he told the reporters that he had no regrets. "I'd do it all over again in the same identical way. I wouldn't change a blessed thing." He then changed into his street clothes, took one last look around and walked out into a new world; a world without boxing. He shook hands with his former opponents and officials, and as he walked outside the Garden he felt sad. He drove his station wagon to his sparse apartment. "What do I do now?" he thought. His mind was in turmoil. He had no money and didn't know how he could earn any.

25.

The Retirement Years

IN 1965, SUGAR RAY received an invitation which thrilled him. He and his partner Millie were invited to attend Queen Elizabeth's 39th birthday party, held at Buckingham Palace. He had met the Queen and her husband, Price Philip, in 1951 when he was in England for the Randy Turpin fight. He said that they were beautiful people after he had enjoyed a long conversation with Prince Philip about events that were making headline news in America, including riots, racial issues and crime. The Prince was a great advocate for Youth Clubs and sporting activities designed to help the younger generation and he suggested that with his charisma and reputation of being able to command respect around the world, he should put his name to good use. This chat caused Robinson to think seriously about getting involved in youth work.

On the 17th May 1966, less than six months after his retirement, he was shocked and saddened to hear of the death of the third boxer who had beaten him, Randolph Turpin, who had committed suicide by shooting himself. Robinson was dismayed to hear that he was being held partly responsible for this tragic demise.

Crusading journalist, J.L Manning, penned a ferocious article in the Daily Mail, titled, 'Turpin: Two Questions Must Be Answered', in which he stated that "two questions are asked about Randolph Turpin's violent death and wretched life which boxing, in all conscience, must answer." His article asked whether Turpin was "a lingering victim of 'punch drunkenness'" and asked what had happened to the £585,439 of purses which the fans had paid to see during his four world title fights. He also reflected on the tragedy of Turpin's story, a back-street-kid who fought his way to considerable wealth by the age of 23 and yet was declared bankrupt at 34 and dead at 38.

Manning ruminated whether Turpin's death may spell the end of the sport. "Was the medical and social consequences of boxing so harmful that it should be abolished?" he asked, highlighting that between 1945 and 1965, 249 amateur and professional boxers had died from boxing sustained injuries. "In his return with Robinson and in the last forty seconds of the tenth round, he was struck with eleven savage and full-blooded blows on his unprotected jaw while unable to defend himself. Referee Ruby Goldstein stopped the fight with only eight seconds before the end of the round. At once, a controversy was raised by spectators. Some thought he would have recovered in the one-minute interval to win a contest which he led on points". Manning's attempts to suggest that Robinson's blows had directly contributed to Turpin's long-term injuries were undermined by the fact that Turpin had 28 more licensed contests before retiring. During this period, however, his actions did become increasingly irrational. His first marriage broke up, there were stories of assault, all pointing to a diminishing sense of social responsibility. His second marriage was to bring him happiness, but the career of Turpin, Britain's best boxer, never recovered.

After the retirement farewell Ray was at a loose end and started to borrow money to subsidise his high standard of living. His sizeable ego would not allow him to consider looking for a steady job, like other men. He was embarrassed when Millie got herself a job to bring much needed money into their apartment. He hated the thought that his wife had to work and so both he and George Gainford made calls to business people whom they had befriended in his glory years. They both learned the stark truth that, although he had been a great fighter, many of these friends claimed that they could not help him. Robinson took these refusals to heart. People who he had believed were true friends, and to whom he had loaned money, suddenly turned a deaf ear when asked if they could now pay him back. This disillusionment prompted him to move to Los Angeles, where Frank Sinatra, hearing of his plight, arranged for a mutual friend to give Sugar Ray a monthly cheque. Sinatra insisted that his involvement in this generous offering was to remain a secret.

Sinatra did make his assistance known on other matters. He pulled strings to ensure that Ray appeared in a number of films. Although in his forties, he remained in tremendous physical condition and continued to train every day. Ol' Blue Eyes, Tony Randal and Mickey Rooney all publicly declared themselves admirers of him to journalists to ensure that his name remained visible, and privately, they invited him to join their social whirl. He appeared on the Las Vegas stage with Rooney and Randal in 'The Odd Couple' and also acted as a boxer in 'Run For Your Life' before he appeared opposite Sinatra in 'The Detective'. There were rumours that he would fly to Rome to appear with Elizabeth Taylor and Richard Burton, which didn't materialise. His main concern, however, was still focused on making as much money as quickly as he possibly could. Marlon Brando helped and advised him about the film business. But he soon tired of the glitzy world of Hollywood and his acting aspirations diminished.

Did he have cause to regret not accepting Muhammad Ali's earlier offer for Sugar Ray to become his manager or advisor? If he did, he never openly discussed it with anyone, but it is difficult to see how this would have worked in practise. Both men's gargantuan egos, along with their differing and deeply held religious beliefs, would surely have made sustaining an effective working relationship difficult.

It was 1969 when the Sugar Ray Robinson Youth Foundation was established in an old church in Los Angeles. It was a brilliant innovation and Sugar Ray, along with other volunteers, often visited troubled areas, problem schools and other establishments where the youth of Los Angeles tended to congregate. The Foundation opened its doors to a few hundred members, which soon quickly grew by the week.

It had various programmes which allowed and encouraged the youngsters to study the fine arts and the performing arts alongside other pursuits like basketball, music and dancing, although boxing was not on the curriculum. The local county eventually helped out with some funding but Sugar Ray never took any payment at first and neither did his staff. The Foundation appeared to give him a renewed sense of purpose and he organised fund-raising events and boxed exhibitions in aid of it. On one occasion he boxed a three round bout against a promising young middleweight named Mike Nixon in the Valley Gym in Los Angeles. He was near fifty years old but looked like the old Sugarman. The flawless moves brought the huge crowd to their feet and elicited wild applause.

Of course, the crowd had seen him before, either in one of his TV roles or taking bows before a main boxing event in one of the local arenas; there was nothing new about seeing Sugar Ray in one of his flash suits and expensive shoes but there was a collective gasp when he took off his robe. He looked splendid and reminded the older members of the audience of how he looked in his great days. Movie star Fernando Lomas, who was sat ringside with heavyweight contender Oscar Bonavena, suggested, "I don't care if he's 47, 48, 50 or even 60, he could still beat half the rated contenders right now." His exhibition received a share of the arenas total receipts. He had continued to keep himself fit by training in the famous Main Street Gym, which was located in a dingy, skid-row section of Los Angeles. He told fellow gym mates that Millie was cooking him soul food, which he loved to eat, and this was why he had to keep in shape.

Unfortunately, his domestic situation was far from settled. Ralph Willey, the seasoned sportswriter, recalled that his son, Ray Junior, often travelled to Los Angeles to spend some valuable time with his father but felt shunted aside by Millie. Ray's sister, Evelyn, later confirmed that Millie appeared extremely jealous and possessive of her husband and Ray Junior claimed that Millie didn't want any of the family around him "because she thought they would get something from him."

In 1979, Reg Noble, the editor-in-chief of Boxing Illustrated magazine, wrote an interesting article on his choice of the ten best middleweights of all time, which concurred with the influential Boxing Writers of America which placed Robinson as the greatest of them all. This view did not rest easily with some of the contenders.

"Robinson was great but he didn't do the things I did," said former world middleweight champion Carlos Monzon, who was rated as second in both estimations. The Argentinian cited his own winning skein (870) plus his inside-the-distance accomplishments (600) as much better than Sugar Ray's, which was an 866 winning percentage and 542 quick finishes. "I made 14 championship defences compared to Robinson's seven," said the agitated Argentinian. He offered his opinion that Robinson had endured far tougher fights than he had ever been involved in. "I've never been in a real struggle. I'm too good a fighter for any fighter to give me problems." When it was highlighted that Robinson had been undefeated for over eight years, which included 91 contests, Monzon countered that "I was not beaten from October in 1964 until I retired in August 1977 (80 contests)." He also pointed out that although he had lost three and drawn nine times, "I reversed my three defeats with easy victories." He showed some humility by conceding that "I am not denying that Robinson was not a great fighter, indeed one of the best, but I am THE best." Robinson chose not to respond, instead allowing the ratings of veteran observers to speak for themselves. Noble's top ten middleweights were: 1. Sugar Ray Robinson 2. Carlos Monzon 3. Stanley Ketchel 4. Harry Greb 5. Mickey Walker 6. Tommy Ryan 7. Frank Klause 8. Billy Papke 9. Mike Gibbons 10. Les Darcy.

In early 1981, Robinson was devastated by the death of his mentor and manager George Gainford, who was in his early eighties. George was well known throughout boxing as the 'Emperor' and the front man for Robinson. They had enjoyed a love-hate relationship throughout their long and illustrious association together. In some interviews, Robinson would actively demean the man who had remained alongside him throughout his entire amateur and professional career and would then deny he had made these hurtful remarks when he was confronted. He used George to argue with promoters on his behalf and often made him the 'fall guy' for any tough decisions he had to make. Gainford benefited his charge on numerous occasions through his own wiles. During his reign as welterweight champion, he would have huge problems making the weight and Gainford would manoeuvre it so Robinson could weigh-in 'behind closed doors'. He was also unheralded for the canny way he had handled Sugar Ray's early career by avoiding meeting the likes of Cocoa Kid, Holman Williams and Charley Burley in order to obtain the most money at the least risk for his man. He had grown increasingly dismayed by the entourage which Robinson surrounded himself with in his later years but had quietly remained loyal, waiting in the shadows.

It was around this period that Ray was suffering with diabetes and high blood pressure and hypertension. It became noticeable that the once outgoing smiling person who could hold interesting conversations with anyone was becoming increasingly vacant and forgetful. Unbeknown to most people, he was beginning to enter into a darkness for which there was no cure as the onset of Alzheimer's disease began to take a hold. He would meet with old friends, smile when they met but then be completely unable to remember their names or anything about them. Rocky Graziano recalled meeting Sugar Ray and hugging him. Although Ray smiled, he looked mystified as to who he was. Graziano had become a huge star of television and frequently appeared in several national adverts and started talking to Ray about their fight and the state of current boxing but did not receive a coherent response. He recounted that this was when he realised that Robinson was becoming ill. Ironically, only a few years later, Graziano would suffer a similar lapse into Alzheimer's.

By 1981, the Foundation was positively thriving and the membership had helped more than 40,000 youngsters in the Los Angeles and Orange counties. Ray was voted in as the chairman and took real delight in the achievements of his pupils, most notably Florence Griffith Joyner, who won three gold medals in the 1988 Summer Olympics in Seoul. In 1981, Ray travelled to New York for a party which was arranged in his honour by his friend and benefactor, Phil Rosenthal. He looked notably tired and weary. Jake LaMotta, Billy Graham, Willie Pep and Ray Arcel all attended, but Millie had asked that the journalists present didn't interview her husband. The reason for this quickly became apparent as when different people came up to shake Robinson's hand and have a few words, Mille would discretely whisper their name in his ear and a broad smile would then flash from his face.

In 1986, his old nemesis, Jake LaMotta, announced that he was getting married for the sixth time in Las Vegas and he asked Ray to act as his Best Man. Millie accepted on her husband's behalf, declaring that Ray was thrilled to be asked. A small number of sportswriters were also present. Tom Archdeacon was among them. He recalls: "Seeing Sugar Ray in this way was sad. Jake, in his gravely-voice, was telling jokes and stories but it was clear that whilst Sugar Ray kept his style, the real substance of this once great fighter was beginning to slide. Millie hovered over him like a Mother Hen, trying to help him from his dark shadows that engulfed him beneath the smile and silk suit." At the reception, the scrubbed up cigar-chewers and congratulators filed past the two fabled former world champions, only to get a hollow handshake from the smiling but unsure Sugar Ray. LaMotta realized something was not quite right with Robinson and he tried to help matters, quietly taking Sugar Ray under his wing and whispering the names of friends Robinson could no longer recall. Jake knew his old foe was fighting the draining debilitation of Alzheimer's disease. Many asked LaMotta why he made Robinson the Best Man at his wedding. Jake looked at them and laughed. "Sugar Ray was always the Best Man," he said.

'The Real Sugar Ray Faces Toughest Fight': was the headline of journalist Jim Murray's sad, but beautiful article which he wrote a year before Sugar Ray's passing, but which reflected on his legacy:

"The night belonged to Sugar Ray. The saxophones played for him. The lights came on for him. Life was a neon boardwalk. He loved the noise, the action. He had to have people around him. Everywhere he went, he looked as if he were leading a parade or riding in one in a shower of ticker-tape. He was beautiful at what he did. He elevated the art. He brought grace, rhythm, style, even science to a cruel craft. It wasn't a fight, it was a ballet. If Nureyev were a fighter, he would do it this way. He was as handsome, sleek, and swift as a cobra. He made everyone he fought look as if they were encased in wet concrete. He fought 78 fights before he got a title shot. Today, they get title shots after 7, as did Leon Spinks, or 23, as did Sugar Ray Leonard. If you think Sugar Ray Leonard is great, you should have seen the real one. He fought for 25 years in three divisions, 209 fights, yet he didn't have a mark on him when he quit. He looked like a ballroom dancer, which he was, or the stage dancer which he tried to be. They invented the phrase uncrowned champ for him. They also invented the designation pound for pound. Pound for pound - or inch for inch, or punch for punches you name it - Sugar Ray Robinson might have been the best there ever was. Or will be. He lost only one of his first 137 fights, that to Jake LaMotta, whom he promptly beat three weeks later. Ultimately, he beat LaMotta five times altogether. He had a fuchsia Cadillac, night clubs, fur coats, beer distributorships. He put the word entourage on the sports page. He came into town like the circus. Wherever Sugar Ray went, his court jesters followed. His barber, golf coach, chef, manicurists, chauffeurs."

Rest in Peace Champ!

On the 12th April 1989, at the age of 68, the arc lights dimmed and finally went out on the life of the greatest ever boxer, Sugar Ray Robinson. Ironically, he died on the anniversary of the death of his close friend, Joe Louis, who had passed away on the same date in 1981. Millions of people across the world mourned his passing. Newspapers throughout the world had his passing in headlines on their front page editions. He died of heart disease at the Brotman Medical Centre in nearby Culver City. He was survived by his wife Millie, his two sons Ronald and Ray Jr, a stepson, a stepdaughter and a sister.

More than 2,000 mourners, including Elizabeth Taylor, Mike Tyson, Don King, Los Angeles Raiders owner Al Davies and Berry Gordy, the founder of Motown Records, packed into the West Los Angeles Church of God - and hundreds more gathered outside - to hear the words spoken about the man considered by many to have been the greatest prize fighter ever to have lived. Robinson had lived in Los Angeles for the past 27 years and was revered as a hero, both in and out of the ring, by many locals.

The funeral was opened with a stirring 45-minute eulogy by the Reverend Jesse Jackson, who described Sugar Ray Robinson as "an art form whose very presence inside the ring had a way of making the world stand still". He reflected upon "a hero, who rose from disgrace to amazing grace; from the guttermost to the uppermost!" He concluded by describing him as "a man who had the sense to want to have class and dignity and self respect. He was a credit to his nation. He defended and beat the odds. Sugar Ray Robinson is as authentic to America as jazz. He has helped bring racial integrity and a commitment to justice for everyone to the forefront of our nation."

The then world heavyweight champion, Mike Tyson, had to choke back tears as he addressed the crowd. "Some of us have to worry about where we're going when we die. I'm sure heaven is asking Sugar Ray to come in with open hands," he suggested. Boxing promoter Don King spoke of Robinson's ability to embrace all colours and creeds. "His life crossed over and touched black and white alike, Americans and foreigners alike. It is vitally important that we, as black people, have heroes. Sugar Ray Robinson was such a man." The Reverend O.C Smith sang an emotion-charged version of 'Everything Must Change' as fight legends, such as Archie Moore, Ken Norton, Bobo Olsen, Art Aragon, Eddie Futch, along with entertainer Red Buttons and other sports figures such as Elgin Baylor, George Allen, and the Dodgers manager, Tom Lasorda, filed past a portrait of Sugar Ray, framed in flowers, next to the casket. He was then interned at Evergreen Cemetery.

Almost a year after his passing, his former wife, Edna Mae, spoke out with a great deal of affection about him. Their stormy marriage and divorce two and a half decades earlier could not subdue the love and the bond they had shared throughout their 18-year marriage. After their 1962 divorce, Edna Mae quietly went about the business of caring for herself and her young son and never remarried. Edna Mae quietly maintained her love for Sugar Ray until her own death in May 2002, at the age of 86.

Ray settled down with his third wife, Millie, whom he had met on his dancing tour when he first retired. She assumed her late husband's leadership of the Youth Foundation before she died quietly at the age of 77 in 1995.

Robinson's enduring legacy to the fight game he graced is still significant. In 1997, The Ring magazine voted Sugar Ray Robinson as "The Best 'Pound for Pound' Boxer" in the magazine's 75-year history.

Sugar Ray Robinson is still the standard by which all non-heavyweight greats are forever measured.

Epilogue

by Frank DeBlase, September 6th, 2006.

The champ was quick and mean, with just the hint of a smile threatening to crack. He faked a left jab for my head and I blocked it as he got me good in the ribs with his right. I faltered and folded. That's when he socked me on the jaw. I saw stars. I was stunned and a little worried. This fellow had beaten Sugar Ray Robinson, after all. He was a brutal fighter who didnt seem to mind being hit. And now here I was, outmatched and outgunned.

I backed up, but he grinned and kept coming towards me. I was on the ropes. The referee stepped in and pushed us apart. And like that, it was over - my first encounter with the champ, Carmen Basilio. And as much as this sounds like a passage from boxing's glory days, it was last week. There was no ring, there were no ropes; we were in the foyer of Basilio's Rochester, New York home. There was no referee; it was Basilio's wife, Josie. And though Basilio did indeed hit me a few times, the 79-year-old champ hung up his gloves a long time ago. Still, who knows what he would,ve done with me had Josie not stepped in. "Now you can tell 'em an old man kicked your ass," he said with a laugh.

I was there to interview Basilio for Brian Hughes, my pal in England who was doing a book on the life of the late, great Sugar Ray Robinson. Basilio and Robinson had met twice in the ring - once in 1957 and again in 1958 - and Hughes wanted Basilio's take on Robinson for his book. "He was an arrogant prick," Basilio said. "He was nearly 6ft, I was 5ft 1-and-a-half. He had better leverage. He was tough. He was a vicious puncher." Robinson apparently talked trash, too. "There was no love between him and I," says Basilio. "As a matter of fact, he hated me, said he's gonna knock me out, he's gonna do this to me, do that. He didn't scare me."

Still, Basilio respected Robinson. "He was saying he was gonna knock me out but that was understandable," he says. "Because he knocked out a lot of guys out." The two finally came face to face for the middleweight championship title on September 23, 1957 in front of 38,000 fans at Yankee Stadium. The fight was also broadcast to millions around the country and they all watched Basilio win by a decision after 15 rounds.

The two matched up again in 1958 in Chicago where Robinson took back the title in a bloody, 15-round battle. Early in the fight, Basilio got cut. "He hit me in here," he says pointing at his eye, "and my left eye closed. For nine rounds I fought with one eye. I couldn't see." Despite the outcome, Basilio is quick to point out that though he lost, he still walked out of the ring. Robinson left on a stretcher. "I beat the shit out of him," he says. "That's the way it went. Yeah, I walked out but he got the decision. What burns Basilio to this day is the tie-breaker that never happened between him and Robinson. "He would never fight me that third fight," he says. "Because he was afraid of me. I was too tough for him. If he had fought me that third fight we would've made a couple of million dollars apiece that night. He wouldn't fight me. He screwed around and screwed around and that was it." That third fight would also put to rest a lot of speculation. "I would've kicked his ass," Basilio says.

Carmen Basilio fought his last fight in Boston in 1961 and retired with a 56-16-7 record. He went on to teach physical education at Lemoyne College for 30 years. "I was very fortunate," he says of his 13 years in the ring. "The fans loved me and they loved me especially at home. My friends all pulled for me. I gave them excitement. I gave them action. I was very, very aggessive. People came to see a fight and they got a fight when they saw me. 'Cause I never backed up. I went forward the whole time. I'd go get my opponent."

The rec room in his basement is a shrine to his illustrious career, including some amazing shots of his two encounters with Robinson. Basilio watches fights whenever he can but none of the new fighters really knock him out, so to speak. "Nobody impresses me right now," he says. The last fighter to impress him? "My wife."

Professional Boxing Record

1940

October 4, Joe Echeverria, New York City	Won TKO 2
October 8, Silent Stafford, Savannah	Won KO 2
October 22, Mistos Grispos, New York City	Won PTS 6
November 1, Bobby Woods, Philadelphia	Won KO 1
December 9, Norment Quarles, Philadelphia	Won TKO 4
December 12, Oliver White, New York City	Won TKO 3

1941

January 4, Henry La Barba, Brooklyn, New York	Won TKO 1
January 13, Frankie Wallace, Philadelphia	Won KO 1
January 31, George Zengaras, New York City	Won PTS 6
February 8, Benny Cartegena, New York City	Won TKO 6
February 21, Bobby McIntire, New York City	Won PTS 6
February 27, Gene Spencer, Detroit	Won TKO 5
March 3, Jimmy Tygh, Philadelphia	Won KO 8
April 14, Jimmy Tygh, Philadelphia	Won TKO 1
April 24, Charley Burns, Atlantic City	Won KO 1
April 30, Joe Ghnouly, Washington	Won TKO 3
May 10, Vic Troise, Brooklyn, New York City	Won TKO 1
May 19, Nick Castiglione, Philadelphia	Won KO 1
June 16, Mike Evans, Philadelphia	Won KO 2
July 2, Pete Lello, New York City	Won TKO 4
July 21, Sammy Angott, Philadelphia	Won PTS 10
August 27, Carl Red Guggino, Long Island	Won TKO 3
August 29, Maurice Arnault, Atlantic City	Won KO 1
September 19, Maxie Sharpiro, New York City	Won TKO 3
September 25, Marty Servo, Philadelphia	Won PTS 10
October 31, Fritzie Zivic, New York City	Won Pts 10

1942

January 16, Fritzie Zivic, New York City	Won TKO 10
February 20, Maxie Berger, New York City	Won TKO 2
March 20, Norman Rubio, New York City	Won TKO 7
April 17, Harvey Dubs, Detroit	Won TKO 6
April 30, Dick Banner, Minneapolis	Won KO 2
May 28, Marty Servo, New York City	Won Pts 10
July 31, Sammy Angott, New York City	Won PTS 10
August 21, Ruben Shank, New York City	Won KO 2
August 27, Tony Motisi, Chicago	Won KO 1

October 2, Jake LaMotta, New York City	Won PTS 10
October 19, Izzy Jannazzo, Philadelphia	Won PTS 10
November 6, Vic Dellicurti, New York City	Won PTS 10
December 1, Izzy Jannazzo, Cleveland	Won TKO 8
December 14, Al Nettlow, Philadelphia	Won TKO 3

1943

February 5, Jake LaMotta, Detroit	Lost PTS 10
February 19, Jackie Wilson, New York City	Won PTS 10
February 26, Jake LaMotta, Detroit	Won PTS 10
April 30, Freddie Cabral, Boston	Won KO 1
July 1, Ralph Zannelli, Boston	Won PTS 10
August 27, Henry Armstrong, New York City	Won PTS 10

1944

October 13, Izzy Jannazzo, Boston	Won TKO 2
October 27, Sgt Lou Woods, Chicago	Won TKO 9
November 17, Vic Dellicurti, Detroit	Won PTS 10
December 12, Sheik Rangel, Philadelphia	Won TKO 2
December 22, Georgie Martin, Boston	Won TKO 7

1945

January 10, Billy Furrone, Washington	Won TKO 2
January 16, Tommy Bell, Cleveland	Won PTS 10
February 14, George Costner, Chicago	Won KO 1
February 23, Jake LaMotta, New York City	Won PTS 10
May 14, Jose Basora, Philadelphia	Drew 10
June 15, Jimmy McDaniels, New York City	Won KO 2
September 18, Jimmy Mandell, Buffalo	Won TKO 5
September 26, Jake LaMotta, Chicago	Won PTS 10
December 4, Vic Dellicurti, Boston	Won PTS 10

1946

January 14, Dave Clark, Pittsburgh	Won TKO 2
February 5, Tony Riccio, Elizabeth	Won TKO 4
February 15, O'Neill Bell, Detroit	Won TKO 2
February 26, Cliff Beckett, St Louis	Won KO 4
March 4, Sammy Angott, Pittsburgh	Won PTS 10
March 14, Izzy Jannazzo, Baltimore	Won PTS 10
March 21, Freddy Flores, New York City	Won KO 5
June 12, Freddy Wilson, Worcester	Won KO 2
June 25, Norman Rubio, Union City	Won PTS 10
July 12, Joe Curcio, New York City	Won KO 2
August 15, Vinnie Vines, Albany	Won KO 6

September 25, Sidney Miller, Elizabeth	Won KO 3
October 7, Ossie Harris, Pittsburgh	Won PTS 10
November 1, Cecil Hudson, Detroit	Won KO 6
November 6, Artie Levine, Cleveland	Won TKO 10
December 20, Tommy Bell, New York City	Won PTS 15
(Won Vacant World welterweight Championship)	

1947

March 27, Bernie Miller, Miami	Won TKO 3
April 3, Fred Wilson, Akron	Won KO 3
April 8, Eddie Finazzo, Kansas City	Won TKO 4
May 16, George Abrams, New York City	Won PTS 10
June 24, Jimmy Doyle, Cleveland	Won TKO 8
(World Welterweight Title Defence.	
Doyle died later from injuries sustained in the Fight.)	
August 21, Sammy Secreet, Arkon	Won KO 1
August 29, Flashy Sebastian, New York City	Won KO 1
October 28, Jackie Wilson, Los Angeles	Won TKO 7
December 10, Billy Nixon, Elizabeth	Won TKO 6
December 19, Chuck Taylor, Detroit	Won TKO 6
(World Welterweight Title defence)	

1948

March 4, Ossie Harris, Toledo	Won PTS 10
March 16, Henry Brimm, Buffalo	Won Pts 10
June 28, Bernard Docusen, Chicago	Won PTS 15
(World Welterweight Title Defence)	
September 23, Kid Gavilan, New York City	Won PTS 10
November 15, Bobby Lee, Philadelphia	Won PTS 10

1949

February 10, Gene Wilkes-Barre, Buffalo	Won KO 1
February 15, Henry Brimm, Buffalo	Drawn PTS 10
March 25, Bobby Lee, Chicago	Won PTS 10
April 11, Don Lee, Omaha	Won PTS 10
April 20, Earl Turner, Oakland	Won TKO 8
May 16, Al Tribuani, Wilmington	Exh 4
June 7, Freddy Flores, New Bedford	Won TKO 3
June 20, Cecil Hudson, Providence	Won TKO 5
July 11, Kid Gavilan, Philadelphia	Won Pts 15
(World Welterweight Title Defence)	
August 24, Steve Belloise, New York City	Won TKO 7
September 2, Al Mobley Chicago	Exh 4
September 9, Benny Evans, Omaha	Won TKO 5
September 12, Charley Dotson, Houston	Won KO 3

November 9, Don Lee, Denver .... Won PTS 10
November 13, Vern Lester, New Orleans .... Won KO 5
November 15, Gene Burton, Shreveport .... Exh 6
November 16, Gene Burton, Dallas .... Exh 6

1950

January 30, George LaRover, New Haven .... Won TKO 4
February 13, Al Mobley, Miami .... Won TKO 6
February 22, Aaron Wade, Savannah .... Won KO 3
February 27, Jean Walzack, St Louis .... Won PTS 10
March 22, George Costner, Philadelphia .... Won KO 1
April 21, Cliff Beckett, Columbus, Ohio .... Won TKO 3
April 28, Ray Barnes, Detroit .... Won Pts 10
June 5, Robert Villemain, Philadelphia .... Won PTS 10
August 9, Charley Fusari, Jersey City .... Won PTS 15
(World Welterweight Title Defence)
August 25, Jose Basora, Scranton .... Won KO 1
September 4, Billy Brown, New York .... Won PTS 10
October 16, Joe Rindone, Boston .... Won KO 6
October 26, Carl Bobo Olson, Philadelphia .... Won KO 12
November 8, Bobby Dykes, Chicago .... Won Pts 10
November 22, Jean Stock, Paris .... Won TKO 2
December 9, Luc Van Dam, Brussels .... Won KO 4
December 16, Jean Walzack, Geneva .... Won PTS 10
December 22, Robert Villemain, Paris .... Won TKO 9
December 25, Hans Stretz, Frankfurt .... Won KO 5

1951

February 14, Jake LaMotta, Chicago .... Won TKO 13
(Won World Middleweight Title)
April 5, Holly Mims, Miami .... Won PTS 10
April 9, Don Ellis, Oklahoma City .... Won KO 1
May 21, Kid Marcel, Paris .... Won TKO 5
May 26, Jean Wanes, Zurich .... Won PTS 10
June 10, Jan deBruin, Antwerp .... Won TKO 8
June 16, Jean Walzack, Liege .... Won TKO 6
June 24, Gerhard Hecht, Berlin .... NC 2
July 1, Cyrille Delannoit, Turin .... Won TKO 3
July 10, Randolph Turpin, London .... Lost PTS 15
(Lost World Middleweight Title)
September 12, Randolph Turpin, New York City ..... Won TKO 10
(Regained World Middleweight Title)

1952

March 13, Carl Bobo Olson, San Francisco   Won PTS 15
(Retained World Middleweight Title)
April 16, Rocky Graziano, Chicago   Won KO 3
(Retained World Middleweight Title)
June 25, Joey Maxim, New York City   Lost TKO by 14
(World Light-Heavyweight Title)
December 18, Announced Retirement From Boxing

1953 - Inactive

1954

October 20, Announced Return To Boxing
November 29, Gene Burton, Hamilton, Ontario   Exh 6

1955

January 5, Joe Rindone, Detroit   Won KO 6
January 19, Ralph Tiger Jones, Chicago   Lost PTS 10
March 29, Johnny Lombardo, Cincinnati   Won PTS 10
April 14, Ted Olla, Milwaukee   Won TKO 3
May 4, Garth Panter, Detroit   Won PTS 10
July 22, Rocky Castellani, San Francisco   Won PTS 10
December 9, Carl Bobo Olson, Chicago   Won KO 2
(Regained World Middleweight Title)

1956

May 18, Carl Bobo Olson, Los Angeles   Won KO 4
(Retained World Middleweight Title)
November 10, Bob Provizzi, New Haven   Won PTS 10

1957

January 2, Gene Fullmer, New York City   Lost PTS 15
(Lost World Middleweight Title)
May 1, Gene Fullmer, Chicago   Won KO 5
(Regained World Middleweight Title)
September 10, Otis Woodward, Philadelphia   Exh 2
September 10, Lee Williams, Philadelphia   Exh 2
September 23, Carmen Basilio, New York City   Lost PTS 15
(Lost World Middleweight Title)

1958

March 25, Carmen Basilio, Chicago   Won PTS 15
(Regained World Middleweight Title)

1959
December 14, Bob Young, Boston	Won TKO 2

1960
January 22, Paul Pender, Boston	Lost PTS 15
(Lost World Middleweight Title)	
April 2, Tony Baldoni, Baltimore	Won KO 1
June 10, Paul Pender, Boston	Lost PTS 15
(World Middleweight Title)	
December 3, Gene Fullmer, Los Angeles	Draw 15
(World Middleweight Title, NBA Version)	

1961
March 4, Gene Fullmer, Las Vagas	Lost Pts 15
(World Middleweight Title)	
September 25, Wilf Greaves, Detroit	Won PTS 10
October 21, Denny Moyer, New York City	Won PTS 10
November 20, Al Hauser, Providence	Won TKO 6
December 8, Wilf Greaves, Pittsburgh	Won KO 8

1962
February 17, Denny Moyer, New York City	Lost PTS 10
April 27, Bobby Lee, Port of Spain, Trinidad	Won KO 2
July 9, Phil Moyer, Los Angeles	Lost PTS 10
September 25, Terry Downes, London	Lost PTS 10
October 17, Diego Infantes, Vienna	Won KO 2
November 10, Georges Estatoff, Lyons	Won TKO 6

1963
January 30, Ralph Dupas, Miami Beach	Won PTS 10
February 25, Bernie Reynolds, San Domingo	Won KO 4
March 11, Billy Thornton, Lewiston	Won KO 3
May 5, Maurice Rolbnet, Sherbrooke	Won KO 3
June 24, Joey Giardello, Philadelphia	Lost PTS 10
October 14, Armand Vanucci, Paris	Won PTS 10
November 9, Fabio Bettini, Lyon	Draw 10
November 16, Emile Sarens, Brussels	Won KO 8
November 29, Andre Davier, Grenoble	Won PTS 10
December 9, Armand Vanucci, Paris	Won PTS 10

1964

May 19, Gaylord Barnes, Portland	Won PTS 10
July 8, Clarence Riley, Pittsfield	Won TKO 6
July 27, Art Hernandez, Omaha	Drawn 10
September 3, Mick Leahy, Paisley	Lost PTS 10
September 28, Yolande Leveque, Paris	Won PTS 10
October 12, Johnny Angel, London	Won TKO 6
October 24, Jackie Caillau, Nice	Won Pts 10
November 7, Baptiste Rolland, Caen	Won PTS 10
November 14, Jean Beltritti, Marseilles	Won Pts 10
November 27, Fabio Bettini, Rome	Drawn 10

1965

March 6, Jimmy Beecham, Kingston, Jamacia	Won KO 2
April 4, East Basting, Savannah	Won KO 1
April 28, Rocky Randall, Norfolk	Won KO 3
May 5, Rocky Randall, Jacksonville	Won PTS 8
May 24, Memo Ayon, Tijuana	Lost PTS 10
June 1, Stan Harrington, Honolulu	Lost PTS 10
June 24, Young Joe Walcott, Richmond	Won PTS 10
July 12, Ferd Hernandez, Las Vegas	Lost PTS 10
July 27, Young Joe Walcott, Richmond	Won PTS 10
August 10, Stan Harrington, Honolulu	Lost PTS 10
September 15, Neil Morrison, Norfolk	NC 2
September 23, Young Joe Walcott, Philadelphia	Won PTS 10
October 1, Peter Schmidt, Johnstown	Won PTS 10
October 20, Rudolf Bent, Steubenville	Won KO 3
November 10, Joey Archer, Pittsburgh	Lost PTS 10
December 10, Announced Retirement From Boxing	

Total Number of professional contests	202
Won By KO OR TKO	109
Won by decision	66
Lost by decision	18
Lost by TKO	1
Draw	6
No Contest	2

Key to abbreviations: W = Won. L = Lost. KO = Knockout. TKO = Technical knockout, either stopped by the referee or a retirement. Pts = Points decision. NC = No Contest. D = Draw. EXH = Exhibition.

BIBLIOGRAPHY

Anderson, Dave - *Sugar Ray*
Robson Books, London, 1996.
Birtley, Jack - *The Tragedy of Randolph Turpin*
New English.
Downes, Terry - *My Bleeding Business*
Stanley Paul, London, 1983.
Garber III, Angus G - *Boxing Legends*
Magna Books, Leicester, 1993.
Gutteridge, Reg, *The Big Punchers*
Stanley Paul, London 1983.
Hauser, Thomas - *Muhammad Ali, His Life and Times*
Simon and Schester, New York, 1991.
Heller, Pete - *In This Corner*
Dell, New York, 1973.
LaMotta, Jake - *Raging Bull*
Prentice Hall International, New Jersey, 1970.
Myler, Thomas - *Sugar Ray Robinson - The Inside Story*
Relym Publications, RPI, 1996.
Schoor, Gene - *Sugar Ray Robinson*
Greenberg, New York, 1951.
Whiting, George - *Great Fights Of The Sixties*
Leslie Frewin, London, 1967.
Wilson, Peter - *More Ringside Seats*
Stanley Paul, London, 1959.

Author's note

Before we decided to undertake the journey of uncovering and detailing the life of the great Sugar Ray Robinson, we both had to answer the questions why we should write a book on this legendary figure and whether we could add anything new and fresh to the numerous accounts which have already been published about his life. Understanding our answers will give you an insight into these pages.

My father (and co-author), Brian Hughes, has been involved in the fight game as a boxing trainer and craftsman for his whole life and so my brothers and I have grown up steeped in boxing history and an appreciation of its greatest exponents, most notably Sugar Ray Robinson, who sat proudly at the top of his all-time favourites list. We have both written a number of other books about great achievers and yet we wanted to bring our passion, respect and enthusiasm for Robinson to the page and we hope that this is conveyed here.

The research offered us a fascinating insight into a sporting and social era which is beginning to fade away into the pages of history; the halcyon days of boxing and its mass appeal feels like a world away from its current form. Looking at the statistics of Robinson's own incredible record of 173-19-6 is inconceivable compared to today's champions, who can fight for world honours before they are out of double figures. We also wanted to show that mere statistics alone do not explain his greatness and so we have attempted to introduce his opponents and give them some context, which proves that he didn't feast on a diet of hapless journeymen to pad his record but faced the best that his era had to offer. Robinson also offered the template for the modern day superstar athletes to enjoy independence and financial worth which has become their right.

The research also led us to some areas of Robinson's life where he was less than perfect. Although we wanted to write a eulogy to the man, it would have been a disservice to both you, the reader, and to Robinson himself, had we ignored these areas, which include his domestic problems and his army service and mysterious departure. These were insights intended to present a rounded portrait of Robinson as a human being. We trust that this doesn't spoil your enjoyment of this remarkable man.

Finally, I want to pay tribute to Brian Hughes. He has been a tireless voluntary leader of the Manchester inner city youth club, Collyhurst and Moston Lads Club, which has been an integral part in the lives of the local community and within the world of boxing and has written a number of best selling books, which have helped raise funding to ensure that the club remains open and accessible to all. He has been credited as an inspiration to generations of children who have been instilled with a sense of hope, purpose and belief in their own abilities. He has also successfully groomed a number of young men to achieve boxing honours, which include Olympic, domestic, national, European and World successes. It is his passion, drive and enthusiasm which have been behind this book. It is as much a tribute to him as it is to the peerless Sugar Ray Robinson.

Thank you for reading.

Damian Hughes.
Manchester, 2007.